D1522138

NEGLECTED
SKIES

The Demise of British Naval Power
in the Far East, 1922–42

ANGUS BRITTS

Naval Institute Press
Annapolis, Maryland

Naval Institute Press
291 Wood Road
Annapolis, MD 21402

Library of Congress Cataloging-in-Publication Data

Names: Britts, Angus, author.
Title: Neglected skies : the demise of British naval power in the Far East,
    1922–42 / Angus Britts.
Other titles: Demise of British naval power in the Far East, 1922–42
Description: Annapolis, Maryland : Naval Institute Press, [2017] |
    Includes bibliographical references and index.
Identifiers: LCCN 2017019145 (print) | LCCN 2017020019 (ebook) |
    ISBN 9781682471586 (epub) | ISBN 9781682471586 (epdf) |
    ISBN 9781682471586 (mobi) | ISBN 9781682471579 (hardcover : alk. paper) |
    ISBN 9781682471586 (ebook)
Subjects: LCSH: World War, 1939–1945—Naval operations, British. | World War, 1939–
    1945—Campaigns—Indian Ocean. | Great Britain. Royal Navy. History—
    20th century. | Sea power—Great Britain—History—20th century. | Great Britain.
    Royal Navy. Fleet Air Arm—History. | Great Britain. Royal Navy—Aviation—
    History—20th century. | World War, 1939–1945—Naval operations, Japanese.
Classification: LCC D770 (ebook) | LCC D770 .B74 2017 (print) |
    DDC 940.54/25—dc23
LC record available at https://lccn.loc.gov/2017019145

Maps created by Chris Robinson.

25 24 23 22 21 20 19 18 17   9 8 7 6 5 4 3 2 1

First printing

In fond memory of my father,

Marshall Malcolm Gordon Britts,

1923–2016

CONTENTS

MAPS AND TABLES

ACKNOWLEDGMENTS

The author wishes to acknowledge the fulsome support provided by family, friends, and colleagues, and pay particular tribute to Professor James Curran (University of Sydney) who supervised the author's MA thesis, which served as the foundation for this publication. Special thanks is also given to Glenn Griffith, Emily Bakely, and all the dedicated staff at the Naval Institute Press for their kindly and timely assistance in assembling the book, and their support for the historical concept upon which it is based.

Angus Britts
2 April 2017

A NOTE ON THE TEXT

Japanese Names. Japanese participants are referred to by family name first and given name second in accordance with Japanese practice.

Aircraft Identification. Japanese aircraft are identified by type designation or assigned Allied code names (e.g., Type 0 Zeke); German, Italian, and all Allied aircraft are identified by designation or given name (e.g., P-40, Swordfish).

Time References. Time references are provided in 24-hour mode, local time unless stated otherwise.

ABBREVIATIONS

ABDA	American-British-Dutch-Australian
ASDIC	Anti-Submarine Detection Investigation Committee (sonar device named after the scientific committee that invented it in World War I)
ASV	Air to Surface Vessel
ASW	antisubmarine warfare
AWACS	Airborne Warning and Control System
BSY	*Brassey's Naval and Shipping Annual*
CAB	Cabinet Document
CAM	Catapult Armed Merchant
CIC	Commander in Chief
CID	Committee for Imperial Defence
COSWR	Chiefs-of-Staff Weekly Resume
FAA	Fleet Air Arm
FSL	First Sea Lord
H.M.S.O.	Her Majesty's Stationery Office
LDNGZT	London Gazette
MOD	Ministry of Defence
RAAF	Royal Australian Air Force
RAF	Royal Air Force
RNAS	Royal Naval Air Service
SDB	Douglas SBD dive-bomber
TNA	The National Archives
UK	United Kingdom
USSBS	United States Strategic Bombing Survey

Introduction

OVER SIX DAYS IN EARLY APRIL 1942 THE EQUATORIAL waters of the eastern Indian Ocean became the setting for a momentous episode in the annals of modern naval history. Since September 1939, Britain's Royal Navy, ill equipped and thinly stretched as it was, had nevertheless mastered the respective surface fleets of its European Axis adversaries. However, on the morning of 7 December 1941, a new and devastating form of warfare made its presence felt in the skies over Pearl Harbor as the Imperial Japanese Navy's Kido Butai (Mobile Force) unleashed its fearsome state-of-the-art aerial armada. Five months later, Japan's paramount first-strike weapon entered the Indian Ocean seeking to locate and destroy the recently arrived British Eastern Fleet. To the south of Ceylon from 4 to 9 April 1942, maneuver and occasional skirmish characterized a cat-and-mouse engagement between these manifestly unequal combatants. For both the Eastern Fleet—and the Royal Navy as a whole—were almost wholly unprepared to confront an opponent that executed massed carrier-borne air strikes in order to overwhelm and crush its selected quarry. Over a century beforehand at Trafalgar, Admiral Lord Nelson's epic triumph over the Franco-Spanish alliance had established the Royal Navy as the dominant Great Power fighting force. The sinking of the aircraft carrier *Hermes* on 9 April 1942 was the final act in a battle where, for the first time, a major British fleet had been forced to withdraw from the battlefield so as to save itself from utter annihilation, with Nelson's long-standing legacy accompanying *Hermes* to the silent depths forever.

1

The story of this largely forgotten decisive battle is likewise the story of the events and circumstances that came to shape its character, conduct, and consequences. *Neglected Skies* recalls an episode two decades in the making—the operational outcome of an era in which the maintenance of British sea power was to be profoundly degraded by an international limitation of naval arms and by domestic fiscal restraint. From 1921 onward, these two principal factors proceeded to consume British naval policy, setting it upon a course whereby, with war looming in the mid-1930s, the Royal Navy would eventually enter hostilities well short of full combat readiness. On 3 September 1939, all but one of the Royal Navy's serving capital ships and aircraft carriers were either obsolete or obsolescent, while the carrier-borne Fleet Air Arm (FAA) possessed approximately 180 biplane torpedo bombers, just 30 monoplane dive-bombers, and no modern single-seat fighter aircraft. Against the German and Italian surface threats, success was primarily achieved through the skillful battlefield application of available tactical advantages. On the other side of the world, meanwhile, the Japanese had spent the better part of twenty years pursuing the benefits of qualitative sea combat superiority, most particularly within the field of carrier-based and land-based naval aviation. Thus, the stage was set for the only battle of its kind in history, a confrontation between the competing doctrines of British air-surface integration and Japanese air concentration. By nightfall on 9 April 1942, there could be no doubting that Japan had indeed engineered the greatest quantum leap in naval warfare since steam power supplanted the days of sail.

When Winston Churchill subsequently described this episode as "the most dangerous moment of the war," his remarks were directed toward the potentially dire strategic repercussions for the global Allied cause, should the Japanese have acquired active control over the Indian Ocean—a theme repeated in numerous postwar accounts of the Indo-Pacific conflict in its entirety.[1]

These consequences, including the severing of Allied sea communications to the east of Suez, and the exposure of vital territories to future attack, have all been adequately acknowledged. What remains missing, however, is any substantial attempt on the part of the histories to explore the engagement as a major signpost in the evolution of naval warfare. Variously known to Western history as the Easter Sunday Raid, the Indian Ocean Raid, the Battle of Ceylon, and the Nagumo Raid, the battle itself has never commanded the same level of operational importance as that attached to the likes of Cape Matapan and Midway. Donald Macintyre's description of the episode as "only a hit-and-run raid" does reflect a widespread trend among postwar historians that the brief skirmishes between the British and Japanese fleets were little more than a postscript to Japan's initial aeroamphibious blitzkrieg.[2] And at face value, the lack of a major clash of arms on a roughly comparable scale with the battles mentioned above does lend significant credence to Macintyre's shared historical assessment.

However, as the reader will come to observe in the following pages, the battle cannot be assessed based upon this factor alone. What the Japanese designated as Operation C,[3] was, in point of fact, a major strategic operation, involving not only the sought-after destruction of the Eastern Fleet but also a concurrent commerce-raiding mission by Japan's Second Expeditionary Fleet—designed to paralyze sea communications in the Bay of Bengal, thereby securing the left flank of the Japanese land advance into Burma. It was also the only occasion in the Indo-Pacific war where the British and Japanese opposed each other in a fleet action and, as such, serves as the only practicable guide for determining whether the British were capable of prevailing against their former allies in fleet combat. Indeed, this action became something of an occasion for other naval historical firsts: the first battle in which both sides fielded aircraft carriers; the first (and only) fleet action involving differing air-naval tactical doctrines; the largest single assembly of British capital ships and carriers for a fleet action in World War II; and the first-ever commerce-raiding mission in which the raiding fleet mustered a carrier, surface warships, and submarines. But it was the events and circumstances that shaped the episode that lend the greatest weight to its acceptance as the operational equivalent of the other great naval engagements of World War II. Because upon no other occasion within the first four years of the war were the collective sins of interwar British naval atrophy—most particularly in the skies above—so comprehensively exposed: it was the decisive battle that ended the reign of the world's greatest blue-water fighting fleet.

Before proceeding to the opening chapter and an overview of the battle in question, it is necessary to identify the various precedents that became embedded in the development of British naval strength from the 1860s to 1919. On the eve of war with the Central Powers in August 1914, the Royal Navy possessed the biggest surface battle fleet in the world, with some 69 capital ships (battleships and battle cruisers), 120 cruisers, and 270 destroyers then in service. Twenty-five years beforehand, British naval supremacy had become enshrined in legislation, with the 1889 Naval Defence Act requiring the Royal Navy be twice the strength of any other two Great Power fleets afloat.[4] Within this lengthy peacetime period, future precedents were to be established in the formulation of both naval grand strategy and operational doctrine, the evolution of warship technology, and the securing of the necessary level of government fiscal support. The 1904–5 Russo-Japanese War and World War I would establish a full range of operational practices for maritime warfare in the developing internal-combustion age, including, in the latter instance, the first developments in shipboard naval aviation.

From the mid-1860s onward, British naval theorists earnestly debated the respective merits of imperial versus continental grand strategy. The likes of Captain John Colomb and Admiral Sir Alexander Milne considered the apparent need to base Royal Navy squadrons at strategic points across the British Empire, with the provision of coaling stations becoming an especially important factor.[5] Established in 1879 to examine the question of imperial defense, the Carnarvon Commission concluded that warships needed to "be so stationed as to be ready at the commencement of hostilities to deal with the enemy's ships in distant seas."[6] Also at issue was the question of what role Britain's white settler colonies would play in a global naval defense network. Following the 1887 Colonial Conference, the principle applied was that the colonies should contribute materially or financially for localized and external maritime commitments. While no immediate European threat existed, the imperial system held sway. However, in 1904, with growing German naval construction and the appointment of Admiral Sir John Fisher as First Sea Lord, imperial defense began to be superseded by the growing need for a strong British fleet presence in the Atlantic. Fisher did not hesitate to scale down squadron deployments abroad as he commenced the assembly of an enormous battle fleet to meet the emerging German threat in the North Sea.

In a series of lectures delivered at the United States Naval War College from 1887 to 1911, the prominent American naval theorist, Captain (later Admiral) Alfred Thayer Mahan, argued in favor of a decisive battle at the outset of war to ensure naval supremacy for the remainder of hostilities.[7] Whereas Mahan's theorizing primarily related to the command of the seas in an imperial context, Fisher's concentration of the Royal Navy's strength to meet the German High Seas Fleet likewise reflected the mustering of warships for an initial engagement. For the British, close blockade had been effectively employed on any number of occasions during the era of sail. Colomb perceived a similar role for the fleet in the evolving steam age, with large fleets to blockade the English Channel and the Mediterranean while smaller detached squadrons protected the remainder of the British Empire.[8] What Mahan and Fisher brought to the table was not a repudiation of blockade as an operational necessity, but rather the idea that, as Mahan put it, "the sustained concentration of the fighting ships" be the key to achieving naval supremacy at the earliest possible moment.[9] In a steam-powered combat environment, this meant the assembly of a large battle fleet in which ever-larger and ever-faster battleships were to provide the decisive tactical edge.

In terms of the evolution in naval technology, prior to 1889 the British were by no means the leading innovators. Instead they responded to overseas initiatives such as the French ironclad *Gloire* (1859) and the American *Monitor* (1862) through a policy of "wait and see," declining large-scale investment in new technologies that would have rendered their existing fleets obsolete.[10] With the enactment of the 1889 Naval Defence Act, however, a proactive policy was needed in order to sustain Britain's legislated two-to-one naval advantage. Henceforth the Royal Navy benefited markedly from seeking to lead the developmental pace. The commissioning of HMS *Dreadnought* in 1906, the world's first all–big gun (12-inch caliber) battleship powered by steam turbine engines, represented an enormous advance over existing battleships, so much so that all existing battleships in service around the world were reclassified as pre-dreadnoughts. Yet there would be a steep price to pay for the introduction of *Dreadnought* and her successors, including the new battle cruiser class, which Fisher personally championed. Once their initial shock concerning this vessel had subsided, Britain's competitors commenced their own dreadnought-building programs. These in turn generated geopolitically destabilizing international arms races; the British Admiralty, in order to sustain the Royal Navy's supremacy, would have to seek greater fiscal assistance from government to build even larger numbers of dreadnoughts and battle cruisers. Additionally, emphasis on these big ships diverted British attention from other important naval issues, including the overdue modernization of the Fleet's elderly armored cruiser squadrons and the potential future conduct of submarine warfare.

Building a large, state-of-the-art battle fleet, and subsequently deploying it at home or abroad, required government financing on a very large scale.

Funding efforts competed with the War Office during a period in which Britain was waging a series of expensive land-based colonial campaigns, and, from the 1880s onward the growing need for social reform and expenditure upon social services gradually arose as another serious funding competitor. Indeed, in 1906, combined budget outlays on health, education, and social welfare exceeded total defense spending for the first time.[11] From the 1870s, however, the Admiralty employed a variety of lobbying techniques that proved to be highly effective in helping to secure its budgetary position. Appeals to both Parliament and the public at large by influential journals such as the *Pall Mall Gazette* and *Brassey's Naval and Shipping Annuals* were extremely beneficial, especially when they portrayed material deficiencies in the Royal Navy that would place it at a disadvantage against foreign competitors. Also beneficial was the presence of serving and retired naval officers in Parliament itself.[12] Nothing succeeded, however, in arousing political and public attention quite like a naval "scare," be the alleged villains the French, the Russians, or the Germans. A series of Eastern Crises took place in the period 1870–85 over French and Russian naval ambitions in the Pacific, while Fisher's persistent warnings concerning German naval expansionism succeeded in securing the funding required for building up to twenty future dreadnoughts from 1906 onward. As the British naval historian Eric Grove observed, one of Fisher's chief concerns was to sustain Britain's naval shipbuilding industry through a secure stream of new orders.[13]

Among the warships built in British shipyards during the four decades prior to August 1914 were those that would eventually serve in the Imperial Japanese Navy. The Japanese had been supplied with British-built ironclads since 1862, and with the beginning of the Meiji Era in 1868 the relationship between the nations' navies expanded to include training and technical assistance supplied by the Royal Navy.[14] With a mutual distrust of Russia, both nations entered into the 1902 Anglo-Japanese Alliance, an event of profound importance in both of the future world wars, as the reader shall observe in detail shortly. At the outbreak of the Russo-Japanese War on 8 February 1904, the Japanese fleet executed a classic Mahanist first strike against the Russian Pacific Squadron at Port Arthur, forgoing the accepted diplomatic practice of first declaring war. Although the initial attacks failed to destroy the Russian squadron, the combination of a subsequent close blockade and supporting artillery fire from a ground offensive against the base sank the majority of the Russian warships. In retaliation, Tsar Nicholas II ordered the Baltic Fleet to sortie to the Far East. Under the command of Admiral Rojestvensky, the newly named Second Pacific Squadron departed its Arctic bases in mid-October 1904. What followed was the nautical version of *Monty Python and the Holy Grail*. On 21 October, the Russian ships fired upon British fishing trawlers in the North Sea under the unfathomable belief that they were being attacked by Japanese torpedo boats.[15] Rojestvensky's ramshackle command eventually staggered its way to the Tsushima Straits some seven months later where, on 27–28 May 1905, it was annihilated by the well-organized Japanese Combined Fleet under the command of Admiral Togo Heihachiro.

From the numerous precedents set in the fighting of the first large naval war involving steam-powered steel-clad warships, two particular aspects stood out. The first aspect was formidable nature of the Imperial Japanese Navy in battle. Togo and his subordinates were not shy in employing then-radical battle tactics, including massed torpedo attacks by torpedo-boat flotillas, and were greatly aided by recent innovations such as wireless in the command and control of their ships.[16] And if a vital strategic advantage could be secured with a preemptive surprise attack, diplomatic niceties were simply ignored. The second aspect was the implicit danger that lay in the over-possession of obsolete or obsolescent warships in battle: an invitation for disaster. Rojestvensky possessed only four modern battleships and a handful of fast cruisers in a large fleet that contained numerous obsolete ships no longer fit for frontline service. Perhaps he would have been better off if the services of the *Python*'s famed Trojan Rabbit had been available to confound the waiting Japanese, so that the 2nd Pacific Squadron could have steamed unscathed to Vladivostok.[17] Certainly it could have done no worse. Yet nine years later there existed strong grounds to direct similar criticism at the Royal Navy itself. Of the sixty British battleships in service, forty of these were pre-dreadnoughts. Almost all of the Admiralty's eighty-two armored and protected-class cruisers were a decade or more in age.[18] Should the Admiralty make a mess of its forthcoming dispositions against Germany's High Seas Fleet, another Tsushima-style catastrophe remained a distinct possibility.

Once the shooting between Britain and Germany had commenced, an allied Imperial Japanese Navy in the Pacific did provide the Admiralty with a greater degree of flexibility when it came to British naval dispositions beyond the Atlantic. In spite of his determination to confront the German threat head-on, Admiral Fisher had never entirely disavowed the idea of a Pacific fleet, with battle cruisers performing a major role.[19] On 8 December

1914, two of the Royal Navy's British-based battle cruisers engaged and defeated the German East Asia Squadron, under the command of Admiral Graf Von Spee, in the vicinity of the Falkland Islands. Yet when viewed as a whole, the Anglo-Japanese attempts to destroy Von Spee's squadron—the only significant naval episode within the Indo-Pacific theater during the course of the war—provided scarce grounds for self-congratulation. The destruction of the German light cruiser *Emden* by the Australian light cruiser *Sydney* near the Cocos Islands on 9 November 1914 became the high point of an otherwise fumbling effort to locate Von Spee's ships. *Emden* sank or captured some twenty-five Allied merchantmen and two warships before being eventually run down, while the Germans thoroughly trounced the 4th British cruiser squadron off Coronel on 1 November.[20] Following the Falkland Islands battle, naval warfare beyond the confines of the North Atlantic and the Mediterranean sharply declined in intensity, becoming instead a protracted conflict between Allied warships and Germany's highly effective armed merchant raiders.

Aside from ramming home the lessons of Tsushima at Coronel, where the obsolete British armored cruisers *Good Hope* and *Monmouth* were sunk with all hands lost, Von Spee's ill-fated expedition likewise featured the fateful intervention of Britain's First Lord of the Admiralty, Winston Churchill. First appointed to the position in 1911, Churchill's stewardship deviated between brilliance and incompetence. His decision to station an upgraded fleet at Gibraltar the year he took office would prove to be of the upmost benefit to British strategic interests for the next four decades, in spite of his having reneged on a previous 1909 agreement with the Dominions to base such a fleet in the Pacific.[21] Likewise his personal support for building the *Queen Elizabeth*–class super-dreadnoughts—the world's first oil-fueled battleships—from 1912 onward, substantially increased the enormous power of the Royal Navy's battle line. On the flip side, it was Churchill who directed the 4th Cruiser Squadron to engage Von Spee, without providing it with any modern vessels that could stand up to the crack German armored cruisers *Scharnhorst* and *Gneisenau*.[22] Further blunders followed, not least the planning and execution of the naval sortie to secure the Dardanelles, and the resulting disaster at Gallipoli, which forced Churchill's resignation in May 1915. Alongside Churchill, another controversial character emerged from World War I in the person of Admiral Sir David Beatty. Charismatic and a man of action, Beatty's successes on the battlefield were to earn him the position of

First Sea Lord at the start of the postwar era, and alongside Churchill, he became a major influence upon the future fortunes of the Royal Navy.

Beatty first rose to prominence at the battle of the Heligoland Bight on 28 August 1914 and played a principal role in the battles of Dogger Bank (24 January 1915) and Jutland (31 May–1 June 1916) as commander of the Grand Fleet's battle cruiser force. In both of the latter engagements, his vigorous pursuit of the enemy proved to be dangerously risky; at Jutland, three of the British battle cruisers were sunk with the loss of almost five thousand officers and ratings. Nevertheless, the Royal Navy's performance in fleet combat during the course of the war did prove successful because the British were able to consistently drive the Germans from the battlefield. At Jutland, the biggest surface naval engagement in history, the German High Seas Fleet outfought the British Grand Fleet for much of the battle but was still forced to vacate the field in the face of a massive barrage from Grand Fleet dreadnoughts and super-dreadnoughts. Indeed the commander (and principal founder) of the German navy, Admiral Alfred Tirpitz, had never sought to fight the Grand Fleet in a full-scale battle, instead attempting to whittle down the Royal Navy's advantage by what Eric Grove described as "disproportionate attrition"—specifically targeting the British battle cruisers at both Dogger Bank and Jutland.[23] The presence of the High Seas Fleet at Kiel and Wilhelmshaven became the quintessential example of the "fleet in being": the employment of a fleet of sufficient size to prevent the Royal Navy from exercising unhindered strategic movement. Fleet in being was to be extensively employed by both sides in the European theater during World War II.

Although the British may have continued to dominate the fleet naval battlefield, it was their almost complete pre-1917 helplessness in confronting the German U-boat menace that set a dangerous precedent for future wars. For a variety of reasons, including the reluctance of shipowners to have their operating schedules interfered with, the 1879 Carnarvon Commission had not supported the use of protected convoys, and these were not to be introduced until September 1917.[24] Prior to this outcome, the U-boats had decimated Britain's merchant marine to the point that the nation faced the possibility of starvation. Warships too were not immune; the sinking of the obsolete armored cruisers *Aboukir*, *Hogue*, and *Cressy* by a single submarine in the North Sea on 22 September 1914, together with the subsequent loss of other British cruisers and pre-dreadnoughts to submarine attack, starkly demonstrated the consequences for a national navy's profound operational ill-preparedness. In emphasizing the importance of the battleship in the prewar period, the Royal Navy had neglected a form of warfare with particularly dire implications for the survival of Britain itself, even though the Admiralty had access to sufficient destroyers and smaller escorts to provide close convoy escort at the outbreak of hostilities.[25] These circumstances would differ from the events of April 1942, however: British naval aviation in the latter instance did not possess the wherewithal in the first place to deal with the Japanese carrier-air spearhead.

Just as the threat posed by German submariners from 1914–17 presented a largely avoidable crisis for the Royal Navy, the evolution of British naval airpower in World War I presented the Admiralty with the means to dominate future wars at sea providing this advantage was properly exploited. First formed on 1 July 1914, the Royal Naval Air Service (RNAS) proved to be effective as both a land- and sea-based air arm. In addition to its fighter and bomber units serving on the Western Front, the RNAS undertook attacks, including those conducted from seaplane carriers, against coastal targets, submarines, and Zeppelin facilities.[26] During the course of the war, numerous experiments in wheeled aircraft launch and recovery from flush-decked vessels were undertaken, and by the end of 1918 two aircraft carriers, *Argus* and *Furious*, had been completed. On 1 April 1918 the RNAS became formally incorporated into the new Royal Air Force (RAF) under the 1917 Air Force (Constitution) Act, so as to consolidate British Army and naval airpower under a single umbrella.[27] The establishment of the RAF was to cause considerable friction among all three of Britain's armed services during the 1920s, and prior to September 1939 played no small role in hobbling the development of the Fleet Air Arm. Yet at the final cessation of fighting in November 1918, there could be no doubt the Royal Navy held the upper hand in this new and highly promising operational field (although the Americans and the Japanese were likewise demonstrating an active interest in the airplane at sea).

With the guns having fallen silent on 11 November, the Royal Navy prepared to enter another cycle of peace and war, having in hand vital precedents from its recent past. In the five decades preceding World War I, the foundations had been laid for future debate over the respective merits of imperial and continental naval defense. The concept of the decisive battle would likewise remain in the Admiralty's postwar thinking, even though, once the war had commenced, it had come about later rather than sooner. And the need to set the pace in the naval technology race had been starkly illustrated by the destruction of two Russian fleets in the Russo-Japanese War: the Japanese demonstrated their formidability as a first-rate naval fighting power. Most importantly, the need for a sufficient budget to lead in that race would present greater difficulty in peacetime: necessary social services became a major fiscal priority of the government. The wartime experience of the Royal Navy in the years 1914–18 provided grounds for both optimism and foreboding as it sought to retain its mantle as the world's paramount fighting fleet. At times the Admiralty experienced setbacks beyond the North Atlantic, however the presence of the Imperial Japanese Navy in the Pacific allowed the British sufficient force to eventually blockade Germany's High Seas Fleet out of the war.

Two principal participants in the next stage of the Royal Navy's evolution, Winston Churchill and Sir David Beatty, had displayed the positive and negative attributes of their respective personalities and capabilities. And although the British again retained mastery of the surface combat battlefield, they also experienced the naked helplessness that lay in the nearly complete prewar neglect of a new form of warfare. It had taken almost five years of war for the Admiralty to understand the submarine. How long would it now take for Britain's senior service to understand the airplane?

To the casual observer gazing across the roadsteads at Scapa Flow in late August 1939, the Royal Navy's assembled Home Fleet must have presented a truly awe-inspiring sight. Swaying at anchor was the massive, yet graceful battle cruiser HMS *Hood*, along with other large capital ships, several carriers, and a plethora of cruisers, destroyers, and smaller craft. Twenty-three years had passed since the epic showdown at Jutland in which surface gunnery had reigned supreme. When addressing a Lord Mayoral banquet on 9 November 1923 in his capacity as First Sea Lord, Admiral Beatty defined the capital ship as "an inexpungable ship combining the greatest offensive powers with the greatest powers of defence, with the addition of speed and good sea-keeping qualities."[28] For Beatty, the Fleet's battleships and battle cruisers remained the bearers of this mantle; he spoke of the aircraft carrier only as an increasingly important support element for the battle line. And for the following sixteen years, the evolution of the fleet air-weapon plodded along while the imposing might of the Royal Navy began to fade in an unfriendly interwar environment. Yet the service would succeed in defying its aging muscles and sinews to repel two worthy European adversaries, only to be left astounded and humiliated by an opponent whose grasp of the use of naval airpower would prove to be absolutely lethal. And as the British naval historian Paul Kennedy sagely remarked in his summation of the Indian Ocean episode, "Beatty, had he lived to see the sight, would have scarcely believed his eyes."[29]

1

The Battle

31 March–9 April 1942

OPERATION C COMMENCED ON 26 MARCH 1942 WITH THE departure of the Kido Butai from its forward anchorage at Staring Bay in the Celebes. Commanded by Vice Admiral Nagumo Chuichi, the force had been assigned a straightforward task. Japanese naval historian and then-senior aviator on board the light aircraft carrier *Ryujo*, Okumiya Masatake recalled that Nagumo "fully appreciated the tremendous enemy strength which would face him in his attempt to destroy British sea power. . . . The Indian Ocean was fast becoming a British Lake, and Nagumo's orders were to smash this enemy strength."[1] Over the past four months, Nagumo's flyers had inflicted mayhem from Hawaii to Java. In the surprise attack against Pearl Harbor, the Japanese air strikes effectively crippled the battleship arm of the United States Navy's Pacific Fleet and likewise devastated the surrounding airfields. Further strikes followed at Wake, Rabaul, Amboina, and Tjilatjap. On 19 February 1942, Darwin was blitzed by aircraft from four of Japan's six large carriers, with numerous ships sunk and the port facilities left in smoldering ruins. Now it was Britain's turn to experience the attentions of a fleet that seemingly sprang from nowhere and then vanished, that had yet to be sighted, let alone attacked. In distant concert with the Kido Butai was the Second Expeditionary Fleet, under the command of Vice Admiral Ozawa Jisaburo. Ozawa's force was to steam into the Bay of Bengal, having left the Andaman Islands on 1 April, and target enemy merchant shipping in the general vicinity while also staging nuisance air attacks against India's eastern coastline.

These two limbs of Operation C had been deployed to not only expel the Royal Navy from the eastern half of the Indian Ocean—thereby securing the western peripheries of Japan's newly acquired Southern Resources Area—but also to secure the seaward flank of the Imperial Army's advance into Burma, currently under way.[2] The Kido Butai consisted of the large aircraft carriers *Akagi* (Red Castle), *Hiryu* (Flying Dragon), *Soryu* (Deep Blue Dragon), *Shokaku* (Flying Crane), and *Zuikaku* (Lucky Crane), four fast *Kongo*-class battleships, two heavy cruisers, one light cruiser, and eleven destroyers. The Second Expeditionary Fleet consisted of the light aircraft carrier *Ryujo* (Heavenly Dragon), five heavy cruisers, one light cruiser, four destroyers, and five submarines.[3] While Nagumo's carriers had been running riot in the Pacific and north of Australia, Ozawa's fleet acted in a support role for the aeroamphibious invasions of Malaya and the Netherlands' East Indies. Immediately following the surrender of Singapore on 15 February 1942, Ozawa's ships destroyed forty of forty-four small vessels belonging to the last evacuation convoy to depart that beleaguered island, the majority of these crowded with fleeing civilians.[4] Thereafter, *Ryujo*'s forty-eight aircraft provided air support for the capture of Sumatra and Java by persistently harrying the defending ABDA (American-British-Dutch-Australian) cruiser squadrons in the Java Sea.

Whereas *Ryujo*'s aircrews would pursue the destruction of enemy merchant traffic in their forthcoming air operations, Nagumo's five carriers fielded a first-line total of 330 combat aircraft and 63 reserves to attack whatever size of fleet the British were assembling at Colombo and Trincomalee on the island of Ceylon. The bombing component of the Kido Butai spearhead consisted of Navy Type 99 carrier bombers (Allied reporting name, "Val") and Navy Type 97 attack bombers ("Kate"). With its distinctive spatted fixed undercarriage and elliptical wing shape, the Val had proven to be a deadly, efficient dive-bomber, and the slender Kate was equally adept at delivering bombs and torpedoes with great precision. The ace card, however, was the Navy Type 0 ("Zeke"), best remembered as the Zero.[5] With the possible exception of Germany's Focke-Wulf 190, the Zeke in April 1942 was the most dominant fighter aircraft, carrier borne or land based, in widespread frontline service. Possessing the range of a bomber, this highly maneuverable

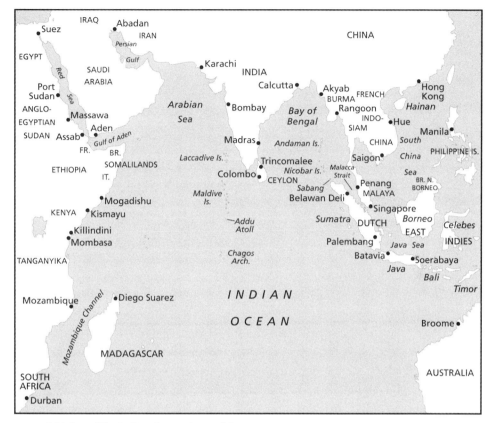

MAP 1. The Indian Ocean Area of Operations

lightweight fighter had thus far easily mastered every Allied fighter type thrown at it. It should be recalled, however, that much of the Zeke's success could be reasonably attributed to the absence of well-organized enemy air commands equipped with sufficient numbers of high-performance fighter aircraft. Nor, for that matter, had the Kido Butai yet engaged an enemy fleet at sea. In a repeat of the Pearl Harbor operation, Nagumo's primary target was the Royal Navy fleet base at Colombo; and if his ships went undetected, no sea battle would be necessary.[6]

Unbeknown to the Japanese, the British had been undertaking frantic steps to bolster Ceylon's sparse aerial defenses after the appointment of Admiral Sir Geoffrey Layton as commander in chief, Ceylon, in early March 1942. Scrounging every aircraft that could be spared from other localities—including two RAF Hurricane fighter squadrons bound for Java as deck cargo on the aircraft carrier *Indomitable*—Layton's command possessed a total of six fighter squadrons, one light-bomber squadron, one torpedo-bomber squadron, and two long-range reconnaissance squadrons. Extra airfields were constructed near Colombo by commandeering the local golf course and racetrack; radar coverage and antiaircraft guns were increased; and air-raid precautions were likewise improved.[7] These preparations were, however, far from complete; Allied "ULTRA" code intercepts indicated the strong prospect of a Japanese naval raid of some sort in the Indian Ocean in early April 1942: time was not on Layton's side. What the British did have to their advantage was Addu Atoll, a coral outcrop at the foot of the Maldives, where the Royal Navy possessed a forward base for the refueling and victualing of the assembling Eastern Fleet. Approximately six hundred nautical miles southwest of Ceylon, Addu's existence as a base was wholly unknown to the Japanese.[8] This factor would certainly aid the recently appointed commander of the Eastern Fleet, Admiral Sir James Somerville, providing him the opportunity to launch a flanking attack against any Japanese force seeking to approach Ceylon from the south or southeast.

Somerville was one of Britain's most experienced and most successful fighting admirals. He had previously commanded Force H operating from Gibraltar into the Western Mediterranean Sea with good effect against the Italians. His ships had also decimated a French squadron at Oran on 3 July 1940, preventing it from falling into German hands following the final surrender of France on 22 June.[9] And in May 1941, Somerville's large aircraft carrier *Ark Royal* performed the pivotal role in the hunt for the German battleship *Bismarck* in the Atlantic: one of her Swordfish torpedo planes scored a hit on the battleship's rudder, disabling her for eventual destruction at the hands of the British Home Fleet. As commander of the Eastern Fleet, Somerville well understood the major strategic objective that both Whitehall and the Admiralty expected him to pursue: "First and foremost, the total defence of the Indian Ocean and its vital lines of communications depended upon the existence of the Eastern Fleet. The longer this fleet remains 'a fleet in being,' the longer it will limit and check the enemy's advances against Ceylon and further west. This major policy of retaining 'a fleet in being,' already approved by their Lordships, was, in my opinion paramount."[10]

Unfortunately for Somerville, the Eastern Fleet he commanded would not have looked out of place at Tsushima in 1905, in terms of his participating warships' relative age and combat suitability. The British fielded two of their most modern large carriers in *Formidable* and *Indomitable*, together with the small (and obsolete) *Hermes*. The battle line consisted of the modernized *Queen Elizabeth*–class battleship *Warspite* and four unmodernized R-class battleships: *Resolution*, *Revenge*, *Royal Sovereign*, and *Ramillies*. Described as "fairly useless" by Churchill, and "my miserable old battleboats" by Somerville himself, these latter four Great War veterans were, despite their very heavy (8- by 15-inch) main armament, almost totally unprotected against air attack and extremely slow (twenty-one knots) by contemporary naval standards.[11] The escort and screening vessels—two heavy cruisers, five light cruisers, and fourteen destroyers—were likewise a mixed bunch, with all of the light cruisers being at best obsolescent. Nevertheless Somerville divided his command into two forces: Force A under his command containing the two fleet carriers, *Warspite*, the two heavy cruisers, two light cruisers, and six destroyers while Force B contained the remainder of the ships, under the command of the experienced Vice Admiral Sir Algernon Willis.[12] On 30 March 1942 the Eastern Fleet departed its anchorages at Ceylon and commenced steaming southward. Far from remaining a distant deterrent to Japanese operations, Somerville intended to lay an ambush for the expected enemy raiding force, even though he did not yet possess any credible intelligence as to the size and composition of that force.

In addition to the less than satisfactory nature of many of its warships, the Eastern Fleet's naval aviation component could only be described as pitiful. Between them the *Formidable* and *Indomitable* carried forty-five Fairey Albacore torpedo bombers, whereas the little *Hermes* possessed just a single squadron of twelve Fairey Swordfish torpedo bombers.[13] Though both of these biplane types had proven to be effective performers in the European theater, they were absolute sitting ducks when it came to interception by any serving Axis fighter. Worse still was the state of the fleet's carrier-borne fighter cover. A grand total of thirty-three fighters—twelve Fairey Fulmars, nine Hawker Sea Hurricanes, and twelve Grumman Martlets—were ranged against more than one hundred Zekes. A two-seat fighter-reconnaissance type, the Fulmar was no match for a Zeke (and would have problems with a Val), while the Sea Hurricane and the Martlet lacked the all-around performance edge required against the Japanese fighter.[14] The Fleet Air Arm's aircrews also lacked experience; Somerville described his Albacore crews "as green as grass."[15] If a large-scale air encounter developed between Somerville's and Nagumo's aviators, the large-scale decimation of the FAA's fighter and torpedo-bomber squadrons loomed as the most likely outcome. And with the withdrawal of the Blackburn Skua from first-line shipboard service in December 1941, the British did not possess a purpose-designed dive bomber, thereby depriving Somerville of a multidimensional strike option.[16] A massed aerial torpedo attack was Somerville's only practical means of inflicting serious damage upon Nagumo's ships, but such an assault would likewise enable the Japanese to concentrate their defending fighters against a one-dimensional threat.[17]

On 31 March, the Eastern Fleet reached a position approximately 200–250 miles south-southwest of Ceylon. Somerville had composed a bold plan to attack the unidentified Japanese force under cover of darkness, seeking to employ similar tactics to those employed with such success by the Mediterranean Fleet against the Italians at Cape Matapan on 28 March 1941:

> The enemy could approach Ceylon from the north-east, from the east, or from the south-east, to a position equidistant 200 miles from Colombo and Trincomalee. This would enable the enemy to fly off aircraft between 0200 and 0400 and, after carrying out bombing attacks on Colombo and Trincomalee, allow the aircraft to return and fly on after the first light (about 0530); forces could then withdraw at high speed to the eastward. I was assuming that the Japanese carrier-borne bombers could have approximately the performance of our Albacores.
>
> 6. My plan was therefore to concentrate the Battlefleet, carriers and all available cruisers and destroyers and to rendezvous ... in a position from which the fast division [Force A] could intercept the enemy ... and deliver a night air attack. The remainder [Force B] to form a separate force and to manoeuvre so as to be approximately 20 miles to the westward of Force A. If Force A intercepted a superior force, I intended to withdraw towards Force B.
>
> 7. On the supposition that the enemy adopted what I considered to be his most probable plan, it was certain that he would have air reconnaissance out ahead.... The success of my plan depended on my force not being sighted by enemy air reconnaissance.[18]

A year earlier, the British Mediterranean Fleet under the command of Admiral Sir Andrew Cunningham, had achieved victory at Cape Matapan through their effective execution of what could best be described as integrated fleet tactics. An initial attack by the FAA's torpedo bombers from *Formidable* crippled a battleship and a heavy cruiser, slowing up the cruiser element of the Italian Fleet and enabling the slower British battleships to pursue, ambush, and destroy three heavy cruisers and two destroyers under cover of darkness.[19] Cunningham's tactics mirrored—as did Admiral Somerville's— the Admiralty's policy as outlined in clause 224 of the Royal Navy's *Fighting Instructions*. Clause 224 dictated that Fleet Air Arm torpedo attacks be conducted primarily against "a faster battlefleet," even if enemy aircraft carriers were also present.[20] Both Somerville and his London-based superiors considered the probable composition of a Japanese raiding force to be a squadron of battleships or cruisers accompanied by a single aircraft carrier, much in the style of British battle formations such as Force H. From dusk on 31 March 1942 until dawn the next day, however, the vista of the Indian Ocean in moonlight remained an otherwise blank canvas for the Eastern Fleet. With no sign of the Japanese, Somerville set course for Addu Atoll to refuel and especially to replenish water supplies on the R-class battleships, all of which lacked adequate onboard desalination facilities for operations in an equatorial climate.[21]

In spite of the extensive patrols undertaken by RAF Catalina reconnaissance aircraft south of Ceylon, no sightings were reported over the following two days. Then, on the afternoon of 4 April, with the Eastern Fleet still undergoing refueling, Admiral Somerville received a flash signal:

> At 1630, I received a report from a Catalina southeast of Ceylon that a large enemy force was in position 00–40N, 83–10E at 1605F, course 315 degrees. Shortly after this report was confirmed by a message from [RAF] 222 Group which gave the course as 330 degrees. This positioned the force 155 degrees from Dondra Head [Ceylon], 360 miles, the distance from Addu Atoll being 85 degrees 600 miles. There was no indication as to the composition of the force.[22]

Frustrated that he had "been had" by the Japanese, Somerville's immediate options for an interception by the Eastern Fleet were severely limited, given that refueling from the few available oilers at Addu was far from complete.[23] At 0015 hours the following morning, Force A eventually departed and set course for a position 250 miles south of Ceylon, with Force B to follow some hours later. Realizing that an interception could not be effected until the morning of 6 April at the earliest, Somerville signaled his two heavy cruisers *Cornwall* and *Dorsetshire* to rendezvous with the remainder of Force A at the chosen position, both ships having remained at Colombo when the fleet originally deployed on 30 March.[24]

Unfortunately for the Eastern Fleet, the Catalina, which had made the first contact, was downed by Zekes before a more detailed report of the enemy force's composition could be transmitted. By 0710 hours, further sightings from other Catalinas provided Somerville with a partial picture of his opponent's strength: two battleships, two cruisers, and some four destroyers located approximately 110 miles south of Ceylon.[25] Forty-five minutes beforehand, however, news from Colombo had added a new dimension to the enemy threat. At 0625 hours the first of 125 Japanese aircraft led by Commander Fuchida Mitsuo began to appear in the skies over Colombo—approximately seventy-five Vals and Kates, with fifty Zekes flying top cover. The Zekes commenced proceedings by surprising and quickly shooting down a number of *Hermes'* Swordfish that had earlier departed Colombo en route to Trincomalee.[26] To the undoubted annoyance of the Japanese flyers, Colombo harbor was almost entirely bare of warships and merchant shipping, so they set about flattening dock facilities as well as targeting the few ships that were present. The British destroyer *Tenedos* was sunk, an armed merchant cruiser set afire, and a submarine depot ship slightly damaged. And for the first time, Nagumo's aircrews found themselves opposed by a powerful, coordinated defending fighter force: over thirty Hurricanes and six Fulmars from the surrounding RAF airfields intercepted the Japanese formations. In the melee that followed, nineteen British aircraft were lost against seven Japanese, six of the latter being dive bombers, before the Japanese squadrons began returning to their parent aircraft carriers.[27]

Any lingering disappointment among Nagumo's aviators over the absence of shipping at Colombo was to be quickly dispelled. As Kido Butai carriers were recovering aircraft, a signal from a reconnaissance floatplane revealed two British warships approximately two hundred miles southwest of Colombo: the *Cornwall* and *Dorsetshire,* which had left Colombo the previous day in order to rejoin Force A. Nagumo dispatched a force of eighty Vals under Lieutenant Commander Takahashi Egusa, which was detected on *Indomitable*'s radar at 1344 hours some eighty miles from Force A.[28] At 1400 hours the Vals spotted the British cruisers and commenced their attacks. Desperate maneuvering by *Cornwall* and *Dorsetshire* proved ineffectual against the fusillade of Japanese bombs; within just fifteen minutes both of the thoroughly pummeled cruisers had been sent to the bottom. Postwar estimates indicate the bombing accuracy achieved lay in the 85–92 percent range—the highest rate achieved in a single air-naval strike at sea throughout World War II.[29] Subsequent British rescue efforts saved two-thirds of the sunken ships' crews, a total of over 1,120 officers and men. This attack had taken place while Somerville was again attempting to position his ships for a night sortie with a Japanese force, which his most recent reconnaissance reports placed east-northeast at a range of 120 miles. Yet Somerville still possessed no clear picture of the composition of the enemy formation he was attempting to intercept.

At 1700 hours that afternoon, Somerville received a further report from Colombo that enemy aircraft carriers were operating in the area, steaming a southwesterly course. From this information he deduced the Japanese were proceeding to attack Addu Atoll and decided to steam south and rendezvous with Force B "so that Forces A and B could close for supporting action at daylight the following morning (6 April)."[30] A further report at 1817 hours indicated the presence of at least two enemy aircraft carriers and several other unknown vessels, however their course was now to the northwest. The admiral altered his course so that Force A would still be in a position to launch a night air attack if required, while maintaining his determination to engage the Japanese the following morning. What Somerville did not realize, however, was that Nagumo had reversed course to the southeast, proceeding in a wide southward arc to approach Trincomalee from the southeast.[31] Adding to the British admiral's difficulties in obtaining accurate information were two shadowing Albacores having been shot down by Zekes just before dusk, again before they could transmit updated reports. No further sighting reports were received that evening, nor during the following morning. At 1400 hours on 6 April, Somerville received a further signal from Ceylon, "a strong Japanese fleet was still somewhere between Addu Atoll and Colombo," so he decided not to return to Addu until the following day at the earliest.[32]

Farther to the north, another series of alarming events were unfolding in the Bay of Bengal. Having departed the Andaman Islands on 1 April, Vice Admiral Ozawa's Second Expeditionary Fleet had divided into three groups. Northern Force—two heavy cruisers and a single destroyer—operated in the vicinity of Calcutta, while the identically comprised Southern Force sought out targets near Cocanada. Central Force, containing *Ryujo*, one heavy cruiser, one light cruiser, and two destroyers, cruised the waters off Vizagapatam.[33] With the Eastern Fleet engaged to the south, no protection whatsoever existed for Allied merchant shipping in the general vicinity of these three groups. Ozawa's ships, submarines, and aircraft were picking off numerous defenseless transports with frightening efficiency, aided by reconnaissance by long-range flying boats based in the Andamans. On the morning of 6 April, *Ryujo's* aircraft descended upon Vizagapatam and Cocanada. Though inflicting little material damage, these nuisance raids along the eastern Indian coast-line fueled panic among the local inhabitants, raising the menace of possible Japanese landings.[34] General Sir Archibald Wavell, recently reinstalled as British commander in chief India, informed Churchill that this "was India's most dangerous hour; our Eastern Fleet was powerless to protect Ceylon or Eastern India; our air strength was negligible." Wavell's summation of the situation was that these raids could be the prelude to what he regarded as the most probable threat: an aeroamphibious invasion of eastern India with ground support from Japanese divisions in Burma.[35]

As Ozawa's rampage in the Bay of Bengal was reaching its crescendo, the Eastern Fleet continued steaming south to Addu. Still believing that the Japanese would attack the atoll base, Somerville as yet had not attempted to return there and refuel, and the sighting of two Japanese submarines to the south of his position on 7 April caused him to further postpone the fleet's arrival. With no further reports from his reconnaissance aircraft of Japanese surface activity, Somerville's warships entered Addu from the western entrance at 1100 hours the following day.[36] While the ships were being refueled, the admiral conferred with his subordinates as to the next course of action. He subsequently determined that Force B should steam to Kilindini (a port harbor in Kenya) and Force A proceed to Bombay. This strategy complied with instructions he received later that day from the Admiralty that the Eastern Fleet avoid returning to Colombo. Winston Churchill subsequently endorsed the withdrawal of the Eastern Fleet in the face of the threat it confronted:

> The experiences of the last few days had left no doubt in anyone's mind that for the time being Admiral Somerville did not have the strength to fight a general action. Japanese success in naval

air warfare were [*sic*] formidable. In the Gulf of Siam two of our first-class capital ships had been sunk in a few minutes by torpedo aircraft [referring to the loss of the battleship *Prince of Wales* and the battle cruiser *Repulse* off Kuantan, Malaya, on 10 December 1941]. Now two important cruisers had also perished by a totally different method of air attack—the dive-bomber. Nothing like this has been seen in the Mediterranean in all our conflicts with the German and Italian Air Forces. For the Eastern Fleet to remain near Ceylon would be courting a major disaster.[37]

Both Force A and Force B steamed from Addu in the early hours of 9 April 1942 and eventually reached their destinations without further incident. This, however, did not signal the conclusion of Operation C. Having doubled back on his tracks following the sinking of the *Cornwall* and *Dorsetshire*, and having thus far failed to locate the bulk of the Eastern Fleet via aerial reconnaissance, Nagumo turned his attention to Trincomalee. At first light on 9 April, approximately thirty Kates with Zeke fighter cover struck the anchorage and the adjacent RAF airfield at China Bay. Once again the anchorage was virtually deserted, so the Kates concentrated their attacks against base facilities, oil storage tanks, and aircraft on the ground, while the Zekes and a mix of Hurricanes and Fulmars fought it out above.[38] Damage inflicted against ground targets proved to be minimal, with three Kates and a Zeke being shot down and the British losing eleven fighters. It was now the RAF's turn to inflict an unpleasant surprise on the Kido Butai. Following the Trincomalee raid, nine Bristol Blenheim light bombers succeeded in catching the Japanese ships almost entirely unawares, with several bombs falling in the near vicinity of *Akagi*. Nagumo's combat air patrol responded with a vigorous pursuit, shooting down five bombers but losing four Zekes.[39] The strike by the RAF Blenheims was the first time the Kido Butai had been subjected to an enemy attack during the course of its five-month, two-ocean offensive.

Yet in spite of the lack of naval targets at Trincomalee, the Japanese were not going to be departing the scene empty-handed. Following a sighting of Nagumo's ships by a snooping Catalina the previous day, the light carrier *Hermes*, previously detached from Admiral Willis' Force B, with two escorts and eight fleet auxiliaries, had vacated China Bay that evening and commenced steaming southwest. Sighted just after dawn some fifty miles south of Trincomalee, the British ships duly attracted the attention of eighty Vals and from 0700 hours came under sustained attack. *Hermes* possessed no fighters and within thirty minutes she had been sunk, along with the Australian destroyer *Vampire*, the sloop *Hollyhock*, and two oil tankers. As had been the case in the sinking of Somerville's two cruisers on 5 April, the dive-bombing attacks were again executed with near perfect accuracy.[40] Okumiya Masatake summed up the sense of achievement evidently felt by the Japanese aircrews following the conclusion of the *Hermes* airstrike: "Our planes were establishing new records and changing the accepted concept of sea-air warfare. At Pearl Harbour a limited number of fighters from this same fleet broke the back of American battleship power; off Malaya for the first time in history our planes sank enemy battleships without the aid of surface vessels; and today, for the first time, our aircraft without the support of surface vessels had sent a carrier to the bottom."[41]

Once all Japanese aircraft had alighted, the Kido Butai altered course to the northeast and steamed away, first to Singapore and then on to Japan itself. Admiral Ozawa's Second Expeditionary Fleet likewise retired, having sunk twenty-nine merchant ships—approximately 150,000 tons in total displacement.[42] The trail of wreckage left by Operation C was immense: one aircraft carrier, two heavy cruisers, three destroyers, two fleet auxiliaries, and twenty-nine steamers sunk and over thirty British aircraft shot down or destroyed on the ground, at the loss of eighteen Japanese aircraft in total. Allied shipping in the Bay of Bengal had been paralyzed and would remain so for several months to come, the vital port of Chittagong rendered vacant as a result; this development contributed to a subsequent 1943 famine that would sweep Bangladesh and claim at least 100,000 lives.[43] The eventual withdrawal of the entire Eastern Fleet to African ports left Ceylon, India, and the western portion of Australia almost entirely at the mercy of the Japanese, should they seek to further expand the western and southern boundaries of their newly acquired empire. The Royal Navy had been expelled by force from the Far East and would not return there again in force until the early months of 1944. By then the strategic picture in the Indo-Pacific theater had changed completely. Following its crushing defeat at Midway and the punishing losses it suffered in the subsequent campaign of attrition in the Solomon Islands, the Imperial Japanese Navy teetered upon a stay of execution. By December 1944 the sentence had been carried out by the most destructive air-naval instrument of the prenuclear age, the U.S. Fifth Fleet. The newly formed British Pacific Fleet was destined to become but a portion of this massive armada during the final American push toward Japan and ultimate victory.

2

Scylla and Charybdis

The Policy Dimension, 1919–39

TWO DECADES BEFORE *HERMES* AND HER CONSORTS PERISHED beneath the swarms of plummeting Vals south of Trincomalee, Great Britain had only just begun to reacquaint herself with the ways of peace following the conclusion of World War I. Great Britain and the wider British Empire had achieved final victory in conjunction with her alliance partners, yet at a terrible cost in blood and treasure. In 1919 Britain stood poised to embrace the prospects for a lasting peace within a new international order, while simultaneously confronting the realities of growing economic impoverishment at home. For the Royal Navy, the years ahead had suddenly become uncertain. Abroad, there existed no credible military menace for the then-foreseeable future, and within three years the Admiralty would be forced to adjust its strategies and policies in order to adapt to the material consequences of multilateral naval disarmament. At home, the continuing maintenance of the world's largest fleet in a weakened domestic economic environment was to soon become impossible, especially given the collective war weariness of the British people and the need for effective social reform. In February 1922 the growing weakening of Britain's economy prompted Lord Balfour, the perennial denizen of cabinet committees, to remark that government was confronted with the choice "between Scylla and Charybdis."[1] Either national and imperial defense would both be inevitably compromised by substantial budget cutbacks, or political and social order would be impacted by possible civil unrest and the spread of extremism, should substantial budgetary steps not be taken in time to curb these potential threats.

For the duration of the 1919–39 interwar period, international naval disarmament and domestic fiscal restraint exercised the greatest influence over formulating British naval policy and, hence, the operational readiness of the Fleet for war in September 1939. The policies pursued by Whitehall and the Admiralty during the 1920s were to fundamentally weaken the Royal Navy by ultimately preventing the effective regeneration of its warship strength and—in concert with the Air Ministry and the RAF—to deny the Fleet Air Arm the opportunity to evolve beyond the level of a fleet-support instrument. With a successful conclusion to the Washington naval limitations negotiations in February 1922, successive British governments, prior to the mid-1930s, were provided with apparently sound justification to substantially reduce naval budget appropriation. In response, the Admiralty's policymaking swung between expansion and contraction: a bold push to reinvigorate the fleet, so as to secure the Far East against a supposed Japanese threat, being superseded in the late 1920s by a resigned retreat marked by steep internal cuts to vital programs, including the development of naval aviation. When Britain needed to pursue naval rearmament from 1936 onward, the neglected state of the Fleet and its supporting infrastructure rendered adequate restoration of its fighting capabilities impossible to achieve before hostilities with Germany commenced anew. Likewise, the need to strengthen the British Army and the RAF, both similarly savaged by interwar budget cuts, would further hinder the Admiralty's belated rebuilding endeavors, especially the priority production of modern carrier-borne aircraft.

An Overview of Government and Admiralty Policy Making, 1919–39

Rejecting the Admiralty's submission for a proposed £10 million addition to budget spending within the 1925–26 Navy Estimates, Winston Churchill succinctly described the major dilemma Britain's armed services confronted in the aftermath of World War I. He contended that large increases in defense expenditure could only be justified upon "the clearest evidence of mortal peril" to British national and imperial security.[2] In June 1919 Germany's High Seas Fleet had been scuttled by its crews at Scapa Flow to prevent its seizure as reparations at Versailles. Given the absence of any obvious European naval threat, the Royal Navy suddenly found itself in a vulnerable budgetary position. This was exacerbated in August 1919 when David Lloyd-George's Liberal-Conservative coalition government instituted the Treasury's Ten-Year Rule, requiring that future defense budgets be formulated on the basis that there would be no major war for a period of ten years.[3] However the hardest funding blows throughout 1919 were reserved for the Army and the RAF, the latter losing over four-fifths of its squadrons as well as being denuded of much of the infrastructure necessary to sustain RAF's existence. As early as January 1919 the secretary of state for Air, Lord Weir, had alerted the Cabinet to the dangers of over-rigorous demobilization; and in November the chief of the Air Staff, Sir Hugh Trenchard, sought Admiralty support for maintaining the RAF as an independent air arm.[4]

An uneasy truce between the services prevailed over the following twelve months as the Admiralty commenced formulating war plans for possible future conflicts involving Japan and the United States.[5] The Royal Navy's capital ship construction program continued apace, completing the 44,600-ton *Hood* on 5 March 1920, thus equipping the Fleet with the largest and fastest warship then in service. In January 1921, however, the Admiralty and the War Office determined to wrest control of the air weapon from the Air Ministry, setting in motion a protracted and bitter interservice feud. As subsequent memorandums from all sides began to ricochet within Whitehall, Lloyd-George's government referred the matter to the Committee for Imperial Defence (CID) for adjudication. Lord Balfour's Standing Defence Sub-Committee issued a preliminary ruling on 26 July 1921 that favored retention of the RAF, but it was stalled when overtaken by more pressing events.[6] In November 1921 Britain joined Japan, France, Italy, and the United States at the Washington Conference, which sought to negotiate a series of naval arms-limitation protocols. These efforts culminated in the signing of the Washington Naval Treaty in February 1922. This historical multilateral agreement succeeded in placing an agreed ratio limit upon capital ship numbers and imposing tonnage ceilings for all other warship classes. Additionally, the negotiated Four Power Treaty between Britain, France, Japan, and the United States on 10 December 1921 replaced the expired Anglo-Japanese Alliance. And from August 1921 the Geddes Committee on National Expenditure had proceeded to formulate a raft of wide-ranging budget cuts for all three British armed services.[7]

Though Geddes' recommendations were weakened by a subsequent Cabinet committee in February 1924, funding for the Naval Estimates had already declined by almost £25 million since 1920.[8] Nevertheless the Admiralty proceeded to form its principal strategic objective, namely the creation of a plan to confront the Japanese in the event of a future Far Eastern conflict. In June 1921 the government had given its preliminary consent to establish a major naval base at Singapore, and it had resolved to permit the expiry of the Anglo-Japanese Alliance within the same year.[9] The Singapore project received official sanction at the October 1923 Imperial Conference, though not without some reservations among Dominion representatives present. Previously, in February 1922, the Admiralty had recommenced its struggle with the Air Ministry over which service should control the future Fleet Air Arm. In March the Cabinet sent the whole question of interservice relations back to the ubiquitous Balfour; after further delays due to the fall of the Coalition government in October, a fresh inquiry in March 1923 eventually produced the Dual-Control system—both services sharing responsibility for the FAA.[10] Adding to the Admiralty's woes, Ramsay MacDonald's Labour government suspended work on the Singapore project, although this decision was rescinded after Stanley Baldwin's Conservatives took office in November 1924. And in early 1925 the Fleet's all-important reconstruction programs suffered a particularly serious blow when they came up for government consideration.

Following heated debate between the Admiralty and the Treasury over the substance of the 1925–26 Naval Estimates, Winston Churchill disallowed the Admiralty's submission, which advocated funding for new cruisers. This rejection of a key component of the Fleet's "tentative Ten-Year Plan," which also included a provision for the construction of four aircraft carriers, was the start of a severe decline in the Royal Navy's peacetime fortunes. Annual naval outlays fell from £60 million in 1925 to an interwar low of £50 million in 1932; following an abortive attempt to revive the cruiser issue in 1927, the Admiralty suspended its ten-year program.[11] After Admiral Lord Beatty's departure as First Sea Lord in 1927, his successors Sir Charles Madden (1927–30) and Sir Frederick Field (1930–33) implemented a series of stringent savings measures because of further economic deterioration. To prevent further erosion of the service's strategic position, Madden and Field both sought to preserve a first-line battle fleet at the expense of almost everything else, including the Fleet's carriers and the Fleet Air Arm.[12] The consequences of these economies were particularly severe: the procurement of fuel-oil reserves was cut in half and the deferment or cancellation of orders resulted in several prominent shipbuilding firms going belly-up. Further, in September 1931 a number of brief mutinies erupted in the Royal Navy, most notably at Invergordon after seamen and petty officers had initiated a strike over proposed pay scale cuts.[13]

With its budget reductions bottoming out in 1932, the Royal Navy reached a peacetime low point in overall war preparedness. However, as the international situation began to slowly decline from 1931 onward, momentum began to build within the recently installed National Government for a modest scale of rearmament, given the nature of rising military threats in both the Far East and Europe.[14] Following the Japanese Kwantung Army's forcible annexation of Manchuria in 1931, the emerging martial sentiment that had accompanied Adolf Hitler's complete seizure of executive power in Germany by August 1934 was to trigger a gradual pattern of foreign expansionism on the part of the European Axis powers. And with this escalation in international tensions, both the Washington Treaty (which had been extended at the 1930 London Conference) and the ongoing Geneva arms negotiations began to collapse. The National Government—despite endeavors to defer general rearmament for as long as possible and an attempt to regulate Kriegsmarine expansion through negotiation of the 1935 Anglo-German naval accord—at last commenced a series of programs in 1936 to reinvigorate the Royal Navy and the Fleet Air Arm.[15] Despite such measures, the combination of foreign appeasement and the urgent need to reconstruct a mothballed armaments industry meant the Royal Navy would eventually confront the dual menace of the modern Kriegsmarine and the Regia Marina in an alarmingly undermodernized condition. And as war beckoned in Europe, the roadsteads at the recently completed Singapore naval base remained an expansive patchwork of empty moorings.

"The trewe processe of Englyshe polycye"[16] 1919–29

Three concurrent factors made the 1920s a unique first in forming policies for defense of the realm: a mechanism for resolving international disputes (the League of Nations), a multilateral naval arms–limitation accord (the Washington Treaty), and the need to finance three peacetime armed services. As of 1919 the Royal Navy easily eclipsed its foreign contemporaries in terms of size and strength; however, from December 1929 its operational capabilities had begun to decline as the then–Labour coalition government sought to achieve adequate national and imperial security at the lowest possible cost.[17] Given the widespread demands on government financing, especially when the British economy remained weakened in the aftermath of World War I, deterioration of Fleet operational capabilities was almost inevitable. The gradual estrangement between government and the Admiralty arose from two incompatible policy postures. Regardless of their differing political philosophies, a succession of coalition governments embraced a pragmatic approach to defense expenditure; in the words of Lord Weir, they attempted to balance "how much *should* the country spend ... and how much the country *can* spend."[18] In response, the Sea Lords articulated a vision of the future that evoked even the remotest of foreseeable threats to justify continuing a large-scale warship-building program and, thereafter, seeking massive investment in Empire defenses in Far Eastern waters.

Although there had been periods of economic downturn within the lengthy peace before August 1914, from 1919 onward the postwar environment challenged more than ever before the Admiralty's task of maintaining the strength of the steam-powered Royal Navy. In the postwar era, with extension of the vote and emergence of the Labour Party, Britain's political landscape experienced a profound transformation. Successive coalition governments were confronted with an unsettled economic outlook: 30 percent of annual government expenditure became earmarked for repayment of Britain's accumulated war debt. Organized labor had become a source of growing social, economic, and political power as exhibited in the 1926 General Strike, whereas the fear of Bolshevist expansion generated growing alarm within the nation's elites.[19] By the middle of the decade legislative agitation grew louder for increased spending on social reform because the nation's economic situation began to further decay; at the same time there was growing Dominion pressure abroad for increased autonomy within the Empire. Within this environment, large-scale defense spending without a clear and present danger would, as Churchill alluded to in January 1925, run the risk of incurring the wrath of the British voter/taxpayer whose already heavy pecuniary burden could not be relaxed if such a course were undertaken.[20] Yet at the same time, such intangibles as national pride and imperial prestige could not be readily ignored by British governments, even if the monetary cost of symbolism became inordinately high.

For the denizens of Whitehall, their deliberations about future national and imperial defenses now included the RAF—the source of a potential leap forward in industrialized warfare—a fact that had yet to be adequately appreciated by its senior service partners.[21] Within a political, economic, and social atmosphere that increasingly embraced collective security and antimilitarism, the respective services had three clear choices for their future policy pathways: They could circle their wagons and present a united front to whatever budgetary onslaught assailed them, follow their political masters' lead and form loose coalitions to ensure the survival of the fittest, or opt for unilateralism and thereby seek to defend their individual fiefdoms from all comers. Yet to choose anything less than a unified standpoint invited nearly certain interservice conflict. Such conflict would inevitably weaken the military's bargaining position—they would be fighting each other as well as the "Treasury Myrmidons" Admiral Beatty so heartily detested.[22] And as John Ferris in particular has noted, the Admiralty capacity to meet ongoing Fleet needs resided in maintaining a finely-tuned partnership with Britain's shipyards, including retaining the latter's skilled workforce. For such had become the interdependence of both entities under the flamboyant Admiral Fisher: throughout the decade preceding August 1914, the Royal Navy and its key industry partners found themselves enmeshed within a self-perpetuating phenomenon similar to what President Eisenhower would one day describe as the military-industrial complex.[23]

From its signing in February 1922, the Washington Treaty became the most pervasive external influence upon the Fleet's operational capacities throughout the following two decades. Of the five participating naval powers, the greatest burden undoubtedly fell on Britain because of the sheer geographic scope of its naval commitments. Yet there can be no logical argument that Britain had any choice other than to sign away its existing two-power maritime advantage because to continue an immediate postwar naval arms race would have been an open invitation for national financial suicide. In 1915 the 31,100-ton super dreadnought *Queen Elizabeth* had cost £2,473,103 on completion; by 1928 this figure was only half a million pounds shy of the final price tag for the 9,750-ton cruiser *Cumberland*. Given that the battle cruiser *Hood* would cost £5,698,946 in 1920, cancellation of three additional ships in her class together with four proposed battleships represented a notable act of political common sense.[24] In terms of capital ships alone, such an undertaking would have presented considerable difficulties within a relatively healthy financial environment, to say nothing of one in which Britain had just lost 6.3 percent of 15-to-40-year-old males, together with 25 percent of its total national assets.[25] Even in the absence of a treaty regime limiting naval armaments, a repeat of the enormous investment in new capital ships after the building of *Dreadnought* in 1906 was clearly out of the question given the onerous economic and social pressures Britain now faced.

With the British fleet reduced in strength and sharing parity with its American counterpart, the decision reached at Washington on 10 December 1921 to enact a Four Power Treaty ended Britain's 1902 alliance with Japan and, with it, imposed the potential burden of a large Royal Navy presence in the Far East should the Japanese become hostile. As historians such as N. H. Gibbs have identified, relinquishment of the Anglo-Japanese Alliance became a landmark in the development of British defense policy; Whitehall no longer possessed the firm alliance relationship that previously gave the Royal Navy leeway to deploy the majority of its assets in European waters.[26] By contrast, the stated objectives of the Four Power Treaty that replaced the Alliance were vague, no firm actions beyond mutual consultation were prescribed in the event of a dispute between the signatories or involving a third-party aggressor. In response, however, the Admiralty intensified efforts to have a government commitment to a substantial Far Eastern naval presence by increasing its budget estimates and formulating specifications for a naval base at Singapore. However, as the Japanese displayed no apparent signs of hostility toward the British Empire and an international naval disarmament regime had been recently implemented, the Sea Lords found themselves upon uncertain ground when debate commenced over the 1925–26 Naval Estimates.

Rejection of the Royal Navy's proposed cruiser program by Prime Minister Baldwin's cabinet in 1925 marked a major schism between the Admiralty and the Exchequer, and much of the blame for this can be attributed to the Admiralty. In attempting to convince legislators of the credibility of the Admiralty's planning, Admiral Beatty had sought to employ the time-honored tactic of a scare campaign to gain public and political support. However, the Sea Lords were negotiating from a position of weakness: whereas Admiral Fisher could point to the proximity of Germany as a naval threat and posit growth in German heavy industrial output to support his successful lobbying for new *Dreadnought*-class battleships, Beatty enjoyed no such luxury. Unlike Fisher, Beatty was operating within a regulated environment on two fronts—Washington and the domestic application of the fiscal Ten-Year Rule. His comment that "in time of peace we have no friends and no influential party supporters" should be viewed as somewhat disingenuous, for the

Admiralty's own campaign to wrest total control over naval aviation cost the service a raft of Cabinet support as early as 1922.[27] And no tangible evidence had been uncovered by the Foreign Office as late as 1929 to suggest any imminent threat of military aggression from Tokyo. Indeed up until 1926 the Admiralty was still conducting an active officer exchange program with the Japanese, while simultaneously providing valuable technical information for Japan's naval designers and shipbuilders.[28]

In January 1925 Winston Churchill concluded that the Admiralty's desire since 1921 to construct a state-of-the-art naval base at Singapore represented "a peg on which to hang the whole vast scheme of scientific naval control of Japan."[29] Regarding the establishment of the facility itself, the MacDonald Labour government decision to suspend the project in 1924 should be regarded as a sensible initiative for two reasons. First, as a number of post-war histories have pointed out, the location chosen was entirely unsuitable for its effective defense; with the bulk of Sumatra to the immediate south, Singapore could only be accessed through the Strait of Malacca or the narrow waters that abutted the Java Sea to the southeast.[30] Were the Japanese able to achieve local naval or air superiority over these access routes, Singapore would be exposed to a geographical fate similar to that visited upon France's Indo-Chinese citadel at Dien Bien Phu in 1954. Second, the Royal Navy would be deprived of an effective forward base because under Washington Treaty terms, Hong Kong had been classified as geographically offensive and therefore unable to be fortified. In the absence of this forward shield, Singapore's defense could only be guaranteed by either the permanent presence of a powerful naval squadron or by the timely disposition of a mobile fleet to the Far East at the outset of hostilities (as previously hypothesized by the 1879 Carnarvon Commission), if the strategic situation permitted the latter course to be undertaken.[31]

Following Sir Hugh Clifford's attendance at a ceremony to inaugurate the new floating dock at the Singapore base in 1929, the Straits Settlement's governor expressed some doubts as to whether he had attended "a christening or a funeral."[32] Given the course of what became known as the Singapore strategy throughout the 1920s, the Admiralty provided the coffin and Stanley Baldwin's Conservative coalition supplied the nails by overturning their predecessors' decision to suspend construction. The principal rationale Lloyd-George's cabinet had accepted from the Jellicoe Committee in granting initial permission for base construction in June 1921 had been that Singapore "not only covered the main entrance to the Indian Ocean from the eastward but flanked the route from Eastern Asia to Australasia, and was of very great importance to the Dominions."[33] By rejecting alternative options such as Ceylon, which possessed a much healthier defensive outlook, both parties undoubtedly compromised future naval operations in the Far East, though it should be likewise acknowledged that planners of the early 1920s could not have foreseen the extent to which airplane capabilities had evolved by December 1941. Yet for the Admiralty, Singapore always represented but part of its wider scheme through which the government would be compelled to fund large-scale modernization programs to meet the supposed Japanese naval threat. As events transpired, however, construction of the base itself would be the only substantial element of the plan realized.

Had the Royal Navy been capable of deploying a credible naval presence to Singapore's roadsteads, where were the British seeking to engage the Japanese at sea? Postwar histories have devoted considerable attention to the Admiralty's campaign for increased expenditure within the parameters of Washington, but less about what precise strategic means the Royal Navy would seek to confront Japan east of Singapore itself. Christopher Bell has addressed this issue, exploring the thoughts of noted British naval strategist Admiral Sir Herbert Richmond and teasing out the Admiralty's inordinate ambition to either impose a general economic blockade in the Asia-Pacific region or wage war in the vicinity of the Japanese mainland. In either instance as Richmond later conceded, success could not be assured in the wake of the negotiated limitations to both warships and base defenses. Despite navy planners contemplating such a course as late as 1929, the Admiralty undoubtedly would have risked the prospect of another Tsushima, had the Royal Navy attempted to deploy its largely obsolescent battle fleet in Japanese home waters.[34] Singapore's only practicable use lay as a defensive shield against possible Japanese incursion into the South China Sea and the Indonesian Archipelago. The greatest failing of the Singapore strategy in the 1920s was, however, its inability to solidify the case for new warship construction in its role as the "peg," as Churchill defined it.

Admiral Beatty and his colleagues, in unsuccessfully pursuing their objectives in the 1925–26 Naval Estimates, had been unable to circumvent the requirements of the Ten-Year Rule. Prior to repeal in 1932, this policy had been necessary to curb general defense expenditure, especially given the then-existing political, economic, and social issues British governments faced.

Yet the pursuit of the Ten-Year Rule was not without substantial risk. The greatest detriment undoubtedly lay in the probability that substantial cuts to the nation's current naval capabilities would leave the Fleet in a precarious strategic position if war arrived before adequate rehabilitation of its operational readiness. A firm majority of historical opinion has placed the domestic responsibility for this situation at the feet of successive cabinets' ambulatory interpretation of the Ten-Year Rule from 1925 onward, which deprived the Royal Navy of the opportunity to effectively address this mounting conundrum.[35] There is considerable merit in this conclusion, particularly in terms of the interwar composition of the service's carrier force. The disallowance of large-scale rejuvenation projects in the 1925–26 Naval Estimates meant no scheduled replacement of the Fleet's three oldest, slowest, and least-efficient aircraft carriers, *Argus*, *Hermes*, and *Eagle*, which together constituted 50 percent of the available contingent.[36] By failing to replace these ships, half of the Admiralty carriers would be unfit for service should war break out before new vessels were constructed. It should be recalled, however, that the Admiralty itself had given priority to replenishment of the Fleet's cruiser assets over the need to reconstruct its aircraft-carrier arm.

While the evolution of Royal Navy aircraft-carrier capabilities became frustrated by the combination of government cutbacks and Admiralty prioritization, the subdivision of authority over the Fleet Air Arm was a dereliction of common sense from the outset. A brief outline of the chosen Dual-Control regime provides some idea of the jumble that cabinet committee processes had imposed on development of the future Fleet Air Arm as of November 1923. Whereas the Admiralty had responsibility for funding, operational specifications, and tactical control of its carrier-borne aircraft, the RAF maintained jurisdiction over flight training, technical development, and supply of the airplanes themselves. Prolonged adjudication of the manning issue resulted in the Air Staff agreeing to supply not less than 30 percent of the pilots, with the Navy providing all observers, with participating officers being seconded to the RAF.[37] Formulation of this model demonstrated government willingness to maintain separate service ministries with no singular coordinating instrument, thereby sustaining an environment in which interservice friction could fester at both political and organizational levels. By rebuffing establishment of an independent MOD (Ministry of Defence), as recommended by the Geddes Committee as early as 1921, the issue had become mired in an exhaustive and often devisive committee process at the expense of a decisive political intervention to resolve the impasse.[38] The formal establishment of the Fleet Air Arm took place in April 1924, but this did not deter the Admiralty from continuing to pursue its campaign to evict the Air Ministry from its shared control of naval aviation.

For their part, during the 1920s the Air Ministry and the RAF sought to prioritize building the vital logistical and educational foundations of Lord Trenchard's "good cottage on the foundations of a castle," but in the process the service invested too little in the technological evolution of the airplane itself.[39] This latter mistake provided the foundation for a dangerous development gap during the 1930s in naval aviation between the British and their overseas competitors, as will be extensively addressed in chapter three. Additionally, Lord Trenchard's pursuit of a no-specialization policy, which emphasized his belief that aircraft use in naval operations produced challenges similar to those of other combat-flying environments, should be recognized as highly significant in two respects.[40] As shall become apparent in the forthcoming chapters, the "one size fits all" design parameters for both land-based and carrier-borne aircraft did not allow for the necessary differences in developing machines appropriately suited for shipboard service. In a similar vein the RAF's failure to propagate a competent shore-based antishipping capability before September 1939 largely denied the Admiralty the crucial assistance of effective land-based air support throughout the first three years of the war.[41] A more far-reaching handicap for the Fleet Air Arm rose out of the determination of both Whitehall and the Air Staff from the mid-1930s onward: to establish RAF Bomber Command as a potent air-strike force to serve as an effective strategic deterrent to the supposed growing power of Hitler's Luftwaffe.

Thus within the decade of peace prior to 1930, government and armed-service policies had been implemented that would seriously corrode Royal Navy operational capabilities and its air arm by the outbreak of hostilities. The Washington Treaty had stripped Britain of her numerical naval superiority and the strategic benefits of the Anglo-Japanese Alliance. Worst of all for the Admiralty, in the absence of a tangible overseas threat Washington strengthened justification for British governments in the 1920s to cut naval budget expenditure. Commencing with the 1925–26 Naval Estimates, these cuts became ever deeper, even though the construction of the new naval base at Singapore had begun. From November 1923, government policy supported the concept of Dual-Control between the Navy and the RAF as the preferred means to develop the fledgling Fleet Air Arm. Admiralty attempts to secure extra funding by emphasizing the danger posed by Japan had backfired, and by 1929 the senior service was struggling to maintain even its most prized assets—the Fleet's capital ships. Although the RAF had made a promising start in terms of infrastructure development, a lack of investment in aircraft technology and no specialized approach toward the particular design requirements for shipboard aircraft were to haunt the FAA for over a decade. So as the 1930s arrived, and tensions within both Europe and the Far East began to bubble anew, Britain's premier fighting service was increasingly but a watery shadow of its former might and power.

1930–39

Addressing the House of Commons on 3 March 1936, Prime Minister Stanley Baldwin warned of the emerging international crises in the mid-1930s, "taking risks for peace has not removed the dangers of war."[42] And for some time a similar message would follow before Adolf Hitler's troops marched down the streets of Prague in March 1939. On 25 February 1936 Baldwin's National Government had authorized a naval expansion program that included seven new battleships, four aircraft carriers, and five cruisers as well as numerous destroyers and submarines. Referring to the progress of rearmament a year later, Minister for Defence Co-Ordination Sir Thomas Inskip advised his cabinet colleagues that while construction of new vessels remained on schedule, the urgent modernization of seven existing battleships would be delayed because of the need to substantially accelerate naval armaments production.[43] Unlike in Germany and Japan, in most Western economies the Great Depression had left armaments manufacture in a fragile state, especially in Britain where severe defense cutbacks were enforced during the early 1930s. For while government sought to negotiate a centrist path during a period of profound social misery, in which the peripheries of party-political expression enjoyed growing public appeal, the Royal Navy's operational readiness declined alarmingly. Simultaneously potential foes in the Atlantic and the Mediterranean began to evoke increasing concern at the expense of the Far East. The risks being taken for peace were very real indeed.

Throughout the 1930s Britain's naval fortunes proceeded through two distinct phases. From 1930 to 1933, government and armed-service policy makers alike continued their scorched-earth campaigns to enforce economies, driving the Royal Navy to the verge of inactivity. As economic circumstances began to ease in 1934, the second phase emerged. National Government support for collective security and arms limitation held firm for as long as such objectives were, in its judgment, feasible; yet it also took increasing steps to bolster the position of the military and the industries it relied on. This route was not without political risk—popular support for collective security and disarmament still existed within the electorate; in 1934 the government lost a series of by-elections to "Peace-Ballot" candidates.[44] Support of the military and supporting industries entailed a serious dilemma: the phased upgrading of industrial output, Stop-Go, would leave the armed forces short of high combat readiness were war to break out before production reached full capacity. Yet in adopting Stop-Go, the National Government was, in essence, conceding that its fiscal cutbacks since 1927 had run down many British defense industries so severely that some had to be reassembled almost from scratch. Add to this the further restrictions imposed by the London Naval Conference, April 1930, on cruiser numbers and cruiser tonnage rations, and it is not difficult to appreciate how onerous a task the eventual rejuvenation of the Fleet became.[45]

Table 1—The World's Principal Fleets in 1930

Type	BRITAIN	USA	JAPAN	FRANCE	ITALY	GERMANY
Battleships	16	18	6	6	4	–
Battle Cruisers	4	–	4	–	–	–
Pocket Battleships	–	–	–	–	–	(1)*
Aircraft Carriers	6	3	3 (+1)*	1	–	–
Heavy Cruisers	20 (+3)*	5 (+5)*	8 (+4)*	6	2 (+4)*	–
Light Cruisers	40	10	21	9	6 (+5)*	6 (+1)*
Destroyers	146 (+10)*	230	120	70 (+10)*	75 (+15)*	25
Submarines	50 (+10)*	100 (+6)*	60 (+10)*	60 (+35)*	65 (+10)*	–

* (building)
Source: G. Bennett, *Naval Battles of World War Two* (Barnsley: Pen & Sword, 2003), 27.

Based upon the above figures, the Royal Navy of 1930 remained a powerful force on paper at least. But as will be demonstrated in the data to follow, the vintage of its capital ships and aircraft carriers in particular was becoming a serious issue. In terms of maintaining both vital infrastructure and personnel, however, the situation had already become dire. From 1930 to 1933 the dramatic downsizing of the Fleet's logistical circumstances—cutting funds to increase fuel oil and ammunition reserves—severely compromised Britain's capacity to respond to any immediate naval crisis.[46] This outcome, along with unrest over proposed pay cuts that led to the disturbances at Invergordon and elsewhere in September 1931, amply demonstrated the perils present when austerity measures were imposed beyond practical limits. In terms of unrest, MI5 had made the Cabinet aware of possible Communist infiltration on the "lower deck," an outcome Whitehall was especially sensitive to—prior mutinies in German and Russian fleets had initiated popular revolutions.[47] The diminution of Fleet capabilities at this time could lead one to conclude that Royal Navy's capacity to operate in strength beyond the Atlantic could, at the very least, no longer be sensibly contemplated in the short term. For as Churchill had warned in February 1922, in the absence of adequate refueling and revictualing facilities to the east of Suez, "we cannot base a fleet capable of fighting Japan on Singapore." By 1931 the situation had become so serious that the chiefs of staff warned that both Singapore and Hong Kong would be captured well before the Fleet could arrive.[48]

Whereas the majority of the logistical shortages were to be alleviated by September 1939, possessing an essentially obsolete battle line became an impossible problem for the British to solve in the remaining years of peace. As Table 2 clearly demonstrates, Britain had fallen substantially behind both Japan and the United States in the reconstruction of commissioned capital ships. The 1930 London Naval Conference's extension of the Washington building holiday most severely impacted the Royal Navy, largely because the Admiralty had been so insistent since the late 1920s about maintaining as large an active battle fleet as possible.[49] With the onset of the Abyssinian Crisis in 1935 and the general heightening of military tensions in Europe thereafter, mass withdrawal of battleships and battle cruisers from operational service for overdue refits and reconstruction could no longer be sensibly contemplated. Without adequate antiaircraft protection, the Fleet's older capital ships were helpless in the face of air attack. The first months of war would emphatically prove Great War–standard anti-torpedo protection to be no match for modern

Table 2—Relative Ages of Existing First-Line Capital Ships as of September 1939

Years Commissioned	BRITAIN	USA	JAPAN	FRANCE	ITALY	GERMANY
1910–14	–	2	2	2	1	–
1915–19	12	6	6	3	3	–
1920–24	1	6	2	1*	–	–
1925–29	2	2*	2*	1*	–	–
1930–34	–	7*	–	1*	–	2
1935–39	3*	–	8*	2*	2*	3

* reconstruction

Source: "List of British and Foreign Ships," in H. G. Thursfield (ed.), *Brassey's Naval Annual* 1941 (BSY 1941) (London: William Clowes, 1941), 216–56.

torpedoes.[50] The operational endurance of most of the Admiralty's big ships had been diminished by a lack of major refits to propulsion systems. This meant that most of these vessels would have severe difficulty in reaching the Far East in good time when required to do so, further degrading future Royal Navy presence beyond the Atlantic and the Mediterranean.

It should be noted, however, that the major reconstructions of American and Japanese capital ships during the 1930s were largely confined to the upgrade of their defensive capabilities. With the exception of the three British battle cruisers and the four Japanese *Kongo*-class battle cruisers converted to fast battleships, the majority of the world's capital ships continued to plod along at speeds of twenty-five knots and under; limited differences remained in terms of main armament carried.[51] Unfortunately for the Admiralty, much of the British cruiser complement paid the price for London's decision to include light and heavy cruiser classes under the renegotiated building embargo. A higher percentage of the Fleet's cruisers had been constructed prior to 1930 than U.S., Japanese, and Italian cruisers; the British did not construct any new heavy cruisers during the 1930s (see Table 3). As early as 1927 the Exchequer had warned the Admiralty of the dangers of obsolescence if ships were built before they were required; this situation had come to pass through the combination of London and the Ten-Year Rule.[52] With a growing percentage of its cruisers verging obsolescence as war approached, the Royal Navy's global capabilities were compromised further: a significant portion of its light cruiser force lacked the endurance required for Far Eastern operations. As Table 3 illustrates, the Fleet's destroyer arm was the only class of warship that grew significantly during the 1930s, from 146 to 192 vessels in service in 1939.

Table 3—Non–Capital Ships in First-Line Service in 1930–39

Vessels 1930–39	BRITAIN	USA	JAPAN	FRANCE	ITALY	GERMANY
Aircraft Carriers	6–7	3–5	3–6	1–1	–	–
Heavy Cruisers	20–20	5–18	8–18	6–7	2–9	0–2
Light Cruisers	40–44	10–19	21–17	9–11	6–12	6–4
Destroyers	146–192	230–214	120–104	70–70	75–112	25–57
Submarines	50–59	100–95	60–57	60–78	65–104	0–57

Source: G. Bennett, *Naval Battles of World War Two*, 27, 35, 37.

In 31 January 1934 correspondence to Sir Phillip Sasson, undersecretary of the Air Ministry, the First Lord of the Admiralty Sir Bolton Eyres-Monsell expressed fears over the absence of a modern aircraft carrier in service with the Fleet: "In view of the present weakness of the Fleet Air Arm, I am firmly convinced that unless we lay down the carrier as part of the 1934 programme the fighting efficiency of the Fleet will be in serious danger. This is an Admiralty responsibility, and one which the Admiralty cannot fail to press."[53]

Eyres-Monsell got his wish; the addition of the *Ark Royal* to the Fleet in 1938 at last provided the Sea Lords with a powerful carrier that possessed roughly the same range of capabilities as its foreign contemporaries. Largely as a consequence of the Admiralty's decision to defer carrier development in order to maintain the operational presence of the capital ships, only the converted battle cruisers *Furious*, *Courageous*, and *Glorious* were otherwise capable of participating in a fast-moving engagement. The Admiralty's capacity to formulate a potent aerial spearhead was thus limited. By 1938 the British had lost their lead in the aircraft carrier race to Japan and the United States; both nations had succeeded in completing additional ships that were both faster and on average carried approximately 50 percent more aircraft than their British contemporaries.[54] The first of four new *Illustrious*-class fleet carriers would not be completed for the Royal Navy until May 1940, equipped with much smaller aircraft complements than compatible Japanese and American ships.

In spite of British leadership in the field of naval aviation at the conclusion of World War I, there was to be no *Dreadnought* moment in the course of the 1930s for the Fleet Air Arm. The effects of the RAF decision to prioritize infrastructure development ahead of aircraft technology were not immediately apparent during the 1920s because aviation science as a whole in this period remained a largely experimental exercise.[55] Prior to 1923, while the other British armed services attempted to seize control of the RAF, both the Admiralty and the War Office highlighted this fact, contending that aviation's future operational potential would be best served by remaining within their capable hands. New advances such as lightweight alloys and improved air engines were consistently generating evolutionary momentum, resulting in smaller numbers of aircraft in active service. During the early 1930s, the FAA was able to keep pace with the foreign competition when the first all-metal airplanes began to enter production.[56] From 1935 to 39, as the principal technological breakthrough in naval aircraft design took place—the introduction of all-metal monoplane types—the British began to fall behind both Japanese and American naval air arms. Whereas the Japanese possessed the advanced Type 96 ("Claude") monoplane naval fighter as early as 1935, the Fleet Air Arm's single-seat fighter program remained committed to the biplane concept.[57] These crucial developments in naval aviation, both in Britain and abroad, are explored in chapter three.

The persistent interservice brawling that initially threatened the future of the RAF itself—before turning to the question of control over the Fleet Air Arm—had abated somewhat in the latter half of the 1920s. Hostilities between the two services reignited in 1936, this time over the issue of manning ratios; and when the Admiralty obtained full control over the FAA the following year, a fundamental weakness of the Dual-Control system became evident. Because many trained maintenance personnel had chosen to return to the RAF, the Fleet's carriers were short by nearly a thousand skilled technicians. To make up these shortages, Dual-Control remained in practical effect until after the outbreak of war with Germany.[58] Operational capabilities of the Fleet Air Arm—once war had commenced—were to be initially compromised by the absence of vital ancillary support. Above and beyond the perils of Dual-Control, however, an initiative by the Air Staff and the National Government from 1934 onward was an even more serious impediment upon the FAA. Germany had pioneered strategic bombing during the previous war, and the prospect of Hitler pursuing the practice in the near future led to calls for a British deterrent bomber force. The 1936 formation of RAF Bomber Command produced serious side effects for production of other aircraft types because the bomber construction came to occupy the majority of Britain's prewar aircraft manufacturing base, imposing delays on procurement of modern fighter aircraft in particular.[59]

The construction of a strategic bombing capability by the RAF was to reap rewards in World War II; Bomber Command, in partnership with the U.S. 8th and 15th Army Air Forces, eventually succeeded in their wholesale demolition of the German war economy. On its own subsequent admission, however, Bomber Command was not properly equipped for strategic operations until May 1942 at the earliest.[60] The aircraft types from British production lines since 1935 were found unsuitable for the task; they suffered such heavy daylight casualties during the first year of conflict they were switched to night attacks, equipped with no means of locating targets with reasonable precision. However it is difficult to characterise the bomber-first policy as clearly negligent because the British, like every other major power, fervently believed that, in Stanley Baldwin's words, "the bomber would always get through."[61] Prior to 1936 the most significant military aviation advances arose through development of fast medium bomber designs. And until early 1939 when monoplane fighter designs began to enter service in sufficient numbers, the majority of monoplane bomber types outperformed the biplane fighters, which still predominated within the various national air arms.[62] By prioritizing bombers ahead of fighters, the British and their foreign counterparts were pursuing a concept of airpower that, like all other forms of military aviation, had yet to be conclusively tested in modern combat.

If significant blame is to be assigned, it lies in the failure of the government and the RAF to understand both the specific nature of the threat posed by the German Luftwaffe and the inherent structural weaknesses within Germany's Air Ministry. This subject is largely addressed in chapter three; it is sufficient to note here the Luftwaffe had discarded strategic bombing as a priority developmental stream in 1936, instead favoring assembly of a ground-support force that would form a key plank in the Blitzkrieg combined-arms offensive doctrine. Whitehall's advocacy for Bomber Command reflected a sharp rise in popular public support for a strong strategic deterrent, particularly in the wake of the horrors visited upon Shanghai and Guernica during 1937. Faced with the prospect of British cities meeting a similar fate, establishment of a deterrent striking force became a political necessity to both counter public anxiety and, if possible, assist in dissuading Hitler from initiating a European war.[63] Aside from impacting fighter production, the development of heavy bombers also diverted funding and factory resources away from strengthening the prewar RAF Coastal Command. With no effective land-based air support, the Royal Navy would be placed in grave danger if the Axis powers were able to establish persistent air superiority over vital coastal seaways and communications routes in the Atlantic and the Mediterranean as well as throughout the wider British Empire east of Suez.

East of Suez, no more vital need for adequate land-based air support existed than the defense of the newly constructed naval base at Singapore, finally completed in 1939. After a vicious fight in 1928 between the Admiralty—with War Office support—and the Air Ministry, the British government determined that the primary defense of Singapore Island would rest with heavy-caliber coastal artillery.[64] And from the 1930s onward, this meant Singapore might be forced to rely upon its Maginot-like defenses for a period of several months, should military circumstances elsewhere prevent rapid deployment of naval reinforcements to the Far East. Ever since the days of the base's initial conception, prominent voices within the Admiralty increasingly questioned Fleet capacity to respond en masse to any serious Japanese threat. In 1932 Admiral Richmond went so far as to describe those who would authorize this potential disposition as "less than fools." Yet at the outbreak of the European war, Whitehall had not abandoned its pledge to the Australian government that in the event of a crisis, the big ships would be sent within a period of seventy to ninety days.[65] But sending the big ships eastward without adequate shipboard air protection, to a destination bereft of sufficient fighters, bombers, and reconnaissance aircraft on its airfields, presented a proposition equally unattractive as no big ships at Singapore at all. The eventual fate of the battleship *Prince of Wales* and the battle cruiser *Repulse* off Malaya on 10 December 1941 became proof positive of this inherent danger.

An assessment of the impact of the Singapore strategy on Britain's naval situation throughout the interwar years may be advanced on financial grounds, though with important reservations attached. The Singapore base cost approximately £60 million upon completion in 1939. An amount that, if not spent on a suspect strategic investment, could have financed a refit of virtually all the Fleet's capital ships and most of its aircraft carriers, and also could have enhanced the Royal Navy's air arm and logistical reserves.[66] On balance, both Whitehall and the Admiralty can be reasonably admonished for continuing to allocate large sums of money for a base that could not be properly utilized because the very funds needed to refit the necessary ships were instead being expended on Singapore. However it must be recalled that within that interwar period, the £60 million in question would have been equally beneficial for naval defense expenditures, not to mention for absolutely pressing domestic social problems that had escalated dramatically from the outset of the Great Depression. What can be said for certain about the Singapore naval base is that its construction was founded almost entirely on a set of then-future strategic assumptions—known to be overly optimistic for almost a decade prior to the base's final completion.

For three of the world's naval Great Powers, 3 September 1939 was the date that the Washington peace became the Washington war. Limitations imposed on the Royal Navy by the Washington Treaty had been exacerbated at London in 1930 by further negotiated restrictions to naval armaments. Likewise the National Government's extension of fiscal restraint over defense spending until 1933 had reduced the Admiralty's war-fighting capabilities to a dangerously low level. There was too little time to fully prepare the Royal Navy for war once British rearmament had recommenced in earnest from 1936 onward. Like the decades of peace preceding August 1914, imperial defense came to dominate both government and Admiralty policy agendas before being superseded by the growing prospect of a major European conflict. Unlike the period 1864–1914, however, the Admiralty's use of a Far Eastern naval scare to secure funding for new warships fell on deaf ears. And the rise of European tensions effectively lowered the status of the Singapore naval base to that of an expensive white elephant. In terms of technological advancement, the Air Ministry and the RAF essentially followed a path similar to that adopted by the Admiralty prior to the 1889 Naval Defence Act: they placed severe impediments on development of the Fleet Air Arm as an advanced air weapon. And with strategic bombing coming to dominate the thought processes of both government and the RAF from the mid-1930s, the FAA's ability to keep pace with its foreign counterparts became an increasingly forlorn hope. Thus on the day the British government announced a state of war with Hitler's Germany, the hopes of nation and Empire at sea rested upon an arthritic fleet and an almost exclusive collection of octogenarian biplanes in the skies above.

These then were the underlying policies that had virtually brought British sea power to its knees as Germany, Italy, and Japan eyed forthcoming wars of conquest. There is a natural temptation to apportion blame, be it toward Britain's interwar governments for excessive cutbacks to defense expenditure, toward the armed services for the manner in which they chose to respond to a growing shortage of money, or toward the deadening blow inflicted on a global maritime empire by negotiated naval limitations. Yet it is perhaps Geoffrey Till's assessment—namely Britain's "whole predicament in defence" following World War I—that comes closest to the truth of the matter.[67] As Lord Balfour had intimated in 1922, the stark choice between defense and social interests would be equally perilous, and so it proved for both the Royal Navy and the Fleet Air Arm. British naval supremacy had been undoubtedly dealt a mortal blow in peacetime. The full effects of the wound, however, would remain shrouded until exposed to the only foolproof test for military weakness, the ultimate rigors of the wartime battlefield itself.

3

In the Outhouse

The Carrier-Borne Air Weapon and the Interwar Royal Navy

D URING ROUTINE EXERCISES IN 1928 A CERTAIN LIEUTENANT Cathcart-Jones proceeded to dive-bomb the battleship *Revenge*, the flagship of Britain's Mediterranean Fleet, with several rolls of toilet paper. In his study of the FAA, Geoffrey Till characterized this as a calculated prank that highlighted a slowly growing sense of frustration within the ranks of the FAA over the subordinate role assigned to naval aviation within the Royal Navy's existent tactical planning.[1] The reluctance of service leadership to fully develop the offensive value of carrier-borne aircraft, especially in the mid-1930s when the first monoplane types were entering service, did not come at an opportune time for British sea power. Thanks to what Admiral Sir David Beatty had described as the peculiar geographical situation of the British Empire, an underpowered Royal Navy would find itself thinly stretched if required to repel simultaneous threats across two hemispheres.[2] Given the aging capabilities of its big ships, any marked flaw in the Admiralty's tactical approach exposed the British to a magnitude of disaster similar to that inflicted upon Admiral Rojestvensky's luckless fleet at Tsushima in 1905. And as a direct consequence of its underdevelopment, the FAA did not possess the means to act as an independent striking force equipped with modern aircraft. Instead its primary role became that of a fleet-support instrument, and it remained so in April 1942, whereas the Japanese by choice, and the Americans through compulsion, had abandoned their previous adherence to this particular operational doctrine.

Our exploration of interwar British naval aviation, and its incorporation within the Royal Navy, spans three principal aspects. First, the technical evolution of the carrier-borne airplane and the aircraft carrier in Britain and abroad and development of the FAA as an organization prior to September 1939. Military historian Louis Casey's four defined "generations" of naval aircraft development, 1915–21, 1922–27, 1928–33, and 1934–39, provide the framework.[3] The second aspect is the integration of air weapon into the Royal Navy's prewar operational structure, with particular attention to airplane involvement in squadron and fleet combat tactics. The third aspect is the composition and fighting doctrines of Britain's Axis opponents in the European theater—the German Kriegsmarine and the Italian Regia Marina— together with a summary of available Allied naval assistance from both the French Marine Nationale and the various Dominion navies. In the course of this approach, three central questions are posed: (1) At what stage during the interwar years did the FAA fall astern of its overseas counterparts, and why? (2) What were the key strengths and weaknesses of the Fleet's integrated warfighting methods as formulated between the wars? (3) How serious a threat to the Royal Navy and its allies were the Germans and Italians at sea, especially given the nations' dissimilar means to seek to wage war, including their utilization of aircraft during naval operations?

Four Generations: The Naval Aviation Race from 1919

By the conclusion of World War I, which included the initial four years of Casey's first generation (1915–21), the British had successfully undertaken conversion of land-based aircraft designs for shipboard service, and likewise introduced the first flush-deck aircraft carrier designs. For its part the RNAS had led the way in the design of offensive naval aircraft, with types such as the Sopwith Cuckoo representing the blueprint for future biplane torpedo-bomber construction. The wartime adaptation of the first British fighters for service at sea proved equally valuable, with advanced types such as the Sopwith Pup and the Sopwith Camel making a smart transition to carrier-borne operations.[4] As a number of the postwar histories have sub-stantially documented, this period in the evolution of naval aviation was characterised by a broad range of methods in competing parties' approach to the best means of deploying the air weapon at sea. In confronting the challenge of operating aircraft from ships, conducting these activities came to include a range of shipboard catapults, "flying-off" platforms, and other ingenious contraptions.[5] Both the British and Japanese appreciated the advantages of a wholly flush-deck aircraft carrier for the launch and recovery of aircraft, temporarily gaining advantage over the Americans who persisted with testing alternative approaches for most of the early 1920s. Whereas the British and Japanese vessels *Hermes* and *Hosho* were specialist designs, the American *Langley* mirrored the earlier British carrier *Argus*, having been converted from an existing merchant ship.[6] In spite of these early advances, there can be no question the balance of power at sea still resided in concentrated employment of surface gunnery throughout the postwar portion of this particular generational phase.

The second generation (1922–27) saw formal establishment of the FAA on 1 April 1924 and the emergence of the first airplanes, in Britain and overseas, that were specifically conceived to meet the needs of aircraft carrier operations. The shift away from purely land-based design conversions resulted in improved structural reliability and more powerful air engines; larger aircraft could be operated with greater range and heavier payloads at sea. The FAA's fighter and torpedo-bomber types continued to parallel foreign contemporaries in performance and modest firepower. The British led the way in acquiring an experimental battlefield-orbiting spotting capability, which in a number of respects became the forerunner of the modern Airborne Warning and Control System (AWACS).[7] As the 1920s progressed, the three existing carrier powers were joined by France with its commissioning of the converted battleship *Bearn* in 1927; the British, Japanese, and Americans increased the size of their carrier fleets in accordance with the provisions of the Washington Treaty. By January 1928 the Royal Navy possessed five commissioned aircraft carriers whereas the Japanese and Americans each fielded three vessels, although Japan's *Akagi* and *Kaga* and America's *Lexington* and *Saratoga* were substantially larger than their British counterparts.[8] Alongside advances in the operational potential of carrier-borne aircraft and the increasing numbers of aircraft carriers in commission, practical employment of the air weapon in combat had already become a matter for vigorous debate within the ranks of the newly formed FAA.

This central issue essentially divided opinion among FAA ranks along service lines. Whereas naval flyers strongly supported using aircraft in a passive spotting/tactical coordination role, RAF personnel favored the offensive air strike option. From the developmental perspective, the favoritism afforded to the "gunnery lobby," as British naval historian Anthony Preston and others have described it, resulted in a significant effort by aircraft manufacturers to produce airplanes that were long-duration spotters such as the Avro Bison.[9] The importance of this trend lay in highlighting not only Admiralty's continuing commitment to surface engagement as the decisive means for achieving victory, but also the extent of the deep divisions that Dual-Control came to exercise. As an anonymous correspondent recorded in *Brassey's Naval Annual 1925*, spotting was strictly a naval gunnery problem "and as such should be carried out by naval officers under the sole direction of the Admiralty."[10] Within a decade, however, spotting would come to seriously impede development of the FAA's fighter arm in particular. Yet it would be substantially incorrect to interpret the Admiralty's attitude toward the operational application of naval aviation in the 1920s as merely an expression of pig-headedness. With the evolution of naval aircraft design still at a very early stage, an accurate assessment of its future possibilities was substantially beyond the reasonable comprehension of both British and overseas experts.[11]

From its outset, the Dual-Control arrangement gave every appearance of a classic shotgun marriage, and the division between the unhappy "newlyweds" requires some necessary social context so as to appreciate the deep-seated forces that gave rise to the professional animosities between them. Beyond the interservice rivalry, the available histories have identified a major cultural divide: the Admiralty's traditional centuries-old links with the British upper classes contrasted with Lord Trenchard's belief in merit-based egalitarianism.[12] Under the Dual-Control regime the requirement for dual-service membership became a considerable difficulty for naval pilot officers especially, as their promotional prospects within the Navy were under constant pressure by senior officers who were opposed to "the evils of Dual-Control." A significant pilot shortage resulted as early as 1927, exacerbated by the Admiralty's refusal to consider recruiting candidates from its lower-deck ranks—another example of the class-conscious attitudes that persisted within the post-1918 Royal Navy.[13] Clearly this situation was an impediment to establishing an elite cadre of pilots and aircrew—the potential adverse impacts on the organization's harmony and morale were considerable. Yet this tension should be viewed as a natural consequence of an imposed compromise that attempted to integrate two entirely different sets of traditions and practices, unlike the situation in Japan and America where both nations continued to retain separate army and naval air forces.[14]

During the waning 1920s, the air weapon's ongoing development gained considerable momentum with the commencement of the biplane's last great phase as undisputed arbiter of the skies. Within Casey's third generation (1927–34) a range of new lightweight alloys and uprated engines drove the biplane configuration to its flying performance limits; operational speeds of over 200 mph became commonplace among British, American, and Japanese carrier-borne fighters. Although the FAA's numbers had begun to fall behind its counterparts because of reduced funding and, with the Geneva disarmament negotiations unresolved, Whitehall's reluctance to authorize mass production, the British maintained their pace in the developmental race. A series of new designs including the Hawker Nimrod single-seat fighter, the Blackburn Ripon torpedo bomber, and the Fairey III spotter remained the equals of foreign counterparts, for widespread use of aluminum and tubular steel allowed for a larger external weapon capacity and heightened structural integrity.[15] Within the same period both the Royal Navy and the U.S. Navy largely discarded several alternative streams of aerial development, particularly in airship design. Several catastrophes on both sides of the Atlantic meant an unhappy end to the proposed use of large airships in maritime operations, thereby entrenching the aircraft carrier as the primary platform for naval air activities.[16] The respective navies still remained undecided as to precisely how the carrier would operate within a fleet setting in which surface firepower continued to be the primary offensive and defensive component.

Throughout this phase both the Royal Navy and the FAA continued to embrace the spotting-reconnaissance platform, an ongoing preoccupation that the operational structure of the FAA reflected. By 1932 the air arm consisted of twenty-seven carrier-borne flights (six to twelve aircraft per flight), nine flights equipped with fighters, seven with torpedo bombers, and eleven designated as Fleet Spotter-Reconnaissance.[17] And with the introduction of a new aircraft, the two-seater Hawker Osprey, Britain's naval air arm began to part ways with the other carrier powers in its attitudes toward the role of the fighter aircraft at sea. Although the British had closely studied the development of single-seat fighters in foreign navies, they turned to the multirole fighter-reconnaissance concept instead. Adoption of this developmental pathway should be regarded as a critical moment in the history of the FAA because the Admiralty was prepared to place such important emphasis on the navigational aspects of the two-seater fighter configuration. In 1935, however, the editor of *Flight* prophetically warned that multirole fighters "would be at a serious disadvantage if pitted against land-based air forces, because of the big loss of performance both in speed and range which the extra crew weight and equipment involves."[18] By 1935 this disadvantage already applied to sea-borne fighters—other carrier powers possessed single-seater biplanes easily capable of outperforming the modest Osprey in most combat situations, and the Japanese were introducing the first batch of their groundbreaking Type 96 Claude monoplane fighters.

Although the monoplane eventually superseded the biplane, that should be viewed as a natural consequence of a progressive science; the biplane had already emerged by the early 1930s as the weapon that could indeed change the face of naval warfare. While acknowledging the performance advantages in converting to monoplane types, Oliver Stewart noted that "the biplane was the type better suited to give the slow flying qualities and good control at low speeds which are essential for deck-flying operations."[19] The effectiveness of the biplane configuration should be regarded as considerable: it could inflict a sufficient level of damage on an opposing force to decisively alter the course of an engagement. Based on post-September 1939 combat records of the Fairey Swordfish and its successor, the Fairey Albacore, the third-generation biplanes represented an obvious menace in the torpedo-bombing role—their performance and general characteristics differed little from these two later designs. In a number of Fleet exercises during the 1930s, simulated torpedo attacks against Royal Navy battleships proved highly effective.[20] From their involvement in various land-based conflicts such as the Sino-Japanese War and the Spanish Civil War, 1930s biplanes proved equally proficient at dive-bombing. And as fighters, their excellent handling capabilities were well enough appreciated from the days of World War I, although their light-weight construction made them vulnerable to battle damage—a menace all biplane aircraft were to face as aerial machine-gun calibers became larger and more destructive.

These weapons advances accompanied the rise of the monoplane, the last of Casey's generational phases from 1935–39, which ultimately removed any lingering doubts over the capacity of airpower to become the leading player in naval warfare. The introduction of low wing monoplanes with all-metal monocoque fuselage structures came to revolutionize all aspects of military aviation, because these advances generally allowed for the installation of more powerful and reliable engines, enhanced fuel stowage, aircrew protection, and more effective offensive and defensive weapons systems than could be carried by biplane predecessors.[21] Of the aircraft carrier powers, Japan took the greatest strides in monoplane production prior to 1939; by 1938 Imperial Japanese Navy carriers were equipped with specialist fighter, dive-bomber, and torpedo-bomber designs. While still retaining biplane single-seat fighters, the United States had likewise introduced monoplanes as the principal strike components on board their vessels. Yet as the postwar histories have noted, a lack of available major manufacturing capacity—because of the priority given to RAF Bomber Command—meant only one significant monoplane design was added to the Royal Navy inventory throughout this period.[22] The appearance of the Blackburn Skua fighter/dive-bomber in 1937 is especially noteworthy for two reasons. First, the Skua reflected the Royal Navy's ongoing infatuation with the idea of multirole aircraft. Second, the primary function of Skua was dive-bombing—a mode of attack the Air Staff had persistently denounced throughout the course of the 1930s and that would be underutilized by the RAF for most of World War II.[23]

The Skua embodied two critical weaknesses that were to severely compromise the Royal Navy's future capacity to deal with Japan's carrier spearhead. Though Geoffrey Till has observed the Swordfish was an inferior design when compared with the American and Japanese monoplane torpedo bombers of the late 1930s, it nevertheless remained a potent weapon.[24] However, in the absence of an equivalent dive-bombing capability, the FAA's strike options lacked the degree of tactical flexibility that both Japan and the United States enjoyed. The Skua would only enjoy a brief operational career, being withdrawn from first-line service in late 1941; fewer than fifty of these aircraft were deployed on board Royal Navy aircraft carriers. Yet the Admiralty was prepared to employ the Skua as the Fleet's principal fighter aircraft; this, more than anything else, exemplified the inferiority of the British approach in developing their onboard fighter capability. Neglecting the cause of the single-seat fighter interceptor rendered Fleet air defenses virtually nil when facing a hostile air strike escorted by single-seat fighters. As Eric Brown and other aviation experts have noted, neither the Skua nor the Fairey Fulmar, a two-seater fighter-reconnaissance type introduced in August 1941, was capable of matching strides with the likes of Germany's Messerschmitt 109 and Italy's Fiat G-50 single-seat fighters.[25] These multirole designs heralded a sequence of wartime British naval monoplane projects that would be so dogged by delays and technical issues that, when the FAA commenced an extensive overhaul of its existing aircraft complements in 1943, the vast majority of the replacements were obtained from the United States Navy.

At the heart of the multirole fighter was one of the fundamental defects of the Dual-Control system. As outlined in the previous chapter, while the RAF supplied the airplanes themselves, they were designed in accordance with the Admiralty's operational specifications.[26] In the case of the Skua and the Fulmar, the Admiralty's ambitions could not be properly fulfilled by the then-existing level of technology. For the Skua and the Fulmar to be at least competitive with single-seater types, both required much more powerful engines than could be produced with mid-1930s engineering. Subsequent Admiralty wartime projects proved equally difficult to master, even following the final wartime disbandment of the Dual-Control system. Aircraft such as the Fairey Barracuda torpedo bomber and the Fairey Firefly two-seat fighter endured lengthy developmental periods prior to entering service in limited numbers. Others such as the Blackburn Firebrand torpedo fighter and the Fairey Spearfish multirole bomber failed to enter service at all.[27] As will be highlighted in chapter four, the Admiralty was eventually compelled to seek RAF assistance in the form of "navalized" Hurricanes and Spitfires in addition to reinforcement from the United States. By the time the British were introducing their first naval single-seat, piston-engine fighter types which were not derived from land-based designs, World War II had ended and the jet age was looming fast, again leaving the FAA well behind its American counterpart in the new post-1945 technological race.

As if the absence of modern single-seat fighters was not enough of a problem for the FAA, the condition of the Admiralty's aircraft carriers presented another steep hurdle to be cleared. For the duration of the 1930s the Fleet's aircraft-carrier resources were in a parlous state. Despite fielding a similar number of carriers to the Americans and the Japanese, the quality of the Royal Navy's vessels left much to be desired. As detailed within the previous chapter, half of the 1920-vintage British carrier force could not compete in a contemporary combat setting due to a lack of speed; and only the *Ark Royal* enjoyed all the benefits of modern carrier design. During this period, the Japanese were adding four fast carriers to their complement, while the United States Navy had commissioned two more fleet carriers after America's 1936 abandonment of the naval disarmament regime. The British found themselves considerably behind the competition when it came to on board aircraft stowage because they had not adopted permanent "deck parks" for their airplanes as had the other aircraft-carrier powers and had only recently stemmed an alarming rate of training fatalities by employing effective arrestor gear for the safe retrieval of aircraft at sea.[28] Given these restrictions, the FAA's deployment as a spearhead force could only be realistically contemplated against opponents with no operational aircraft carriers themselves, until such time as the Admiralty could field sufficient modern carriers capable of carrying at least fifty aircraft per vessel.

As will become apparent, however, size on its own represented no guarantee for combat success unless mixed with skillful airmanship and clever tactical application. In terms of airmanship, the available evidence points to FAA prowess as a highly skilled wartime cadre with exceptional levels of competence in all forms of operations, including the extra demands of night flying.[29] This speaks volumes for the quality of the organization's personnel who had been able to overcome their differing service prejudices, insufficient funding, and scarce maintenance assets to exert the maximum performance from the aircraft they flew. Whereas the Dual-Control era had created internal divisions along service lines during the 1920s over how best to utilize the naval air weapon, these were to be largely resolved once hostilities commenced in September 1939. Whatever the weaknesses of its aircraft, its organization, or its fighting doctrines, the performance exhibited by FAA aircrews during the course of World War II was to be nothing short of exemplary. And when deployed under the command of a fighting admiral who understood how to best exploit the existing British partnership between carrier-borne airpower and surface gunnery, the FAA would become the Admiralty's critical offensive player in a fleet- or squadron-scale engagement.[30] Once the shooting commenced, it would prove fortunate for the Royal Navy that three of its fleet commanders, namely Admiral Sir Andrew Cunningham, Admiral Sir John Tovey, and Admiral Sir James Somerville, were to emerge as particularly skillful exponents of integrated fleet combat.

At what stage during the interwar years did the FAA fall astern of its overseas counterparts, and why? The answer to the first question posed in this chapter is that the FAA commenced its decline during the fourth of Casey's generational phases (1935–39), and it did so because British naval aviation lacked the ability to adequately transition from the biplane to the monoplane before war with Germany had commenced. As long as the biplane held sole ownership of the skies, the FAA remained an equivalent force to both the

Japanese and American naval air arms. Once the evolution of the naval monoplane had commenced in earnest, however, the effects of the events and circumstances of the 1920s returned to haunt both the Royal Navy and the RAF. The Admiralty's unrealistic operational specifications for multirole fighter aircraft in particular were unable to be met effectively; the RAF's designers and manufacturers did not possess the then-requisite technical capabilities to address these strenuous requirements in a satisfactory fashion. Given the prior lack of funding for technical development within the RAF, together with the production prioritization afforded strategic bombing in the mid-1930s, the Fleet found itself deprived of the modern aircraft types it required, most notably single-seat fighters. Yet even if an adequate transition to the monoplane had been possible, the antiquated condition of the Fleet's aircraft-carrier contingent would not have permitted the British to develop the naval air weapon as a stand-alone, fleet combat spearhead. As such, the FAA was compelled to remain in a fleet-support role until it possessed the necessary aircraft and aircraft carriers to do otherwise.

A "Balanced Force": The War-Fighting Tactics of the Post–Jutland Fleet

From Salamis to Jutland, all of the great naval engagements had shared one common aspect: combat on site required combat on sight. Over the course of three millennia, the maximum firing range that separated combatant fleets had expanded to little more than ten miles. Whereas the capital ships that dueled at Jutland on 31 May 1916 possessed artillery that could strike the enemy at ranges up to twenty miles, their targeting capabilities were governed entirely by the visual limits of onboard sighting apparatus. Given these circumstances, the protagonists were directly exposed to the risk of severe damage or destruction of their respective formations at such narrow intervening distances. However with the advent of the airplane, the opportunity existed for this exposure to be substantially reduced, if not eliminated altogether. And this enormous potential advance in the conduct of naval warfare likewise presented the opportunity for the equality, indeed the superiority, of forces that would have been otherwise deemed an inadequate match within a purely surface-orientated environment. For the Royal Navy in particular, bearing in mind the global nature of its responsibilities and the degrading effects of various interwar maladies upon its fighting prowess, the aircraft carrier presented just such a solution. Faster, modern surface opponents could be sufficiently neutralized through crippling carrier-borne air strikes before the accompanying, often slower British capital ships, inflicted their salvos upon a battered and disorganized enemy fleet or squadron. As long as the British could control the terms of the combat in this fashion, their fighting supremacy upon the naval battlefield remained intact.

An analysis of the incorporation of the air weapon into the Royal Navy's plans for fighting the enemy as of September 1939 is greatly enhanced by using the Admiralty's published *Fighting Instructions 1939* (C.B.04027) as a template.[31] Derived from the prevailing Navy War Manual QU5394, these instructions set out the conduct of naval activities as falling within one of two categories: Fleet Actions and Minor Operations. The concept of the fleet action revolved around a major engagement between the two principal combatant battle fleets on a basis similar to that experienced at Jutland, whereas all other forms of engagement were classified under Minor Operations. Yet the conduct of the naval war for which these instructions were prepared was to assume a far broader tactical basis than had been contemplated within the Admiralty's prewar thinking. By the conclusion of hostilities in August 1945 the plethora of operational methods would range from the mundane to the bizarre, from massed air strikes to suicide sorties undertaken by individual personnel piloting aircraft, fast motorboats, and even converted torpedoes. Bearing this fact in mind, it becomes possible to appreciate the sheer complexity of the Royal Navy's efforts to maintain Britain's command of the sea in such a diverse operational environment. For the likelihood of successfully maintaining control over the Empire's vast network of maritime communications no longer resided in the bosom of Winston Churchill's "supreme sea battle," but lay instead in the combination of minimalist force dispositions wherever possible, effective interservice cooperation, and superior battlefield leadership.[32]

Whereas Jutland ultimately represented the *Götterdämmerung* for surface naval combat involving very large numbers of capital ships, the fundamental tactical principles that governed the Royal Navy's actions on that occasion remained unchanged throughout the following two decades. In charting the sequence of an engagement, the Fighting Instructions emphasized the division of battle into three distinct phases—approach, contact, and action.[33] The principal objectives of the two opening phases were to locate, shadow, and weaken the enemy force, depriving it of air support and screening forces before the Fleet's battleships would directly engage their opposite numbers in the action phase. Within this paradigm the FAA would sight and shadow the enemy, establish air superiority by sinking any opposing aircraft carriers, wound the opposing battle fleet, and conduct real-time orbital spotting for its own battleships.[34] In the event of a smaller-scale confrontation (i.e., anything less than the commitment of the bulk of the respective combatants' battle fleets), these fighting principles continued to apply. And in strategic circumstances whereby the Admiralty would be compelled to disperse its assets, the deployment of a "balanced force" became the decisive operational factor. As defined within the Fighting Instructions, a balanced force consisted of "capital-ships, cruisers, destroyers and perhaps an aircraft-carrier, irrespective of the number of each type."[35] What is particularly noteworthy about the wording of this definition was the apparent preparedness of the Admiralty as late as September 1939 to still regard carriers as optional extras within a modern combat setting.

For each of the Great Power navies, the employment of the air weapon in an observing role had been undertaken by the conclusion of World War I, and this trend continued to enjoy strong support throughout the interwar period. This passive employment of aircraft included fleet reconnaissance, shadowing and spotting duties with the correspondent "Zetes" noting as of 1936 that reconnaissance remained the principal task for the FAA to undertake during combat.[36] Naval powers across the globe came to recognize that extensive reconnaissance and shadowing by aircraft and submarines served to greatly enhance the tactical maneuvering of a fleet or squadron in order to secure the most advantageous approach for a forthcoming engagement.[37] As for the use of spotters during subsequent gunnery exchanges—the primary function of the air weapon in the minds of the powerful gunnery lobby (which Arthur Hezlet has described as the "Go-It-Alone" school)—the advantage for the battle line was significant. Coordination of gunfire and increased accuracy allowed for ranges to be extended beyond the limits of range-finding optics on the capital ships and cruisers. Thus the paramount role of the battle line would continue to be preserved if the majority of the participating aircraft were earmarked for observation and spotting duties as their primary functions.[38] And during the course of the 1920s, when numerous aspects of naval aviation science had yet to be explored let alone solved, allocation of most FAA multiseat aircraft to passive missions by the Admiralty represented the most practicable use of a weapon that was still in its relative infancy.

Even with the advantages that aerial reconnaissance and spotting provided in a fleet or squadron action, a faster-moving opponent could still outmaneuver the Royal Navy's battle line unless this advantage was removed by preemptive damage. As the introduction of stronger and more reliable biplane bomber types proceeded in the early 1930s, torpedo bombing became the Admiralty's preferred solution for this problem. This form of attack was ideally suited to the prevailing belief that aircraft could at least slow down a faster adversary, though the battleship remained an unsinkable aerial target in the minds of many within the Great Power navies. Whereas their armored bulk provided reasonable shielding against bomb hits, the capital ships remained at their most vulnerable when exposed to torpedo strikes because of the torpedo's capacity to directly penetrate vital areas such as engine rooms and associated propulsion spaces.[39] And until such time as radar-controlled rapid-fire anti-aircraft weapons were readily available, surface warships would continue to lack the proper means to generate an effective antiaircraft barrage. However, the lack of a more extensive dive-bombing capability deprived the FAA of the opportunity to conduct two-dimensional sorties that would have likely inflicted even greater damage on the enemy force as a whole. And worse still, if the opponent possessed carrier-borne or land-based fighter cover, the defending fighters would concentrate all of their efforts on shooting down the dawdling torpedo planes instead of being presented with the conundrum of combating separate attacking formations.[40] At Midway on 4 June 1942 the Imperial Japanese Navy experienced this dilemma firsthand as its fighters massacred the American torpedo bombers, only to leave their parent carriers totally unprotected against a devastating strike by the enemy's dive-bombers.

The presence of torpedo bombers also provided the British and their overseas competitors with another tantalizing prospect, namely the destruction of an enemy force before it could put to sea. As early as 1918, Admiral Beatty had seriously contemplated a massed attack by carrier-based Sopwith Cuckoos against Germany's principal naval bases.[41] Further experiments along this line were conducted by the FAA during the interwar period. The results obtained from such an exercise at Singapore in February 1937 amply demonstrated that a surprise attack with concentrated carrier airpower at the outset of hostilities could deliver an annihilating blow against any hostile fleet.[42] Utilizing aircraft in this manner would validate Alfred Mahan's belief that a fleet that possessed a first-strike capability was well placed to seize command of the seas from the outset of hostilities. The crippling of three Italian battleships at Taranto by the FAA on 11 November 1940 led an Italian naval officer, Captain M. A. Bragandin, to record that "it was as if we had lost a great naval battle, and could not foresee being able to recover from the consequences."[43] Yet while the Admiralty was favorably disposed toward the deployment of the FAA in such a role, it was still reluctant to take the greater leap forward. Attacking warships at anchor in an enclosed area such as a harbor represented but one advantage supplied by a concentrated aerial spearhead. Fighting an opposed naval engagement with a tactical regime that contemplated the destruction of the enemy fleet through airpower alone was a development that the Royal Navy of the 1930s had yet to accept philosophically, and was unprepared to do so materially.

Within the FAA's fleet-support role, the fleet fighter was to primarily provide offensive fighter support—at least in theory. Since the late 1920s, advocates of the fleet fighter concept had envisaged aircraft that would seek out and destroy the opposing fleet's air strength through long-range fighter sweeps. Aircraft such as the Osprey, the Skua, and the Fulmar, were considered suitable for this role as they possessed not only the necessary range, but also a second crew member to handle navigation over lengthy distances.[44] Employed solely as bomber destroyers, two-seater fleet fighters were potentially worthwhile assets in either an offensive or defensive capacity, provided of course that the enemy fielded no single-seat fighters. The weaknesses of these airplanes in combat with single-seat types have been addressed previously, however, one aspect of interwar British doctrine equally demonstrates the Admiralty's attitudes toward close fighter protection. A number of senior officers, including Admiral Sir Ernle Chatfield, First Sea Lord (1933–38), believed that antiaircraft fire on its own to be a far more adequate means of close-in protection than fighter interceptors, as the correspondent Volage (a pseudonym) explained in *Brassey's 1936*: "The general inference is that while aircraft do constitute a practical method of attacking surface warships, they only become a serious menace when their numbers, range and striking power exceed some arbitrary figure in relation to the defensive equipment of these ships."[45] Admiral Sir Thomas Phillips was one adherent who maintained his faith in antiaircraft fire, even after early wartime reverses such as those in the Norwegian campaign had proven otherwise. He would eventually pay for this intransigence with his life, and those of many others, in the sinking of the *Prince of Wales* and the *Repulse* off Malaya on 10 December 1941.

Whereas the Royal Navy's aircraft carriers were an operational trump card for the service against its European opponents with no carriers, for much of the interwar period their physical location in either a fleet or squadron tactical setting rendered them extremely vulnerable to attack from the very vessels they were supposed to target. As Observer (a pseudonym) commented in *Brassey's 1938*, the Royal Navy's senior tacticians were still divided over how Fleet carriers should be properly incorporated into the wider force setting and over the competing merits of close protection versus an escorted "stand-off" position some thirty to forty miles from the battle line. Within the Fighting Instructions, however, there at last emerged the acknowledgment that the Fleet's aircraft carriers must operate in a detached fashion once combat was joined, though they were expected to remain as part of the battle line when cruising.[46] The critical future consequence of the Admiralty's preexisting preparedness to permit the aircraft carrier to remain in the proximity of a surface engagement, and indeed (during the 1920s) become an active participant, will be found in the designs of the four *Illustrious*-class carriers that had been authorized for construction in 1936. Once operational in wartime, these ships sported armored flight decks and interiors—a concept that was intended to allow the vessels to withstand bombs *and* surface gunfire, but at the ultimate cost of a greatly reduced aircraft complement. This meant that a single carrier of this class within a battle squadron faced a far tougher task if deployed against a similarly equipped Japanese force during the course of operations in the Far East.[47]

Given the comparatively small size of its aircraft-carrier complements, the Royal Navy required the presence of strong land-based air support to supplement its activities wherever possible, especially in the execution of long-range antisubmarine and convoy-support missions. This had become a divisive issue between the Admiralty and the Air Staff in the early 1920s when the Balfour Committee resolved to place the control of all land-based naval air support in the hands of the RAF.[48] By September 1939 RAF Coastal Command (as it was now known) found itself in a particularly sorry state. With the Air Staff immersed in their pursuit of a strategic bombing deterrent, Coastal Command's resources amounted to a handful of flying-boat squadrons and some inadequate light bomber units that were equipped with converted trainers such as the Avro Anson. Despite the excellence of the Short Sunderland flying boat as a convoy-defense and antisubmarine platform, too few were in service to meet the Admiralty's needs. Until the RAF could be persuaded to assign fighters and some of its more capable medium and heavy bombers for coastal service, the British lacked the capacity to provide effective protection measures beyond their coastal waters, leaving the majority of convoys bereft of such assistance for the balance of their dangerous passages.[49] This resulted in the Royal Navy having little option but to assign elements of the Fleet's aircraft-carrier assets for the performance of these tasks, thereby exposing the larger carriers to the increased risk of submarine attack in a convoy-protection setting.

What were, then, the key strengths and weaknesses of the Fleet's integrated war-fighting methods as formulated between the wars? The answer to this question covers the three distinct stages of aircraft involvement. In the first stage, the passive reconnaissance-spotting era during the 1920s, the tactics utilized by Britain, Japan, and the United States were basically those of World War I. On their own, reconnaissance and gunnery spotting from aircraft would have greatly expanded battlefield intelligence, tactical maneuver and firing accuracy for all concerned, in terms of both physical distance and command-control procedures. From the British perspective, the slower comparative speed of at least two-thirds of the Admiralty's available capital ships still counted against a wholly successful interception, unless air searches provided the opportunity for an ambush. And for each of the four aircraft-carrier powers, the relatively close proximity of the carriers to the battle line directly exposed these vessels to punishing surface fire.[50] During the second stage—the last great biplane era from 1930 to 1934—integrated fleet tactics allowed the Royal Navy in particular to compensate for its battleship mobility difficulties through the offensive air strike methods explained previously; the carrier placement issue, however, remained unresolved. From 1935 onward—and the third stage, the evolving monoplane era—foreign monoplanes became the central problem. With the lack of specialized single-seat fighters on their carriers and enjoying only limited land-based air support, British naval operations became far more hazardous when conducted in areas where modern enemy aircraft were present in numbers. This liability certainly applied—at least in theory—to naval combat with the German and Italian fleets, both of whom had rejected Mahan's concept of great decisive battles in favor of other ways to counter the British at sea.[51]

Foes and Friends: The European Axis Navies
and Britain's Allies Afloat

Despite being the smallest of the Axis navies, the Kriegsmarine posed by far the widest geographical challenge to Britain's global naval position. In the event of war the Germans could undertake operations from the Barents Sea to the Pacific through their employment of a four-pronged offensive capability perfectly tailored to the needs of a *guerre de course* (a war against trade). This course of action included use of surface warships, armed merchant raiders, U-boats and land-based aircraft. The Kriegsmarine big ships exercised a range of significant advantages over their older British counterparts, possessing superior speed, range, and fire-control apparatus. In the case of Germany's three pocket battleships, a massive cruising range of 26,000 km allowed for these vessels to operate throughout the Indian Ocean with the aid of prepositioned tankers and supply ships.[52] Armed merchant raiders were another source of discomfort for the British Empire as a whole, given their ability to undertake raiding and mining sorties as far east as the Central Pacific and astride Australia's coastlines. German U-boats also enjoyed the benefit of limited British interwar preparations for a submarine-based offensive against convoy traffic, a factor that has been extensively highlighted in postwar histories.[53] And if employed in the antishipping role, the Luftwaffe's range of modern medium-bomber designs was well suited for carrying out attacks with bombs, mines, and aerial torpedoes. Had all limbs of Germany's offensive seaborne capability been competently coordinated, the Royal Navy would have been hard-pressed to maintain the security of Britain's vulnerable maritime lifelines.

Fortunately for the British, the Kriegsmarine suffered from a series of deep-seated political and administrative maladies that effectively prevented the Germans from properly exploiting their advantages. Following Hitler's accession to full executive and titular power in August 1934, the nature of relations between the various branches of the Wehrmacht had become increasingly dominated by personal friction and intrigue at the highest levels. As head of the Reich's economic Four-Year Plan, the Luftwaffe and much else besides, Hermann Goering refused to countenance any naval authority over the Luftwaffe. Goering steadfastly opposed Grand Admiral Eric Raeder's advocacy for an independent naval air arm and successfully lobbied Hitler to delay and eventually postpone the completion of the newly launched aircraft carrier *Graf Zeppelin*.[54] This course of action robbed the

Kriegsmarine of the enormous advantage of possessing a carrier that could support raiding sorties by surface warships within the North Atlantic. Hitler's preoccupation with waging a future series of land campaigns in Europe also impacted Germany's naval fortunes on the factory floor. In spite of the Fuhrer's grandiose Plan Z, a scheme to eventually eclipse the Royal Navy's superiority through the construction of a greatly enlarged battle fleet, the Germans entered hostilities with only a fraction of the resources available to the Royal Navy.[55] Until such time as U-boat production received high priority within an economy that had been placed on a full war footing, the Kriegsmarine could not exercise its full potential, though it did possess sufficient initial means to inflict heavy losses on British merchant commerce.

In the absence of a large-scale German fleet presence, the Royal Navy would be instead compelled to prevent sorties by individual or paired surface warships through their interception within the North Sea before they could break out into the North Atlantic shipping lanes. With RAF Coastal Command providing adequate reconnaissance, the composition of an interdicting battle squadron dispatched from Scapa Flow could be tailored to achieve the destruction of enemy ships with minimal apportionment of available resources. In the Mediterranean, however, the Admiralty confronted a more traditional form of maritime adversary. Under Mussolini's patronage, the Regia Marina had emerged as a formidable fighting force equipped with fast and well-armed modern warships. Its latest *Littorio*-class battleships, which eventually reached service in 1940, were far superior in most respects to their British counterparts, although they lacked radar equipment. The Italians also possessed a large submarine arm, and the elite *Decima Flottiglia MAS* naval special forces would prove to be deadly efficient when attacking surface targets within heavily defended harbors.[56] For air support the Regia Aeronautica fielded a range of bombers that were competent performers in an antishipping role. Operating from airfields in southern Italy, Sicily, and North Africa, Italian aircraft were capable of interdicting both hostile merchant traffic and offensive operations undertaken by the British Mediterranean Fleet in the vicinity of Malta and Sicily.[57] These advantages made the Mediterranean a probable hornet's nest for the Admiralty, especially if the Regia Aeronautica was able to be centrally concentrated in support of the Italian fleet.

Similar to the Luftwaffe, the Italian air arm's strike aircraft were frequently required to perform ground-support operations, and its dedicated maritime assets were largely confined to reconnaissance aircraft. Italian airplanes were also plagued by a lack of high-performance engines, which often hindered their combat effectiveness.[58] However it was through the combination of geography and operational strategy that the Regia Marina came to suffer its most critical failing. Both Mussolini and the Italian Naval Staff had refused to sanction construction of an aircraft-carrier capability; they believed the ready accessibility of airfields would adequately provide for the demands of fleet air support. And by 1938 the Italians were pursuing an overall operational strategy known as Plan B, a strictly defensive outlook that emphasized the existence of a fleet in being at the expense of a more aggressive posture that had been discarded. Instead of utilizing its considerable advantage in speed and maneuverability as an offensive tool, the Regia Marina's principal task was to act as the defensive shield for Italian convoys plying between metropolitan ports, Sicily and North Africa.[59] By permitting its warships to operate in this defensive setting, the Italian Naval Staff were in effect providing the opportunity for the Royal Navy to assume the initiative as the aggressor in the case of a fleet- or squadron-scale engagement. And in the absence of Italian fighter support, the FAA's torpedo bombers were positioned to cripple the faster Italian warships and leave them at the mercy of subsequent British surface fire.

The British would not find themselves alone in waging the impending European war at sea, with the Admiralty enjoying the companionship of France's not-inconsiderable Marine Nationale. Spearheaded by two brand-new *Dunkerque*-class battle cruisers, the French possessed powerful cruiser and destroyer arms; the carrier *Bearn* proved to be too slow, however, for offensive operations, as were a number of the French fleet's World War I–vintage battleships.[60] Aside from augmenting the Royal Navy's strength in the Atlantic, the French Mediterranean Fleet represented a powerful counterweight to the Regia Marina. The presence of French naval forces in the Western Mediterranean not only served as an important buffer against any Italian incursions toward the vital British naval base at Gibraltar but also provided the British with the flexibility to rapidly dispatch some of their assets in the Eastern Mediterranean to Singapore via Suez if so required. Unfortunately for the Marine Nationale, the general high quality of its surface forces and submarines could not disguise the largely substandard quality of its land-based air support. The French aero industry had descended into chaos during the course of 1937 as a consequence of nationalization, with strikes and woeful productivity delaying service debuts of the bulk of the Armeé de l'Air's most potent fighter and bomber designs.[61] And with two new carriers yet to be launched, the French were wholly committed to surface-to-surface operations unless their warships were absorbed within British battle squadrons.

Generous naval support from the Dominion nation-states was also forthcoming. Between them, Australia and New Zealand could contribute two heavy and six light cruisers along with a dozen or so destroyers and other light escorts. Similarly the Canadians were able to make a modest initial contribution of a dozen destroyers and smaller craft; by the end of World War II, the Royal Canadian Navy possessed one of the largest escort-centric fleets in service worldwide. Though the Dominion flotillas were subject to the authority of their respective naval establishments and governments, in practice they would operate under the strategic direction of the British Admiralty as they had done in the previous war.[62] The participation of the Canadians in the Atlantic would prove to be of enormous benefit to the Royal Navy in the forthcoming struggle between British merchant convoys and the German U-boats. Likewise, the presence of Australian and New Zealand warships in the South Atlantic and Indian Oceans would provide important support against German surface raiding activity, and the Royal Australian Navy would come to distinguish itself in the Mediterranean. It should be recalled, however, that willingness of the Australian and New Zealand governments to permit deployment of their warships in this manner was based on Whitehall's often-stated commitment that a British fleet would be deployed to Singapore should the Japanese seriously threaten the Empire's security in the Far East.[63]

How serious a threat to the Royal Navy and its allies were the Germans and Italians at sea, especially given the dissimilar means through which each of these nations would seek to wage war? The Germans certainly posed a widespread geographic menace when considering the danger posed to British sea communications and that the Admiralty could not afford to allow the sea lanes in either the South Atlantic or the Indian Oceans to remain entirely unguarded. The German surface fleet, however, was simply too small to offer battle on a large scale against the Royal Navy's Home Fleet. The Italians could also inflict severe damage on British sea communications in the Mediterranean with their large submarine fleet, and unlike the Kriegsmarine, the Regia Marina was capable of challenging the local British and the French surface fleets in the Mediterranean. Airpower presented itself as the decisive factor. Both the Germans and the Italians had been extremely foolish in not equipping their respective fleets with carrier air support, so assistance gained from land-based aircraft would become vitally important. If the Luftwaffe and the Regia Aeronautica were able to supply consistent air support where and when required, the British and their allies would become exposed to very heavy losses if their warships operated in coastal waters where the enemy possessed air superiority. The European Axis naval cause would be doomed from the outset without such assistance, including the effective coordination of command and control between the fleet and the air force in each nation, and between both nations in the Mediterranean.

The Washington peace had come to a close. Following two decades during which the carrier-borne air weapon had become integrated within the Fleet's interwar operational structures, the Royal Navy was to go to war while in possession of a second-tier naval air arm. Fundamental misjudgments by the Admiralty and the RAF had undoubtedly degraded the capabilities of the FAA compared with its Japanese and American contemporaries. As was the case in the previous chapter, however, an objective allocation of responsibility is not a straightforward exercise here. The policies and developmental streams pursued by the two British services were themselves shaped by the circumstances of naval disarmament and fiscal restraint as explored previously. And prior to September 1939, no wartime precedent existed for offensive strike sorties by carrier-borne aircraft within an opposed naval combat setting. As such, any comprehensive apportionment of blame will necessarily remain incomplete until an appraisal of the relevant wartime outcomes has been undertaken. That said, however, the prospects for the FAA in combat possessed evident limits. Were the Luftwaffe and the Regia Aeronautica absent, or at least not present in sufficient strength, integrated fleet tactics would give the Royal Navy a distinct advantage over the German and Italian surface fleets. If the opposite were true, the FAA would likely experience a hard time in protecting the British warships against air attack, especially without effective single-seat fighter cover. It is likewise sobering to note that both of the European Axis air arms combined possessed but a fraction of the dedicated naval air resources controlled by the third future signatory to the Tripartite Pact.

For the first time in history, the participating Great Power navies were to fight a war preceded by a lengthy naval arms limitation regime. Unlike the situation preceding World War I, the practical demise in 1936 of the

Washington-London protocols left too little time for anything like full-scale naval rearmament to be achieved prior to the outbreak of hostilities.[64] For the British especially, this meant their conduct of operations on a global scale could be undertaken with only the most stringent dispositions of the Royal Navy's first-line fighting strength. To prevail within this environment, what may be best described as decisive minimalism—the ability to achieve effective outcomes in the field with the bare minimum of material resources—became the only practicable strategy for the Admiralty to pursue. Accordingly the importance of the FAA's contribution—especially in engagements in which elements of the aged British battle fleet were required to corner and destroy German or Italian surface forces—became the essential difference between success and failure. Even though possessing an aircraft complement which, like the ships it flew above, had yet to be adequately modernized, the FAA could wreak havoc against the carrier-less European Axis navies through the absence of coordinated, land-based Axis air support. Most important of all for British hopes, the Royal Navy would have to demonstrate its ability to adapt and modify campaigning procedures to defeat dissimilar opponents in dissimilar combat situations throughout the broad oceans and narrow seas, vital arteries for nation and Empire alike.

4

Broad Oceans, Narrow Seas

The Test of War against Germany and Italy,
September 1939–April 1942

A T 0445 HOURS, 1 SEPTEMBER 1939, ABSENT A FORMAL declaration of war, Adolf Hitler authorizes the execution of Operation Fall Weiss (Case White). Fifty-three German divisions begin their attacks at various points on the Polish frontier while air strikes are mounted against airfields and communications; the pre-dreadnought battleship *Schleswig Holstein* shells the Polish naval arsenal at Westerplatte. Following the expiry of the Anglo-French ultimatum on 3 September, RAF Bomber Command mounts concerted raids against German warships at Wilhelmshaven; strikes on 4 September inflict only minimal damage as the unescorted bombers are savaged by the Luftwaffe's fighter defenses.[1] Within ten months the German Wehrmacht sweeps all before it, eventually controlling the Atlantic coastline from Norway to the Spanish frontier. Italy's entry as an active belligerent on 10 June 1940 expands the naval war to the Mediterranean where the Royal Navy must confront the Italian fleet without French support. Fearful that the Axis navies would seize control of the Marine Nationale's Mediterranean Fleet in the wake of France's capitulation, the Royal Navy destroys or neutralizes French warships at their North African bases on 3 July. With the daunting prospect of conducting a naval war extending from the Barents Sea to Bass Strait, the absence of the French fleet induces an unprecedented level of strategic maritime vulnerability for Britain and the British Empire alike. By November 1940 the Admiralty's efforts to sustain British naval supremacy have become, in the judgment of the émigré German naval theorist Herbert Rosinski, "the dominant fact of the present conflict."[2]

With the war in Europe approaching its ninth month, First Lord of the Admiralty Winston Churchill outlined his concept of British naval supremacy to the House of Commons on 11 April 1940: "When we speak of command of the seas, it does not mean command of every part of the sea at the same moment, or at every moment. It only means that we can make our will prevail ultimately in any part of the seas which may be selected for operations, and thus indirectly make our will prevail in every part of the sea."[3]

Five months later during October 1940, Herbert Rosinski authored an essay titled "Mahan and the Present War," first published in *Brassey's 1941*. A German scholar whose expertise extended throughout the fields of military and naval affairs as well as international relations, Rosinski journeyed to Britain in 1936 after he was barred from lecturing in Germany because of his Jewish ancestry. He lectured at Oxford until 1939 and, having been briefly interned as an enemy alien, subsequently relocated to the United States and secured an academic position at Princeton before becoming the principal military analyst for *Voice of America* in 1944.[4] Largely forgotten within the postwar histories, his essay identified a number of key subject areas through which the progress of the war at sea could be assessed. Examination of these areas through both the testing of Rosinski's period conclusions as well as the ongoing relevance of his interpretations throughout the following eighteen months of conflict (November 1940–April 1942) between the British and European Axis navies, documents the extent to which the Royal Navy was able to achieve Churchill's stated goals.

Prior to specifically addressing the outcomes thus far from the war at sea, Rosinski provided a more general commentary as to the continuing applicability of Alfred Mahan's strategic theories. He commenced by noting that the one-hundredth anniversary of Mahan's birth (1940) marked the climax of a process in strategic naval thought that had been in progress since the end of World War I. He explained that while Mahan's concepts of maritime strategy were still revered "in ritual" they were no longer regarded as a major influence on British and American naval thinking and the Germans and the Italians had come to regard him as an "outdated old fossil" whose teachings favored the imposition of Anglo-American sea power. Rosinski then proceeded to examine what he considered to be Mahan's limitations as a strategist, in particular the theorist's reluctance to integrate his insights into "a systematic analysis of the whole complicated and paradoxical structure of naval warfare." Accordingly Rosinski concluded that Mahan understood the concept of sea power but apparently did not appreciate what was required for a nation to exercise "superior sea power." In framing the range of issues to be covered in his essay, Rosinski stated that his analysis did not extend to Mahan's wider interpretations of the relationship between command of the sea and the concept of homogenous nation-states for which Mahan had been denounced by "economic" historians throughout the course of the 1930s.[5]

Rosinski then turned to Mahan's two central strategic principles, the indivisibility of the sea and the supremacy of sea power over land power. In the first instance he set out Mahan's dictum that a sea power was always advantaged over its land competitors because of its ability to traverse unfortified and borderless seas and oceans. Mahan's concept of maritime supremacy revolved around the offensive use of naval power; the requirement to either fight an immediate battle or impose a blockade so as to force the opponent into battle.[6] In setting out Mahan's interpretation, the author noted that throughout the course of naval history the inferior power had been compelled to retaliate by the employment of *guerre de course* against the superior power's lines of communication, a course of action that could never be entirely neutralized but which was insufficient to wrest naval supremacy from the opponent's battle line. In turning to the supremacy of sea power, Rosinski explained that the superior mobility of warships provided the opportunity for the maritime state to exhaust its opponent's greater land-based resources by forcing campaigns in distant theaters as had been the case in the Russo-Japanese conflict of 1904–5. He further contended that the Royal Navy's dominance in the seventeenth and eighteenth centuries had arisen through its ability to isolate the weaker European sea powers by cutting their overseas communications, although this did not extend to the United States because the concentrated base of American strength lay beyond its effective reach.[7]

Whereas Rosinski acknowledged that Mahan's basic principles explained the rise and maintenance of the British Empire, he asserted that in the absence of a proper analysis, Admiral Alfred Tirpitz had based Germany's pre–World War I naval strategy on what he [Rosinski] described as Mahan's overgeneralization of sea power. In his view, the error in Tirpitz's thinking was to attempt to gain parity with the British by way of bluff through the construction of a fleet in being strong enough to totally paralyze the Royal Navy's Atlantic dispositions. Subsequent naval failure in World War I led to Germany's repudiation of Mahan in the postwar era, with Italy following a similar path. It is relevant to note that Rosinski referred to the Italian embrace of qualitative superiority in combination with Fascism's cult of willpower, a situation analogous to that in Japan, although the more offensively minded Japanese still sought to achieve their aims through the fighting of a decisive battle against the United States Navy.[8] In his summation of the emergence of "new" strategic theories through the interwar years, the author asserted that Germany and Italy would not pursue maritime supremacy, but seek instead to inflict as much damage as possible on British sea communications because both Axis nations believed that modern weapons systems, particularly airpower, would limit naval warfare to a *guerre de course* alone. Rosinski regarded this concept as unrealistic and sought to disprove it within his subsequent interpretation of the wartime situation.[9]

Chronology of European Theater Naval Events: September 1939–April 1942[10]

1939
3 September: Winston Churchill appointed as First Lord of the Admiralty; 17 September: aircraft carrier *Courageous* is sunk by a U-boat; 14 October: battleship *Royal Oak* is sunk by a U-boat; 13–17 December: Battle of the River Plate.

1940
17 February: Seizure of the German supply ship *Altmark* in Norwegian waters; 9 April–8 June: Norwegian campaign; 28 May–5 June: evacuation of Dunkirk; 10 June: Italy enters the war; 3–4 July: French Mediterranean Fleet neutralized by Force H; 9 July: first escorted convoy to Malta, Battle of Calabria; 17 October: first U-boat "wolfpack" attack against Convoy SC7; 11 November: FAA air strike against Taranto cripples the Italian battleships *Littorio, Caio Duilio,* and *Conti de Cavour* ; 27 November: Battle of Cape Spartiveno.

1941
11 January: Fliegerkorps X (Luftwaffe) commences operations from Sicily; 15–16 March: German battle cruisers *Scharnhorst* and *Gneisenau* sink sixteen

merchant ships from various dispersed convoys; 28 March: Battle of Cape
Matapan; 29 April–3 May: evacuation of Greece; 14–29 May: Battle of Crete;
20–27 May: pursuit and sinking of the German battleship *Bismarck*; 21 August:
first Royal Navy convoy to Russia; 13 November: aircraft carrier *Ark Royal*
is sunk by a U-boat; 25 November: battleship *Barham* is sunk by a U-boat;
17 December: First Battle of Sirtre; 18–19 December: Italian naval special
forces cripple the battleships *Queen Elizabeth* and *Valiant* in Alexandria
Harbor; 20 December: first employment of an escort carrier *Audacity* for
convoy protection (Convoy HG76).

1942
11–12 February: the "Channel Dash" by the German battle cruisers *Scharnhorst* and *Gneisenau* from Brest to Wilhelmshaven; 20–23 March: Second
Battle of Sirtre.

"The Present War"

Under the first of his analytical subheadings, Rosinski outlined the principal
factors that he saw as the obstacles for the Royal Navy after a year of fighting to sustain its command of the sea. These factors included the respective policies of the European Axis navies to avoid a major naval battle and
seek instead to interdict Britain's lines of communication, the debilitating
impact of reductions to the Royal Navy's strength during the interwar years,
and Germany's conquest of France's Atlantic coastline. These observations
reflected Churchill's own conclusion that the Fleet "had to face enormous
and innumerable difficulties rather than an antagonist," and the events of
the period September 1939–October 1940 certainly confirmed this fact.[11]
So far only one fleet-scale engagement had taken place: a tactical victory for
the British over the Italians at Calabria on 7 July 1940. The Royal Navy had
been expending the majority of its time and effort in a wide variety of operational situations, including convoy escort, amphibious assaults, evacuation
of ground forces, and pursuing surface raiders. Its casualties were heavy, with
two large aircraft carriers and a battleship sunk, while the Fleet's cruiser and
destroyer arms had been roughed up by the Luftwaffe on several occasions,
most notably in the waters off Norway and Dunkirk. And losses in merchant
shipping tonnage to attacks from the U-boats were steadily climbing; well
over three million tons having been sent to the bottom. If the Admiralty

was to successfully implement Churchill's stated strategy, especially in the absence of French support, it would have to pursue what Stephen Roskill described as "flexibility in the application of [British] maritime power and the concentration of its instruments."[12]

Turning to the operational methods Rosinski believed would ensure success for the Royal Navy, he emphasized the importance of a range of technical devices effectively coordinated with existing weaponry through superior, quality leadership. His inference regarding new technologies that were necessarily "shrouded in mystery" undoubtedly referred to the development of radar, ASDIC sonar detection, and other means of remote detection, all of which would indeed play an enormous role in securing Allied success in every maritime theater.[13] Radar provided the crucial edge in the detection, redetection, and sinking of the *Bismarck* in May 1941 as it had for the British at Cape Matapan in March of the same year. The combination of radar, ASDIC, and airpower has been widely acknowledged as the key factor in the final defeat of the Kriegsmarine's U-boat campaign in mid-1943; conversely, Admiral Sir Andrew Cunningham believed that a different complexion upon the "air bombing menace" arose from use of radar on board aircraft carriers as it provided a far more coordinated deployment of the Fleet Air Arm's protective fighter screens.[14] Although the Germans too had pursued radar and radio detection-finding technology during the 1930s, their research in these particular fields never succeeded in matching that from across the Channel. This inability to achieve scientific parity with the Allied powers did not necessarily reflect a lack of ability on the part of the leading German scientists, but rather the dysfunctional nature of decision making within the Third Reich itself.

The scientific development of new technologies within the Nazi state suffered at the hands of the same byzantine power apparatus that frustrated the German armaments industry as a whole. In postwar interviews and published works, Albert Speer, Grand Admirals Eric Raeder and Karl Doenitz, and Luftwaffe general Werner Baumbach, individually expanded upon a range of impediments, especially the effects of intrigue on the part of senior leaders such as Goering and Himmler to gain Hitler's favor for their pet armament projects. Baumbach additionally recalled that Hitler, in disallowing a prewar proposal for a separate naval Luftwaffe, explained his decision by stating that "no one is in a position to say that he will fight with land aircraft on land and with naval aircraft at sea," an echo of the sentiments expressed by Lord Trenchard a decade before.[15] Yet the German scientists, admirals, and technocrats were not alone in being pestered, prodded, and frustrated by the head office. When it came to the means and methods of waging war, Winston Churchill was a dedicated naval enthusiast (which Hitler was not), carrying his experience of a second stint as First Lord of the Admiralty into Downing Street when he became prime minister. The extent of Churchill's prime ministerial influence within the Admiralty at both the strategic and tactical levels has remained a contentious topic in British historical circles throughout the postwar period, with Stephen Roskill and Arthur Marder having a particularly testy published exchange of views over the issue.[16]

Though the substance of the dispute between these historians lay in the veracity of their respective primary sources when addressing the issue of relations between Churchill and the Admiralty, it was the operational-level commanders who bore the collective brunt of this decision-making process. Churchill's direct intervention in military affairs mirrored that of both Hitler and Josef Stalin, yet Churchill did not appear to contradict professional advice as readily as Hitler in particular. On the question of the Admiralty's influence over events at sea, Roskill made the salient point that unlike the Air Ministry and the War Office, the Admiralty exercised both administrative and operational control over the Royal Navy so there can be little surprise regarding its persistent encroachment at the tactical level.[17] This encroachment became an object of resentment among senior fleet commanders such as admirals Cunningham, Somerville, and Tovey; Tovey succeeded Admiral Sir Charles Forbes as commander in chief Home Fleet in the wake of Forbes' being sacked for his alleged poor performance in the fumbling Norwegian campaign. Somerville was compelled to face a Board of Inquiry over his conduct during the Battle of Cape Spartiveno because of the apparent necessity to placate those in authority who were impatient for decisive results. Cunningham too had his difficulties. In a letter to the then–First Sea Lord, Sir Dudley Pound, he complained of feeling "rather harassed" by Whitehall and the Admiralty. It did not appear that either entity fully appreciated the difficulty of carrying out offensive operations in the absence of sufficient screening vessels and naval air reserves.[18]

Yet in spite of this sometimes fractious relationship between senior and subordinate levels of command, the Royal Navy's operational successes against its German and Italian opponents arose largely through the quality of its fleet-level and squadron-level leadership. The principal British battlefield commanders, namely Cunningham (Mediterranean Fleet), Somerville (Force H), and Tovey (Home Fleet) achieved excellent results because they understood how best to utilize the often minimal forces at their disposal. These admirals recognized the value of the air weapon in modern naval combat and were forthcoming in attributing British success in episodes such as Matapan and the pursuit of the *Bismarck* to effective aerial reconnaissance and air strike capabilities.[19] Their faith in the FAA as a vital strike instrument was rewarded when positive outcomes were achieved with a minimum of available aircraft. Fewer than fifty airplanes participated in each of the events noted above; also, Cunningham's daring strike against Taranto in November 1940 involved just twenty-four Swordfish torpedo bombers. In referring to the subsequent action off Cape Spartiveno, Somerville observed that it was desirable wherever possible that the carrier act independently of the battle line; this remark provided some wartime conclusions for the preexisting debate as to how aircraft carriers would best "fit" into the Royal Navy's wartime tactical dispositions. In addition, the majority of serving British admirals quickly came to recognize that effective carrier-borne fighter support—a rarity in the first three years of hostilities—had become an absolute imperative when carrying out fleet- or squadron-scale activities.[20]

Although Rosinski lauded the impact of new technologies in the Royal Navy's successful prosecution of operations prior to November 1940, he remained convinced the role of the battleship remained unchallenged, as did Churchill, the Admiralty, and its fleet commanders.[21] In engaging both the Regia Marina and the Kriegsmarine, British admirals were committed to the interwar concept of integrated battle tactics, seeking to slow down their quarry with air strikes before the final blows at the hands of the accompanying surface forces. At Cape Matapan, Cunningham sought to initiate these strikes at a maximum range of fifty miles so his capital ships and cruisers could quickly close the range and attack Admiral Angelo Iachino's fleet before it had the chance to utilize its superior speed and escape. However Cunningham, Somerville, and Churchill also bemoaned the fact that the Fleet's R-class battleships in particular were incapable of making effective contributions in such circumstances because they were too slow to maintain touch with their own forces let alone the enemy's.[22] Though the strike against the Italian battleships at Taranto confirmed that capital ships could be sunk by aerial torpedo attacks, the crippling of the three vessels took place while they were secured in a relatively shallow anchorage. As of 9 December 1941 no capital ship had been sunk at sea by aircraft alone, and this remained the case throughout the course of European hostilities until the 9 September 1943 sinking of the Italian battleship *Roma* by an air-launched German guided missile.

"Limitations of Airpower"

In considering airpower, Rosinski commenced his assessment of its limitations by asserting that while use of the air weapon had modified certain aspects of sea warfare, it had not succeeded in shaking the foundations of naval strategy. The author subsequently addressed the issue on three bases: (1) the employment of aircraft in coastal and offshore waters, (2) the value of aerial reconnaissance, and (3) his adjudication that the attainment of naval supremacy now depended on a solid partnership with "a not too profoundly inferior air force."[23] Notably, however, Rosinski's interpretations regarding airpower were largely confined to land-based air activity, as he made no reference to either the employment or relative effectiveness of the aircraft carrier in British naval operations. Yet this omission was understandable in that prior to October 1940, the aerial contribution of the Fleet's carriers had been negligible in terms of damage inflicted on the Axis navies. Instead, the initial outcomes of carrier sorties were comprehensive disasters: the loss of *Courageous* while hunting U-boats without an adequate screening force and the sinking of *Glorious* by the German battle cruisers *Scharnhorst* and *Gneisenau* during the Norwegian campaign because of a similar lack of surface protection. In the latter instance the *Glorious*, without active aerial reconnaissance for reasons which have never been ascertained, had been ambushed by the German ships before her torpedo planes could be launched and was sent to the bottom with fewer than fifty survivors out of more than eight hundred personnel on board.[24]

Had the Royal Navy forfeited its capability to provide effective surface cover for both its big ships and vital merchant convoys, it would have likely lost the war at sea itself. Within a prewar memorandum from the British chiefs of staff concerning the protection of wartime trade, the authors noted that a balance needed to be drawn between the needs of the Fleet and those of convoy protection when it came to the allocation of screening vessels such as light cruisers and destroyers.[25] Waging a conflict that involved differing operational strategies placed an enormous strain on the Admiralty's capacity to provide the necessary protection for both entities. Whereas the events off

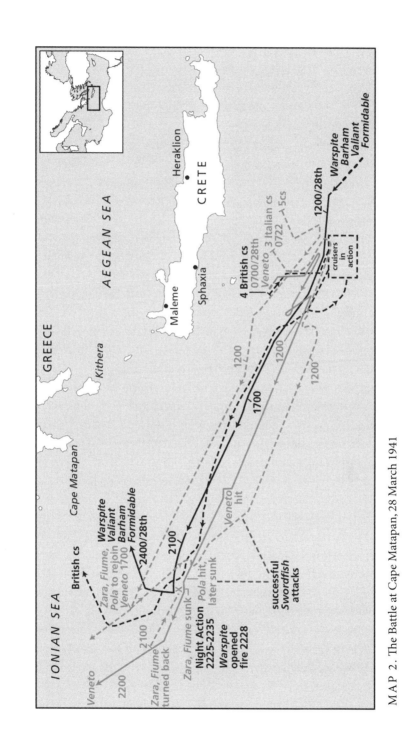

MAP 2. The Battle at Cape Matapan, 28 March 1941

Norway and Dunkirk did not include the loss of any of the Fleet's capital ships or aircraft carriers to air attack, the heavy casualties that were sustained within British destroyer squadrons—along with alarming cruiser and destroyer losses during subsequent operations in the Mediterranean—seriously impeded the Royal Navy's ability to protect both its fleet units and convoy traffic.[26] Fortunately for the Admiralty, this conundrum in the Mediterranean did not assume terminal proportions as Werner Baumbach recalled, "At quite an early stage England's position in the Mediterranean could have become most precarious if there had been co-operation in those strategic designs between the German and Italian air forces—with expert leadership. . . . But the complications of dual command in the Axis were always giving the British sufficient breathing space until American support arrived and sheer weight of material decided the issue in the Mediterranean."[27]

Nevertheless the lessons were clearly apparent from the Norwegian campaign: in the absence of sufficient fighter support, naval power as a whole would be severely compromised if operations were carried out within range of hostile land-based aircraft; and if the opponent could complement its aerial striking power with persistent high-performance fighter escort, the effects of this problem would be dramatically escalated. As Vice Admiral Sir Bertram Ramsey commented in his dispatch following the evacuation of Dunkirk, the massive concentration of the Luftwaffe's available firepower literally overwhelmed the RAF such that the embarkation of troops had to be at first suspended and then limited to dawn and dusk in order to ensure protection of the vessels involved.[28] And Rosinski's assertion that, throughout the first twelve months of war the effectiveness of aerial reconnaissance had not lived up to prewar expectations, proved to be substantially correct—a point that both the participants and the postwar accounts have acknowledged as a major impediment to the Royal Navy maintaining its blockading activities.[29] His observations about the employment of the Luftwaffe in offshore commerce-raiding were similarly accurate, especially given the subsequent impact on the Atlantic and North Russian convoys. These long-range operations were an example of the value of qualitative superiority when a meager handful of long-range Focke-Wolf *Kondor* aircraft had succeeded in sinking almost 500,000 tons of merchant shipping by the conclusion of 1940, a factor Churchill readily acknowledged in his postwar histories.[30]

By April 1942 the RAF bore testament to the credibility of Rosinski's broad proposition that command of the sea resided in an effective partnership between a fleet and an air force, even if the air arm was (at worst) modestly inferior. The central question to be addressed here is whether the RAF met Rosinski's stated prerequisite, and if not, why did it eventually succeed? In support of his argument, Rosinski cited the instance whereby the Royal Navy had maintained control over the Channel following the Dunkirk evacuation, and a German maritime invasion of Britain had been prevented by the combination of sea command and adequate fighter cover.[31] Within British coastal waters and the North Sea both the Fleet and the merchant convoys could generally rely on a large fighter force together with the vast majority of the RAF's bomber and reconnaissance elements. The situation in the Mediterranean, however, was another story altogether. There is no hint to be found in Cunningham's dispatch concerning the engagement at Matapan as to whether he intended relief or sarcasm to color the observation that this had been "the first time [March 1941] that our bombing aircraft had co-operated with the fleet at sea."[32] If sarcasm, his attitude would have been entirely appropriate because, until June 1942 at the earliest, the RAF's material presence in the Mediterranean could only be described as profoundly inferior in terms of all classes of airplane and especially lacking in modern fighter interceptors that could effectively disperse Axis air strikes against shipping.

Given the tactical superiority the Luftwaffe and the Regia Aeronautica were capable of exercising in the Mediterranean, the failure of both Axis air forces to decisively sweep away British and Allied shipping represented a costly mistake on their part. Baumbach's explanation about the perils of dual command represented but a portion of the equation, as he additionally noted that a sustained air campaign in the Eastern Mediterranean would have potentially dealt the British Empire a mortal blow by neutralizing the Suez Canal as a transport and communications link.[33] This point illustrates the critical problem that neither the German nor Italian air staffs were able to manage, namely sustainability. Although the Luftwaffe's elite Fliegerkorps X antishipping unit periodically terrorized the British east of Sicily, the frequent dilution of its fighter and attack units for service on the Eastern Front seriously dented the German unit's capacity to press home its advantage to the fullest extent possible.[34] Likewise the Italians suffered from pressing commitments in North Africa and the Eastern Front and similarly failed to utilize their aerial resources as they should have. Accordingly the Royal Navy managed to maintain its presence at Gibraltar, Malta, and Alexandria but barely so in the latter two instances. Yet the situation would begin to change from mid-1942 onward: the British produced increasing numbers of high-quality fighters and fighter bombers such as the Bristol Beaufighter and the de Havilland Mosquito, which, with American assistance, eventually exercised land-based air superiority throughout the Mediterranean maritime theater.

Within a 1935 Admiralty memorandum concerning the planning for a future war in the Mediterranean, some of the Royal Navy's strategists predicted it could be necessary to conduct operations from external locations "until the test of war can prove what the threat from the air really amounts to." In correspondence with Admiral Pound following the evacuation of Crete in May 1941, Cunningham drew the following conclusion: "As I have always feared, enemy command of the air unchallenged by our own Air Force and in these restricted waters with Mediterranean weather is too great odds for us to take on except seizing opportunities for surprise and exercising upmost circumspection."[35]

If the events off Norway had not provided adequate proof of the need to exercise the "upmost circumspection" when conducting operations in hostile airspace, the toll of four light cruisers and four destroyers sunk or heavily damaged during the evacuation of Crete (plus the battleship *Warspite*'s heavy damage) finally did. During this episode, it was Germany's fearsome Junkers 87 *Stuka* dive-bomber that inflicted the heaviest losses, as it had done at Norway and Dunkirk.[36] Just as menacing, especially for merchant shipping, were the attentions of Axis medium bombers such as the German Heinkel 111 and the Italian Savoia-Marchetti 79; both proved to be proficient torpedo bombers. The Germans and Italians were found wanting, however, in their lack of long-range single-seat fighters. Without an airplane that matched the range of the Japanese Zeke, their bombers, absent a single-seat fighter escort, found themselves in serious trouble when attacked by the FAA's two-seater fighter types.[37]

"Sea Communications Maintained"

Rosinski's analysis of the state of British sea communications as of October 1940 encompassed each of the principal areas in which the Royal Navy had had to resist Axis efforts to sever Britain's maritime lifelines. First, in Rosinski's appraisal of the assault on British shipping in the Atlantic by Germany's U-boats, he proposed that new methods would need to be found to combat the submarine threat so as to prevent it from becoming a serious menace.

In his comments about the relative success of surface raider activity, Rosinski assessed the impact of the Kriegsmarine's warships as limited and far less effective than the activities of merchant raiders that had led Churchill to express unease over the state of British defenses in the "outer oceans."[38] Rosinki then turned briefly to the effects of German naval activity in the English Channel before discussing the reduced effectiveness of the Royal Navy's blockade because of the Reich's access to resources through its European conquests and the Molotov-Ribbentrop Pact between Germany and the Soviet Union.[39] From this point he commenced a preliminary examination of the relative position of sea power within an evolving wartime environment that reflected increasing dominance of land-based military mobility, an exercise that Rosinski expanded upon under the next subheading. The principal issue that arose presently, however, was whether the Royal Navy possessed the operational means to maintain its supremacy in defiance of an extended period of overall Allied strategic inferiority.

Upon the basis of the available evidence, it is this author's contention that September 1939 through April 1942 should be regarded as the evolutionary phase of the conflict between the Royal Navy and the U-boat. Throughout this time the combatants acquired the necessary tactics and weapon types to prosecute their operational intentions; however neither side yet possessed the required volume of firepower to inflict a crippling defeat upon its opponent. From the Axis perspective the Italian submarine campaign contributed little, due largely to poor intelligence and operational tactics together with a growing fuel shortage that had begun to limit all aspects of Italian naval operations from mid-1942. By contrast the Kriegsmarine's U-boats had sunk an estimated 4.8 million tons of merchant shipping by December 1940 and would sink an additional 8.4 million tons throughout the remainder of the specified period.[40] Working in partnership with the long-range Kondors and on occasion raiding warships such as the heavy cruiser *Hipper*, the submarines profited from Doenitz's introduction of wolf-pack tactics in October 1940 when seven of them sank half of the thirty-four ships in Convoy SC7 without sustaining any losses. However, as Doenitz explained in a 1973 television interview, less than half of Germany's U-boats were available for direct deployment on the convoy routes because of defensive commitments in various coastal locations; also, the production of new boats had still not assumed a sufficient priority status in the Reich armaments industries by April 1942 thanks to Hitler's preoccupation with the Eastern Front at that time.[41]

Although a potential defeat by the U-boats seemed ominous in early 1943, the British were able to summon enough of a technological advantage, together with a growing number of escort craft and the assistance of the Canadian and American navies, to eventually prevail. The Admiralty had begun the war with the incorrect assumption that, even in the event of Germany conducting unrestricted submarine warfare, only limited attacks would take place outside British home waters.[42] The Admiralty then made a fatal blunder by employing hunter-groups in a vain attempt to track down U-boats in the Bay of Biscay, which resulted in the loss of the fleet carrier *Courageous*. By the time Rosinski was applying pen to paper, the U-boats already constituted a most serious menace for the Admiralty, in part because the British had still to fully recognize the primary role of airpower in this field of operations. The solution was eventually found, thanks to two low-cost innovations—first the Catapult Armed Merchant (CAM) ships and second, in December 1941, a converted merchantman used as the escort carrier *Audacity* in Convoy HG76. In partnership with the expanding resources of Coastal Command and American assistance in the form of very long-range B-24 Liberator bombers, the employment of escort carriers and new aggressive antisubmarine tactics won the day.[43] For in spite of Doenitz eventually winning Hitler's approval to prioritize submarine construction, by mid-1943 the Allied antisubmarine aerial umbrella had become unchallengeable for Germany's U-boat force.

Rosinski's reference to the lack of decisive results achieved by Germany's surface warships against British sea commerce remained a credible assertion from November 1940 onward, although the Germans did conduct several successful Atlantic operations throughout the first six months of 1941. The neutralization of the threat posed by Hitler's big ships did not, however, arise from a stream of interceptions by the Home Fleet, indeed quite the opposite. The battle cruisers *Scharnhorst* and *Gneisenau*, the pocket battleship *Admiral Scheer*, and the cruiser *Hipper* were all able to "break out" from their North Sea bases unmolested and subsequently evade engagement with the British squadrons pursuing them. Yet thanks to the Admiralty's assigning the Fleet's older battleships and aircraft carriers to convoy escort wherever possible, the Germans exercised great caution in choosing their targets, often preferring to pick off ships that were steaming independently. Following the sinking of the *Bismarck* in May 1941 and the return of the *Scharnhorst*, *Gneisenau*, and *Prinz Eugen* to Wilhelmshaven following their successful Channel Dash of 11–12 February 1942 from Brest, the direct threat posed to the Atlantic

convoys from German surface forces effectively passed.[44] Instead the surviving Kriegsmarine warships shifted attention to the North Russian convoy
routes where combined operations with U-boats and the Luftwaffe inflicted
serious losses in the latter half of 1942. For the Germans, the vital missing
piece in the Atlantic puzzle always remained the aircraft carrier. A number
of postwar accounts have rightly speculated how the course of the entire
Atlantic campaign could have been dramatically altered had the *Graf Zeppelin*
accompanied Hitler's capital ships on their raiding sorties.[45]

Confronting a German battle squadron, which enjoyed the support of
modern fighters and strike aircraft launched from the *Graf Zeppelin*'s flight
deck, represented a potential nightmare that, most fortunately, the Admiralty
did not have to contend with. Instead, the vast majority of British surface
actions took place within the Mediterranean against the Regia Marina, itself

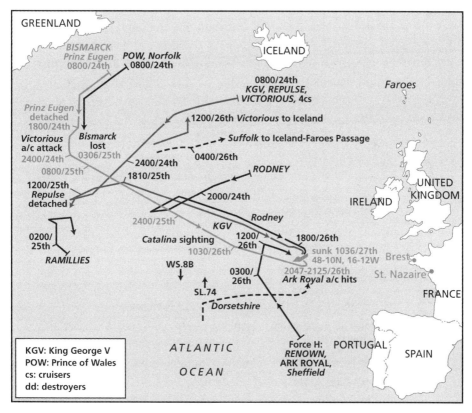

MAP 3. The Pursuit and Sinking of the *Bismarck*, 24–26 May 1941

a formidable opponent due to the large array of modern warships fielded by the Italians. Yet as explored previously, the Royal Navy's integrated battle tactics provided the vital edge because the Italian fleet did not possess an aircraft carrier and Italian commanders invariably attempted to break off an engagement once aware of a carrier within a British force. The positive results the British obtained at Calabria and Cape Spartiveno were achieved more through deterrence than the infliction of major punishment because the high-speed Italian warships were virtually impossible to catch if they evaded the FAA's torpedo attacks.[46] Cunningham's victory at Cape Matapan became the classic illustration of what the Royal Navy could achieve when the Regia Marina's ships were decisively engaged; his battleships demonstrated their mastery of night surface battle, combining clever maneuvering and radar-controlled gunnery at close range, thereby sinking three enemy heavy cruisers and two destroyers. Likewise the superiority of British tactics succeeded in repelling Italian sorties that sought to interdict convoys, even when the Italians held sway in both numbers and firepower.[47]

Rosinski maintained that Germany's disguised armed merchant raiders had accomplished more than the Kriegsmarine's big ships during the first year of war; in terms of bringing mischief to Churchill's outer oceans, this appraisal was justified. Less than a dozen of these "auxiliary cruisers," each heavily armed with guns, torpedoes, and mines, succeeded in generating havoc throughout both the South Atlantic and Indian Oceans. Prior to being sunk by the heavy cruiser *Devonshire* on 22 November 1941, the *Atlantis* had destroyed over 140,000 tons of shipping by preying on unescorted merchant traffic. Another raider, *Pinguin*, sank over 160,000 tons during a voyage lasting 357 days, sustained by a network of prepositioned supply ships and tankers.[48] Shells were lobbed into a British wireless station on Nauru and mines laid off Auckland and in Bass Strait, while combined operations with U-boats in the South Atlantic produced rich pickings for these solitary hunters. The raiders also represented a deadly menace for unwary warships, the Australian light cruiser *Sydney* being sunk with all hands on deck by the *Kormoran* on 19 November 1941. Eventually the Royal Navy's patrolling cruisers were able to track down and destroy three of their number; only two of the remainder survived the war.[49] Although the overall level of damage wrought by these ships proved to be insignificant when compared with the carnage generated by the U-boats, they were responsible for the Royal Navy having to assign valuable resources to the Empire's peripheries in order to maintain control of the shipping lanes.

The activities of the disguised raiders provided a pertinent example of Rosinski's contention that the Germans and the Italians had set out to inflict "at least the maximum destruction" on British sea communications, rather than to wrest command of the sea itself.[50] Sorties by Axis light forces against coastal shipping in the English Channel and the Mediterranean proceeded in a similar vein, with the Kriegsmarine's motor torpedo E-boats causing considerable damage. Most noteworthy of these efforts were attacks mounted by Italy's Decima Flottiglia MAS because the Italians, contrary to derogatory postwar impressions of their valor and commitment, were prepared in this instance to sanction a range of methods clearly semisuicidal in nature. The catalog of assaults undertaken by the Regia Marina's explosive motorboats and semisubmersible manned torpedoes could not, however, redress the inherent disadvantage of a navy that remained entirely devoted to the fleet-in-being concept; nor could the Kriegsmarine hope to prevail in the Atlantic without the sustained coordination of surface, submarine, and air assets.[51] Stretched as it was, the Royal Navy retained its supremacy due to Axis navies' incapacity to deliver a knockout blow and to the Admiralty and field commanders conjuring the required level of operational flexibility to counter the various seaborne threats deployed against them. At the same time, the Royal Navy displayed its offensive capabilities in seeking to blockade German and Italian sea commerce, albeit with mixed results.

With the German occupation of Norway in 1940 and the Luftwaffe's presence in the North Sea and the Norwegian Sea, the Royal Navy's role in the active blockade of enemy shipping undoubtedly suffered a major setback. Sorties conducted by cruiser and destroyer flotillas yielded only modest results throughout the period in question, whereas a daylight attack against merchant shipping at Kirkness and Petsamo on 12 September 1941 proved to be a disaster for the FAA: it inflicted only minimal damage at the cost of over half the attackers lost to defending fighters and flak.[52] Attacks from Britain's smaller submarine arm likewise yielded only modest results, which were miniscule compared with those achieved by the U-boats; by December 1942 the Royal Navy's boats had sunk just 250,000 tons of merchant shipping—thirty-six ships in all. However, better fortune was to be found in the Mediterranean where the combined RAF and FAA operations, the surface attacks and submarine activity, decimated the Italian merchant marine, with the submarines alone sending an estimated 585,000 tons (195 ships) to the bottom. The solution for the initial lack of British success along the northern seaboard lay with the increasing strength of Coastal Command; by 1944 the RAF had throttled much of Germany's iron ore shipments through the combination of laying mines and low-level strikes by Coastal Command's fighter bombers.[53] Yet the overall effects of sea blockade against Germany were to be overshadowed by the fundamental nature of the European conflict itself, especially from June 1941 onward when Germany commenced the waging of a vast war of economic pillage against the Soviet Union.

"New Limitations on Sea Power"

Under this final subheading, Rosinski concluded his study by returning to the broader strategic struggle for supremacy between sea power and land power. Given the outcomes of the war prior to November 1940, he reasoned, sea power could be nullified through domination of the European plain by mechanized forces and airpower. In support of his contention, Rosinski cited the Norwegian campaign as an example of the modern difficulties sea power experienced when attempting to isolate land-based objectives by great naval campaigns; and he predicted a similar fate for Greece in the event of a future German land invasion.[54] When considering the pre-June 1941 period of the European conflict in isolation, the eventual military outcomes in both Greece and Crete largely validated his assessment, based as it was on the thus far unchallenged success of Germany's blitzkrieg warfare. With the evolution in complexity of the European war following the German invasion of the Soviet Union, however, a broader basis for determining the strategic contest between sea and land became necessary. Within the voluminous postwar analysis that exists, a general consensus has arisen that three particular elements came to shape both the character and conduct of this war from June 1941 onward: the Eastern Front, the strategic bombing of the German war economy, and the massive scale of American military intervention.[55] In rounding out our exploration of the Royal Navy's performance in the European theater, an overview of the various impacts of these three elements on Fleet operations completes the picture as to how and why Britain was able to master the European Axis naval threat.

Hitler's decision to unleash Operation Barbarossa against the Soviet Union on 22 June 1941 became the crucible for the ultimate defeat of the Wehrmacht on the battlefield and hence the defeat of Germany itself. In the vast campaigns that raged across the Russian steppe, the innate strength of the German army was first absorbed, then repulsed, and eventually broken by the sheer size and power of the Russian land-based military machine. For the Royal Navy, the Eastern Front presented a double-edged sword. British aid to the Soviets in the form of northern convoys to Russia further thinned the Fleet's already stretched resources, especially in a combat environment in which German surface warships, bombers, and U-boats were complemented by weather that favored successful convoy interdiction.[56] Rosinski believed the British naval blockade would provoke a food crisis in Germany because the Reich was burdened with captive peoples; this was proven incorrect. By applying what A. J. P. Taylor described as "autarky without restraint" on a massive scale in the East, the Germans were able to mitigate this problem through the systematic malnourishment—and often subsequent extermination—of what they viewed as an inexhaustible supply of foreign slave labor.[57] As detailed previously, the most substantial long-term benefit for the Admiralty arose through the steady transfer of the majority of the Luftwaffe's tactical-support, bomber, and long-range reconnaissance elements to the East, thereby dooming whatever opportunities that may have existed for the German and Italian navies to fulfill their strategic aims.

During the latter half of the 1930s the Admiralty's planners had acknowledged the need to neutralize the Luftwaffe through what was described as the "air counter-offensive" against Germany itself.[58] With the defeat of France in June 1940, and no possibility of an invasion of Europe within the then-foreseeable future, a strategic bombing campaign against the Reich's war industries presented as Britain's only viable option for waging a direct offensive war against Germany. By April 1942 the effects of RAF Bomber Command's attacks against the Ruhr had been negligible; the British bomber force did not yet possess the technology and techniques for effective night bombing of industrial targets. Even with the welcome addition of the U.S. Eighth Army Air Force during the final months of that year, a round-the-clock combined bomber offensive would remain largely ineffective until the Luftwaffe was defeated in its own airspace. As events transpired, it was not until May 1944 that the Allies were able to neutralize the German fighter force. By July 1944, punishing results were beginning to be achieved through the targeting of Germany's synthetic oil production and land transport infrastructure.[59] Prior to this point, the influence of strategic bombing on Royal Navy operations had been mixed at best. Due to the escalating demands of the bomber offensive, until mid-1943 at the earliest RAF Coastal Command did not possess enough long-range aircraft to combat German U-boats within the so-called Atlantic Gap. Nor for that matter did the bombing of U-boat production facilities—a stated strategic priority at the January 1943 Casablanca Conference—produce a tangible fall in submarine production before 1944, by which time the Allied navies had already succeeded in substantially defeating the U-boat threat at sea.[60]

The strategic bombing campaign did produce a decisive edge for the Admiralty at sea through its acquisition of radar and radio direction-finding technology, distinct from the material damage inflicted by the bombing itself. ASV (Air to Surface Vessel) airborne radar proved to be a useful first step; however it was the introduction of H2S shortwave radar in 1943 that made possible the large-scale detection and destruction of U-boats on the surface.[61] The provision of H2S, however, initially suffered from the same lack of interservice collaboration that had hampered the Royal Navy for most of the first four years of hostilities in Europe. During this period, a prolonged battle was waged within Whitehall as to whether strategic bombing or the struggle in the Atlantic should be afforded first priority in men and materials. Sir Arthur Harris, Bomber Command's new leader from February 1942 onward, forcefully argued the case for his command to be assigned the leading role in the defeat of Germany.[62] Once an acceptable level of cooperation had been reached between the services in mid-1943, the wholesale neutralization of the U-boat menace could at last begin in earnest. As for the presence of the Kriegsmarine's remaining surface warships, where the Royal Navy had thus far failed, Harris' aircraft succeeded in destroying the threat the battleship *Tirpitz* posed to the Admiralty's Russia-bound convoys. After repeated carrier-borne air strikes and a daring attack from X-craft submersibles, the giant *Tirpitz* was finally sunk at her moorings at Tromso on 12 November 1944 by Avro Lancaster aircraft armed with 12,000-pound demolition bombs.[63]

Following the sinking of the *Scharnhorst* by the British battleship *Duke of York* and her consorts at North Cape on 26 December 1943, the loss of the *Tirpitz* finished the career of the Kriegsmarine's surface fleet. In truth, the war it had fought was effectively lost when the first Japanese bombs were released over Pearl Harbor two years before. With the entry of the United States into the war and the subsequent decision by President Franklin Roosevelt to give priority to the defeat of Germany, the Allied cause in Europe could not realistically fail.[64] Yet neither could it succeed without the Atlantic sea-lanes being first secured, and it was the Royal Navy that had established the initial foundations for this. Trial and error in the first three years of the war against the U-boat had provided the British with the formulas to defeat the submarine. The provision of American naval support on an increasingly large scale permitted both navies to take the offensive in the Atlantic, aided as they were by the welcome presence of very long-range aircraft such as the B-24 Liberator supplied by the United States. When the Western Allied powers staged Operation Overlord on 6 June 1944, such was their level of naval control over the English Channel and its northern and southern approaches that the few attempts by German U-boats and light surface forces to stage any sort of meaningful incursion were contemptuously repulsed. America's intervention in the European naval war made it inevitable that the Allied fleets would eventually succeed in fulfilling Winston Churchill's stated April 1940 policy by making their collective will prevail in every part of the sea.

From September 1939 to April 1942, the Royal Navy had been compelled to fight one of the most arduous wars imaginable against its European Axis opponents. It had entered the war with an undermodernized battlefleet and aircraft carrier arm, an underdeveloped FAA, and little in the way of guaranteed land-based air support from RAF Coastal Command. Deprived of French support in July 1940, the Admiralty found itself involved in the most multidimensional naval conflict in history, with the challenge to provide effective solutions for each new operational situation encountered. In addition to what would be described as purely naval-centric activities, the Royal Navy had also been required to participate in four enforced evacuations of British and other Allied ground forces; but in spite of suffering heavy losses to Luftwaffe air attack, the Royal Navy succeeded in successfully evacuating the vast majority of troops involved. By April 1942 in the Atlantic and the oceans beyond, previous success and failure had equipped the British with the know-how to defeat Germany's *guerre de course*, though final victory itself still lay over a year away. The price for obtaining this advantage was grievous: 13 million tons of merchant shipping sunk as of June 1942 and the loss of several capital ships and carriers, the largest being the battle cruiser *Hood*, sunk by the *Bismarck* on 24 May 1941 with the loss of all but 3 of her 1,400-strong complement. In the Mediterranean, meanwhile, both the Mediterranean Fleet and Force H prevailed in a series of surface engagements with the fast and well-armed Italian squadrons. The value of naval airpower was emphasized with outstanding results at Taranto and Cape Matapan.

Similarly, success in the Mediterranean was bought dear; the mauling dealt the Mediterranean Fleet by the Luftwaffe in the 1941 evacuations of Greece and Crete merely solidified the lessons from Norway and Dunkirk the year before. For all its impressive results as an offensive torpedo-bomber force, the FAA's fighter defenses were a continuing source of weakness, with too few modern single-seat aircraft to adequately control the Fleet's own operational airspace. It had been fortunate indeed for the Allied cause in the Mediterranean and would so remain, that the Axis air arms found it impossible to provide the consistency in air support that would have prevented the Royal Navy from exercising any meaningful authority over those narrow waters. Still, with highly competent battlefield leadership and sensible use of vital advantages such as naval aviation and radar, the various British naval formations were usually able to prevail where and when required. To the east of Suez on 7 December 1941, however, another navy, and another way of fighting at sea, had announced its presence in no uncertain terms. In the balmy equatorial waters of the Far East, British naval supremacy was about to collide head-on with the most powerful array of naval air firepower yet assembled in war.

5

Niitaka Yama Nobore!

The Imperial Japanese Navy, 1920–41

A s Nagumo's charges proceeded along their stealthy eastward course through the murk and squalls of the bleak North Pacific on 1 December 1941 the commander of Japan's aircraft carrier spearhead received a flash coded signal from Imperial General Headquarters (IGHQ) in Tokyo. *Niitaka Yama Nobore!* (Climb Mount Niitaka!) commanded Vice Admiral Nagumo Chuichi to proceed with a surprise aerial attack on the morning of Sunday 7 December against the United States Pacific Fleet at Pearl Harbor. Meanwhile within a myriad of roadsteads across Southeast Asia and the Central Pacific, bulging Japanese troop transports were weighing anchor, en route to a series of invasion objectives stretching from Wake Island to the Malay Peninsula; massed bomber and fighter formations squatted ready on the aprons of Formosan and southern Indochinese airfields. Three adverse factors—an acrimonious and at times violent relationship with the Imperial Japanese Army, frequent internal factionalism, and material restrictions imposed by the need to preserve the Imperial Japanese Navy's existing stocks of fuel oil and aviation gasoline—had not succeeded in dissuading the navy from seeking a truly remarkable triumph. While Nagumo's carriers steamed toward the onset of their subsequent two-ocean rampage, the fleet's biggest battleships continued to swing serenely upon their moorings in the Inland Sea. Given the geographic immensity of an initial assault that stretched from

Hawaii to Singapore and the daunting necessity for precise coordination of a multitude of operations over such vast distances, Japan's aeroamphibious blitzkrieg staked a deserved claim as the single greatest offensive endeavor in recorded military history.

In his summation of the future course of the European war, Herbert Rosinski believed the British Empire in India and the Far East would be threatened by what he described as "new super war machines."[1] The assembly of Japan's six largest aircraft carriers into a single striking force—the Kido Butai—marked the creation of such a machine. On 7 December 1941, no other navy in the world possessed a single formation that could deal out the same level of aerial devastation as could Nagumo's command. Likewise, the Japanese had contrived the assembly of the most advanced land-based naval air arm in existence, specifically configured to exercise air superiority over vast distances. Understanding how and why Japan's naval air advocates were able to contrive such an imposing carrier-borne and land-based aerial capability is not founded alone on basic appreciation of command-and-control, strategy, tactics, and operational resources. By exploring these aspects individually, the wider montage reveals a unique coalescence of technology, pragmatism, patriotic pseudomysticism, and militarist geopolitics that guided the evolution of these formidable instruments during the interwar era. Through the recollections of the Imperial Japanese Navy's senior surviving participants the Western observer comes to absorb the complexity of Japanese naval thinking and practice: the wholehearted desire to pursue the offensive at all costs with very limited margin for error. In spite of these inherent flaws, Japan's premier strike weapons wielded a level of destructive power that could only be ultimately overcome by an equivalent commitment to the airplane at sea within the United States Navy.

Command and Control

On 7 December 1941 the command and control of the Imperial Japanese Navy resided in a multilevel structure under the supreme leadership of Emperor Hirohito. As Generalissimo of Japan's armed forces, the Emperor exercised his authority through a Supreme War Council, known from 1937 as the Imperial General Headquarters–Government Liaison Conference. This body formulated policy decisions at the highest level, invariably upon the advice of the Imperial General Headquarters (IGHQ), which represented the interests of both services and counted among its members the army and navy chiefs of General Staff, the war minister, and the navy minister.[2] Subordinate to the IGHQ were the Naval General Staff and the Navy Department; the former being responsible for all operational tasks the latter primarily responsible for administrative functions. Subordinate to the Naval General Staff, the Combined Fleet served as the umbrella strategic instrument for six major fleet commands including the carrier-borne First Air Fleet and the land-based Eleventh Air Fleet. Like their British and American counterparts, both the Naval General Staff and the Navy Department fell under the delegated authority of the navy minister, whose presence conveyed the outward impression that the navy was subject to cabinet-government and Japanese Diet (parliament) dictates.[3] Unfortunately, the Meiji Constitution contained no credible provisions for government oversight, as understood by Western democracies.

The considerable range of Royal Navy guidance and material assistance provided to the Imperial Japanese Navy after its formation in the 1870s, noted Arthur Marder, did not extend to inculcating the Japanese with Western concepts of the role of the military in a democratic political system. The Meiji Constitution provided for a Western-style parliamentary system; however, its framework reinforced the authority of the traditional warlord military factions, its Articles XI and XII placing the armed services under direct sovereign authority. This enabled the Imperial Japanese Army to assume the dominant role in national politics. Only by means of imperial decree was an independent Naval General Staff established in 1903.[4] Under this constitution the civilian government exercised no binding authority over the military, with the war and navy ministers being appointed from the ranks of serving officers. The conventions and practices of Japanese government and administration were based on the Prussian model; the Imperial Japanese Army had chosen the Prussian state as its exemplar throughout the post-1850s reconstruction of the nation's civil and military institutions. Western history has generally portrayed the emergence of ultranationalist sentiment in the early 1930s as the catalyst for Japan becoming a militarist state: the wherewithal for army dominance in national politics had, however, been established over several decades with enactment of the Publication Law in 1893 paving the way for subsequent legislative erosion of civil rights and liberties.[5]

While the absence of executive government control over the armed services would benefit the Japanese navy's evolution as a first-line maritime power in certain respects, direct military subordination to the Emperor did not remove a serious obstacle to that service's peacetime ambitions. As Hirohito consistently displayed a marked reluctance to impose his views on the "advisory" Supreme War Council/Liaison Conference, policy debates within this body were waged along service lines. Thanks to the Japanese Army's higher standing in the political arena due to growing public support from ultranationalist organizations during the late 1920s, it usually got its way in forming domestic public policy.[6] The navy as a fleet undoubtedly benefited from the continuation of its various Replenishment Plans in the wake of the establishment of the Washington naval disarmament regime; however, the command structure it operated under revealed a number of glaring flaws. Considering itself sole guardian of all military and naval planning, the IGHQ refused to share its formulations with civilian representatives in the Liaison Conference while also refusing any naval strategy advice or assistance from the Combined Fleet's senior commanders. And though Navy Department influence had been supposedly negated through creation of the Naval General Staff, Chihaya Masatake described the department's Military Affairs Bureau as the "centre of propulsion" for the navy as a whole because of its overarching jurisdiction in the vital areas of procurement, supply, and day-to-day fleet administration.[7]

As the 1930s progressed, lack of an effective third-party buffer between the Japanese armed services only served to exacerbate an increasingly volatile relationship between them. Whereas disputes between British services were usually confined to a slew of memoranda and bouts of tut-tutting within the echelons of higher command, the Japanese reality bore greater resemblance to the settling of underworld scores in New York and Chicago. Violence and intimidation were often used by young radical army and navy officers toward their conservative superiors. A number of politicians were assassinated for "crimes" such as supporting the Washington Naval Treaty or pursuing friendly relations with the Western democracies. Both Admiral Yamamoto (CIC Combined Fleet) and Admiral Yonai (Navy Minister) received direct threats because of their opposition to Japan's entry into the 1940 Tripartite Pact with Germany and Italy.[8] Germany's naval attaché Vice Admiral Paul Wenneker noted in his postwar interrogation that senior-level joint army and navy planning was undertaken only when absolutely necessary, while endemic corruption ran rampant at many administrative levels in the IGHQ command structure. And beneath the everyday hurly-burly of interservice relations lay a fundamental schism in army and navy strategic thinking: the army's commitment to imperial expansion on the North Asian mainland was at odds with navy plans to seize critical resources in Southeast Asia. The major consequence of this divide was the constant threat of deadlock in ongoing policy deliberations.[9]

Quite aside from descending into increasing conflict with army militants, the navy's command structure suffered a number of serious internal divisions, further weakening its position in the wider Japanese political landscape. From the February 1922 signing of the Washington Treaty, a major rift had developed between the so-called Fleet (Naval General Staff) and Treaty (Navy Department) factions. A number of Staff officers denounced the agreement as a national disgrace and publicly berated then–navy minister, Kato Tomosaburo, for agreeing to sign it. With Tomosaburo's death in 1923 the Fleet faction gained increasing influence over the service as a whole.[10] Then in 1933 the appointment of the pro-German Osumi Mineo as navy minister triggered a large-scale purge; numerous senior admirals were denounced and cashiered as supportive of the treaty regime and Western-orientated in their outlook. This event exposed within the officer corps an open geopolitical breach— many junior-grade officers were beginning to reject traditional links with the Royal Navy in favor of new bonds with the German and Italian fleets. Indeed many young officers had joined the "bandwagon," as Oi Atsushi described the surge in patriotic public support for the nationalist-militarist movement. This momentum led to another split in 1939 within the senior ranks, this time over Japan's proposed admission to the Tripartite Pact.[11] The signing of the pact in September 1940 represented another victory for the radicals, and a further distancing of the navy from its long-standing British exemplar.

Although radicals within the navy were determined to relinquish British traditions and practices that had been established at the Etajima Naval Academy since 1888, one philosophical bond remained firmly in place: *Kenteki Hissen* or "Fight the Enemy on Sight." This concept lay at the heart of the navy's philosophy, for the Japanese both admired and sought to emulate the Royal Navy's principle of taking the fight to the enemy as quickly and decisively as possible. This concept fit with the ideal of *Nihon Seishin*, "Japanese spirit," which emphasized Japan's moral and spiritual superiority over its Western opponents and, in turn, created what Arthur Marder described as the "Tsushima-Jutland syndrome" within the navy's senior leadership.[12] Aside from the individual impact these philosophies had on operational, tactical, and material initiatives (to be explored shortly), their presence created what Ohmae Toshikazu considered to be an overemphasis "on the offensive in our naval thinking and our War College training." For the navy the consequences of an ultraoffensive mentality were ultimately disastrous in two central respects.

First the command structure totally ignored the need to secure wartime trade and commerce through a convoy system; indeed a separate Escort Fleet command did not eventuate until 1943.[13] With no effective means of protecting the critical conveyance of raw materials, most especially fuel oil, the Japanese merchant marine would be systematically massacred by American submarines throughout the course of the war. This demise of Japan's mercantile shipping, which drastically curtailed the operational scope of the navy's endeavors due to a lack of fuel oil, came to represent but one consequence of the navy's reckless obsession with the offensive at sea.

The second consequence is in what Vice Admiral Kurita Takeo subsequently described as the lack of "a sure touch, a sure treatment of planmaking" within the ranks of the Naval General Staff. Numerous Western accounts have seized upon the Japanese penchant for overly elaborate battle planning. Donald Macintyre provides this sage summary, referring to the fateful Midway campaign in June 1942: "The ingenious and elaborate Japanese plan, with its division of the fleet into a number of independent task forces, could only justify its disregard of the principle of concentration of force if secrecy were preserved and surprise was achieved."[14]

Macintyre's interpretation highlighted the fundamental weakness within the Japanese command system. Individual fleet commanders were prevented from exercising influence over IGHQ and Naval General Staff planning procedures. These inherent disconnects effectively compromised the navy's capacity to use the Combined Fleet's naval and aerial capabilities to their fullest extent, a malady that would not become evident until May 1942 during the Coral Sea engagement. For the present, however, the core failings of Japan's naval command were largely subsumed against a backdrop of strategic policy, which, if sensibly executed, held out the prospect of an incredible success against American and British naval might.

Strategy

In spite of prevailing factionalism within naval ranks, the leadership remained committed to a perimeter-defense strategic posture for the balance of the interwar period, its centerpiece being the theory of Kantai Kessen (Decisive Battle). This Japanese concept emerged in the writings of two of the foremost naval strategists, Akiyama Shinshi and Sato Tetsutaro. Akiyama's early 1900s publication, *Kai Sen Yomu-Hei* ("Essential Instructions on Naval Battles"), became the strategic bible for senior naval planners.[15] As Vice Admiral Ozawa Jisaburo explained in his postwar writings, from 1905 the United States became regarded by the Naval General Staff as Japan's foremost future naval adversary, and by 1920 planning was in place for a Jutland-style confrontation east of the Philippines. This engagement was thought to be the logical consequence of initial amphibious attacks against Guam and the Philippines that would bring the U.S. Navy's Pacific Fleet steaming to the aid of these distant dependencies in much the same manner as the Tsar had dispatched the Baltic Fleet to Port Arthur during the 1904–5 Russo-Japanese War.[16] Not until 1938 did the Japanese begin formal planning (and only in a most perfunctory fashion) for the possibility of waging a simultaneous naval war against the United States and Britain. Yet as Captain Watanabe Yasugi noted in his postwar interrogation, prewar instruction at Etajima did cater to this possibility: "In Japanese tactics we were told when we have two enemies, one in front and one in the back, first we must cut in front by sword. Only cut and not kill, but make it hard. Then we attack the back enemy and kill him. Then we come back to front enemy and kill him."[17]

Watanabe's blunt interpretation of the solution to Japan's probable two-ocean dilemma neatly illustrated the Imperial Japanese Navy's chosen strategic formula in December 1941 at the outbreak of hostilities with the Western powers. War with the United States would commence with a surprise attack against the Pacific Fleet at Pearl Harbor by the Kido Butai's massed carrier-borne spearhead. Immediately after this attack the navy's land-based Koku Kantai (Eleventh Air Fleet) was to perform two critical tasks: seek out and destroy any capital ships and aircraft carriers based at Singapore and annihilate American aircraft at Clark Field sixty miles north of Manila. Once these targets were neutralized, Combined Fleet resources were to lend their support to a series of aeroamphibious thrusts through the Central and Southwest Pacific and the Indonesian archipelago.[18] With the boundaries of the newly conquered Southern Resources Area secured, the Kido Butai would meet and defeat any attempt by the Royal Navy to intervene from the Indian Ocean, reverse course and finally settle its score with the Americans in the long-planned Kantai Kessen, and negotiate a subsequent settlement to secure Japan's new imperial frontiers.

The Imperial Navy's domination of Japan's strategic policy at the eleventh hour should not be interpreted as the result of a long-standing systematic enterprise on its part. For as Ohmae Toshikazu and other Japanese participants have suggested, planning for a naval-centric war in East Asia commenced only in 1938, with periodic revisions until final approval by the IGHQ Liaison Conference in November 1941.[19] The changing tides of geopolitical fortune from June 1940 onward created the circumstances for a major U-turn. With the signing of the Tripartite Pact and the subsequent conclusion of a nonaggression treaty with the Soviet Union, the Imperial Army had readily surrendered its primary ambition to combat the Soviets. So the Imperial Japanese Navy was actually able to take the initiative in policy making by benefiting from an Axis alliance that the majority of the service's most senior officers had come to view with intense vexation during the interwar period.[20] Central to the maintenance of Japan's long-term security in the eyes of the naval planners was the establishment of a perimeter shield stretching from the Malay Barrier to the Aleutian Islands. If the existing Western presence in Southeast Asia and the Pacific could be rapidly overcome, the fortification of chosen strongpoints, both astride and within this perimeter, would make Japan's newfound economic gains practically unassailable.

The particular geography in the assigned perimeter of the Southern Resources Area presented the most powerful argument for the navy's chosen strategy. West of Rabaul the various access points to waters beyond the Malay Barrier were both narrow and well covered by a myriad of airfield sites, providing the Japanese with the priceless advantage of local, land-based air cover; their opponents, however, would be compelled to seize territory in order to furnish a similar level of support. Within the Japanese Empire's eastern boundaries lay a series of island chains that could be rapidly utilized by its warships and aircraft in the event of a retaliatory thrust by the Pacific Fleet. The location of these islands enabled the construction of several concentric rings of defense of Japan itself.[21] Any American or British attempt to force this lengthy perimeter with substantial naval forces would likely risk entering seas and straits festooned with a veritable hornet's nest of aircraft, warships, submarines, and mines. However the annexation of southern Indochina in July 1941, a major jumping-off point for the navy's initial southward thrust (and the resulting American embargo upon Japanese oil supplies), must be viewed as an important caveat on Japan's perimeter strategy. With the Japanese navy's existing fuel reserves standing at eighteen months' full supply as of November 1941, timetabling the process of assault and consolidation became the critical issue.[22]

Sato Ichiro's assertion in *Brassey's 1927* that the Japanese navy's strategic posture was strictly defensive rang true in terms of fuel-oil supplies, for even the Fleet's prewar exercise regime suffered from cutbacks because of shortages. Lack of a guaranteed wellhead supply source was the major impediment to any Combined Fleet attempts to enforce its supremacy beyond the proposed imperial boundaries.[23] If the navy's principal objective, the oilfields within the Netherlands East Indies, could not be successfully secured, further naval and air activity would be severely curtailed, exposing Japan's perimeter and interior defenses. Chief of Naval General Staff Admiral Nagano Osami, in his submission to a Liaison Conference meeting on 23 October 1941, warned the assembled military leadership that the Japanese fleet was already consuming an hourly average of four hundred tons of fuel oil; thus, offensive action could be undertaken only within the next few months.[24] The poor state of Japan's existing Pacific defenses created additional pressure on navy planners. Chihaya Masatake chronicled a litany of uncompleted works at vital strongpoints in the Caroline, Marshall, and Mariana Island chains—a situation due, in part, to the Japanese government's reluctance to openly contravene Washington Treaty prohibitions of fortifying advanced bases. Further complicating the situation, Japan's merchant marine did not possess the capacity to simultaneously support offensive activity, convey captured resources, and provide for the urgent upgrading of existing Pacific facilities.[25]

Aside from these structural weaknesses, the essential problem for the Japanese lay in actually luring America's Pacific Fleet into this labyrinth to engage and destroy it. Under the pre-April 1941 planning regime, opinion remained divided as to whether the Americans would launch an immediate effort to relieve the Philippines or would adopt a more systematic "island-by-island" campaign.[26] From the American perspective, Hector Bywater had warned that when "the United States relieved Spain of the Philippines, she gave hostages to fortune in a sense that the American people never fully realised." Sensibly the Americans had removed the early advance concept under that nation's War Plan Orange protocols during the mid-1930s. Those Japanese officers who had assumed the length of a Pacific conflict to be in the order of two to three years were proven correct in one sense—within three years of Pearl Harbor, the Japanese fleet had been effectively decimated as a fighting force.[27] Despite the possibility of a destructive blow at Pearl Harbor, Admiral Nagano warned his IGHQ colleagues that there was "no set of steps that would guarantee our checkmating the enemy," and Yamamoto had expressed similar fears given his firsthand knowledge of American industrial expertise. Therefore, at the outset, the scale of devastation wrought upon the Pacific Fleet would have to be such that the United States would have no other option than to seek an early settlement, thus creating the time required to secure Japan's future strategic position.[28]

While the Pacific Fleet occupied the forefront of Japanese strategic thinking throughout the majority of the prewar era, the presence of the Royal Navy came to be regarded as somewhat less menacing. By 1939 the Naval General Staff had correctly assumed that the British Admiralty would be unable to initially assemble a large fleet in Far Eastern waters because of the evolving situation in Europe, thereby permitting the Imperial Japanese Navy to destroy any advance force based at Singapore before dealing with a subsequent British fleet presence in the Eastern Indian Ocean.[29] Although Yamamoto was persuaded to assign a separate escort force to protect troop convoys during passage to their assigned Malayan beachheads, he believed the squadron that the Admiralty eventually dispatched to Singapore in November 1941 would be located and destroyed by the elite land-based 22nd Air Flotilla flying from Indochinese airfields. Once the Indonesian archipelago was secured, the Kido Butai was to replicate its activities over Hawaii with similar air strikes against the main British fleet anchorages at Ceylon.[30] Operating as an independent first-strike weapon and equipped with its train of oilers and other fleet auxiliaries, Nagumo's force provided a practical solution to a vital Japanese problem, namely the need to subdue two enemy fleets in two separate oceans. If the fast-moving Kido Butai was able to strike each of its opponents at anchor, or at sea, it possessed the required aerial firepower to inflict losses the Americans and the British would be unable to recoup for many months, if not years. The entire Indo-Pacific theater would be at Japan's mercy.

Tactics

From the outset in the 1870s, the Imperial Japanese Navy's officer corps recognized that in the absence of industrial superiority, Japan would have to match the larger Great Power fleets through supremacy in quality. Ozawa Jisaburo set out the formula the Japanese sought to adapt in the form of the equation $F \propto M \times E \times S$. Fighting strength ($F$) was to be determined by the combination of mechanical strength (*M*), efficiency (*E*), and mental strength (*S*).[31] In concert with the positive effects of the significant range of training and technical assistance provided Japan by Britain, America, and France from the 1870s, this equation came to the fore during the 1904–5 Russo-Japanese War. The combination of the one-two punch that still characterized the navy's strategy as of December 1941—the initial surprise attack and a resulting decisive battle—had been revealed with devastating force at Port Arthur (February 1904) and Tsushima (May 1905). In both engagements Japanese forces clearly demonstrated their capacity to carry out a series of lightning thrusts into the heart of the Russian fleets through superior reconnaissance, signaling, mobility, and firepower. For the first time in naval history Admiral Togo's fleet at Tsushima used the wireless to coordinate rapier cuts into the slower Russian formation, which was fatally handicapped by its chaotic procession of obsolete warships no longer fit for first-line service.[32]

Whereas the Russians, like the Chinese before them in the 1894 Sino-Japanese War, were not in the same class as the other Great Power navies, the Japanese had nevertheless displayed their mastery of surprise and speed, particularly in the prosecution of night engagements. Ozawa regarded this emphasis on night operations "a very favourable method for the side which had the [numerically] weaker force," and the Imperial Japanese Navy took special note of the havoc that torpedoes could cause in a close-combat environment.[33] Yet development of Japanese tactical doctrine continued to follow that favored by the Western navies during the 1920s, with the battle-line remaining the core of Imperial Japanese Navy fighting strength. Led by Vice Admiral Koga Mineichi, the so-called battleship faction continued to exercise a powerful influence even after the success at Pearl Harbor. In his informative postwar essay, Oi Atsushi described the rationale behind this thinking regarding development of the monster battleships *Yamato* and *Musashi* during the 1930s: "The fact that the Japanese Navy had *Yamato* and *Musashi* is believed to be partly, if not primarily, responsible for making the Japanese admirals so obsessed with a 'battleship first' idea. Then why did the Japanese navy build these mammoth battleships? Because the superiority of the U.S. Fleet over the Japanese naval forces was so great that the Japanese Naval General Staff . . . tried to discover various sorts of tactical methods to reduce this U.S. superiority before a final fleet encounter was fought."[34]

In step with its Western counterparts, throughout the 1920s the navy considered the aircraft carrier an auxiliary to the battle fleet for scouting and striking purposes. Admiral Ozawa, as one of Japan's foremost interwar advocates of naval airpower, offered commentary on the interaction between battleship and carrier that clearly highlights the tactical weaknesses of this relationship prior to 1934.

> In usual cases the carrier division used to stay, generally as a group, within the visibility limit of the battleship group on the latter's noncombat side. Its aim was to give air cover over the latter as well as over itself, in addition to its own mission of attacking the enemy. Another reason for keeping the carrier division quite near the battleship group was not to let it separate from the main force, while making flexible movements as a carrier group in accordance with the prevailing wind, lest it should be offered a chance of being attacked separately. But this school of tactics had a disadvantageous aspect which before long was uncovered through further subsequent studies. This disposition of a carrier division in fact contained the battleship's movement too; the latter came to lose its flexibility of movements for the decisive engagement. Moreover on many occasions both the battleship group and the carrier division were simultaneously discovered by the enemy, thus increasing the chance of the vulnerable carriers being attacked [by] almost 100%. The method of giving one fighter cover over both the battleship group and the carrier division also proved not so effective.[35]

Whereas the Japanese aircraft carriers had been organized into separate divisions (each division containing two carriers and screening forces) from 1928, it was not until 1934 that studies were undertaken as to the feasibility of carriers acting independently from the battle fleet. Yet until April 1941, each of the carrier divisions continued to be attached to a corresponding battleship division. In adopting this course through the latter half of the 1930s the Japanese pursued a line of thinking similar to that of the United States Navy, which had also been experimenting with independent carrier-air tactics while still placing its carriers at the disposal of the battleline.[36]

In April 1941, however, the efforts of Ozawa, Yamamoto, and Admiral Inoue Shigeyoshi were rewarded: the First Air Fleet was established, which in due course became known as the Kido Butai. From Yamamoto's

1940 appointment as commander in chief (CIC) of the Combined Fleet, intensive exercises had also been conducted combining carrier-borne and land-based airpower because from 1932 the latter had been regarded as a critical way to offset Japan's numerical inferiority in surface warships.[37] The formation of the Kido Butai marked the first occasion in naval history that a nation determined to field all of its large aircraft carriers within a single striking fleet. Further, at the outbreak of war the navy's land-based Eleventh Air Fleet deployed the elite *Genzan* Air Corps, a veteran of Chinese operations and the most powerful specialist day/night antishipping unit then in existence.[38]

The absence of analysis in both Japanese and Western sources of what the outcome of an early engagement might have been between the Kido Butai and the Pacific Fleet *at sea* does leave a gap in history's understanding of this remarkable naval air force. Use of aircraft and submarines to reduce the American fleet before the set-piece decisive battle highlighted the multidimensional nature of Japanese planning and tactics. An attack mounted by Nagumo's carriers in the absence of the Combined Fleet held out the prospect of an appalling disaster for the United States Navy. Had the Japanese sought to conduct their southern thrust without an initial strike against Hawaii, a clash between these enemy forces would have exposed the Pacific Fleet with its carriers providing support to the battleline as a slow-moving target for the crack Japanese naval aviators. A concentrated air strike mounted against an ill-prepared American opponent with its carrier assets divided, and not yet possessing aircrews with combat experience, would have contained all the ingredients for a potential massacre. The total number of big ships lost at sea plus a corresponding escalation in casualties outside the shallow depths of Pearl Harbor could have instigated the knockout blow Yamamoto and his subordinates were attempting to achieve. One of the principal reasons why the staccato encounter between the British Eastern Fleet and the Kido Butai off Ceylon in April 1942 assumes such importance is because these skirmishes were the only occasion when Nagumo's carrier force—operating independently—clashed with a fleet-scale opponent.

The presence of the carrier spearhead provided the necessary mechanical strength to defeat Japan's Western adversaries; yet this tactic represented but part of the equation in the Japanese navy's mindset for achieving naval supremacy. Operational efficiency and mental strength were likewise considered to be prerequisites; however, in terms of field command both Japanese and Western historical sources have emphasized the lack of quality leadership at this level. Japanese accounts have highlighted the enforced retirement of officers for pro-Western sympathies as a major catalyst, whereas both Arthur Marder and Fuchida Mitsuo have highlighted what Marder described as "the absence of independent rational judgement" as a flaw in both naval and national character.[39] The British and Americans were able to produce a series of gifted fleet commanders such as Cunningham, Somerville, Halsey, and Spruance, but the Japanese remained somewhat limited in this area. Ozawa was considered to be a standout as an accomplished fleet tactician, though doubts existed over the competence of Nagumo, as will be explored in the following chapters. At the subordinate fleet levels, leaders including Admiral Mikawa Gunichi and Admiral Tanaka Raizo were responsible for some of the navy's most notable Pacific successes, especially night engagements. Both Oi and Takata Toshitane believed a lack of high-quality officer cadets, combined with the inherent conservatism of their superiors, was the principal reason fewer Japanese officers possessed less expertise at fleet command and subordinate levels than their Allied counterparts.[40]

Several British postwar studies have independently concluded that the standards of Japanese seamanship were generally excellent, with Marder noting that the Imperial Japanese Navy petty officers were the best of their kind, with outstanding specialist skills in many areas. This level of competence has been largely attributed to the ferocious training regime the Combined Fleet undertook during the interwar period in spite of restrictions imposed by fuel shortages.[41] The simulation of actual battle conditions in training (including the frequent use of live ammunition) honed the navy's crews with an extra edge in their skills—a policy not without considerable cost. Peacetime exercises resulted in a high number of sailor and aircrew casualties; numerous fatalities were sustained during exercises in a 1936 typhoon. The Imperial Japanese Navy and Air Force training regime produced a highly experienced first-line cadre but very little in the way of trained reserves. Many among the armed-services leadership believed that through rigorous training the "moral spirit of Japan, the land of the Gods, will shine on this occasion," as Army vice chief of staff Tsukada Ko emphasized at a Liaison Conference on 1 November 1941.[42] The concept of mental superiority became enshrined in this notion of Japanese spiritual leadership, emphasized as it had been through the cult of *Bushido* where self-sacrifice for the Emperor became recognized as the highest national virtue. This belief structure persisted throughout the course of the war, eventually creating the rationale for the official adoption of kamikaze suicide tactics in late 1944.[43]

Operational Resources

Japan's impressive prewar array of capital ships, heavy cruisers, light cruisers, and destroyers reflected a combination of British and indigenous design influences, most visible in the four capital ship and numerous light cruiser classes constructed during the pre-Washington period. Post-1922 cruiser and destroyer concepts, however, showed a sharp shift toward wholly Japanese naval design. Responding to restricted capital ship numbers, the Japanese began developing a series of heavy cruiser and destroyer classes designed to be superior to anything the Western navies could field, albeit with a considerable amount of fudging of official tonnage limits imposed on these classes of vessel.[44] The construction of Japanese heavy cruisers continued unabated during the 1930s, although the Imperial Japanese Navy's refusal to share design details of their new *Furutaka*-class heavy cruisers with the Royal Navy in 1926 led to a hefty scaling back of design cooperation between the fleets. The most notable shift in Japanese thinking about qualitative superiority came in the mid-1930s with the construction of the massive *Yamato*-class super-battleships. Equipped with enormous 18-inch guns, the Yamato class could outshoot any capital ship afloat while packing a formidable array of antiaircraft weaponry. So secret was the process of design and construction for these ships that the British considered early reports of their size exaggerated; and the Americans knew virtually nothing of their operational specifications until the end of the war.[45]

Aside from the speed and size advantages that Japanese heavy cruisers and lethal *Fubuki*- and *Kagero*-class destroyers enjoyed over their Western counterparts, the most powerful Imperial Japanese Navy surface weapon was the Type 93 surface-launched torpedo. Known as the Long Lance, these formidable liquid oxygen–powered weapons were carried on all Japanese cruisers and destroyers, and many of the pre-Washington light cruisers were refitted as large torpedo boats.[46] With dimensions similar to those of a modern cruise missile, the Long Lance could reach speeds of forty knots with a maximum combat range of up to twenty-four nautical miles—the approximate equivalent of the primary surface batteries on capital ships. These torpedoes were wakeless—and their volatile fuel mixture and their massive warheads could easily tear apart any warship up to the size of a heavy cruiser (ten thousand tons) with a single hit; Allied capital ships and carriers were also extremely vulnerable against their striking power. Designed for use by submarines, the Type 95 torpedo was also capable of extreme speeds; however the Japanese failure to employ its submarine fleet in a commerce-raiding capacity proved to be a costly strategic blunder.[47] Whereas British cruisers and destroyers were equipped with torpedoes, American cruisers were not; this contributed to a number of disastrous results for the United States Navy throughout the Solomons campaign. As Japan slid toward defeat in late 1944, manned versions of the Long Lance were employed as *Kaiten* suicide weapons.[48]

Japanese advances in aircraft carrier design were significantly aided in the early 1920s by sensitive Royal Navy technical data provided by Lieutenant Commander Frederick Rutland who had been co-opted by the Japanese in an elaborate espionage campaign to obtain British design secrets.[49] The initial conversion of the fast capital ships *Akagi* and *Kaga* was followed in 1934 by the construction of the light carrier *Ryujo* and in the late 1930s by the commissioning of *Soryu* and *Hiryu* as purpose-designed fleet carriers. In 1941 the two *Shokaku*-class vessels *Shokaku* and *Zuikaku* entered service; prior to the appearance of the American *Essex*-class in 1943, these ships were considered by many Western experts to be the most advanced carrier designs in the world.[50] Aided by tanker refueling capability from 1927 onward, the performance of *Soryu*, *Hiryu*, and the two *Shokaku*s exceeded that of their British and American counterparts. Through the use of turbine assemblies similar to those used on the navy's latest destroyers, which meant operational speeds of 33 knots or better for all four ships, the Japanese had produced a series of vessels with excellent handling characteristics. This combination of speed and extended range allowed the Kido Butai to voyage beyond the boundaries of the Empire's proposed defensive perimeter, creating a formidable first-strike instrument.[51] Moreover, the employment of a force of this nature allowed the Combined Fleet to retain the majority of its older and slower battleships within Japanese home waters—a consequential savings in terms of the navy's critical fuel reserves.

Rutland's treasonous disclosures to the Japanese apparently failed to prevent a serious flaw within all of the Japanese navy's prewar carrier designs, with disastrous wartime results. Unlike the majority of British and American carriers, the Japanese vessels incorporated the storage tanks for aviation gasoline (avgas) within the actual hull structure itself. Even if a torpedo or bomb failed to detonate the avgas upon impact, the resulting concussion often fractured the tanks and their associated pumping apparatus, allowing the fuel to vaporize and spread throughout the ship, turning it into a floating time bomb.[52] Lack of armor protection, efficient ventilation, and firefighting equipment provided all the necessary ingredients for subsequent catastrophic explosions that invariably destroyed the ship with enormous casualties. Three fleet carriers and five of the navy's eight escort carriers were thus sunk, following torpedo attacks by American submarines. This mode of attack revealed another notable weakness in Japanese naval research, namely the failure to properly develop advanced electronic aids such as radar and associated antisubmarine warfare (ASW) detection equipment. Both Japanese and Western sources have outlined the navy's desire to create a fleet was almost entirely devoted to offensive activity at sea; the outcome meant Japanese ships lacked proper defensive capabilities, rendering the carriers and many surface warships especially susceptible to battle damage. This oversight likewise prevailed in the skies above.[53]

The Imperial Japanese Navy's land-based air arm owed much of its post-1919 development to another triumph of espionage, this time through classified material provided by William Forbes-Sempill, otherwise known as Colonel the Master of Sempill. Leader of the RAF's first "unofficial" mission to Japan, Sempill handed over secrets while his compatriots provided the Japanese with first-rate tuition in a myriad of areas, including establishing training facilities and instruction in flying procedures on aircraft carriers. At the heart of the British Air Ministry's tacit approval for the mission lay the desire to monopolize influence at the expense of the Italians and French, thereby creating a future market for British aviation firms such as Gloster and Handley Page.[54] Yet it was the Japanese who played the British for fools by reaping all the rewards. Japanese aircraft and their associated heavy and manufacturing industries were the principal beneficiaries of the acquisition of brand-new infrastructure for developing their own indigenous designs, an enhanced understanding of aviation science, and a doggy-bag full of license contracts, particularly for the production of British-designed air engines, Throughout the 1930s large industrial entities including Mitsubishi Jukogyo, Nakajima Hikoki, and Kawanishi Kokuki established a domestic monopoly, reinforced in 1938 by government control over licensing and aircraft specifications.[55] In a rare instance of general cooperation between the armed services, manufacturers were permitted to design and build aircraft for each service's air arm, with the larger firms generally producing a wider variety of aircraft types than their British counterparts.

By 1936 both Japanese armed services had sought increasing technical interaction with the Luftwaffe and the Regia Aeronautica, with the Japanese army taking a particular interest in German and Italian design trends. With Yamamoto's establishment of a series of design teams upon his 1932 appointment as head of the navy's aeronautical Technical Division, the Imperial Japanese Navy, equipped with information and advice obtained from British, American, and French firms, embarked upon a wholly indigenous path.[56] The results of this ambitious program began to emerge from 1936 on. Three new monoplane aircraft, the Type 96 fighter (Claude), the Type 96 attack bomber (Nell), and the Type 97 attack bomber (Kate), entered general production in 1936; these were followed by the Type 99 bomber (Val) in 1939 and in 1940 by the Type 1 attack bomber (Betty). With the exception of the Claude, a sprightly little carrier-borne fighter, which could easily outperform its mid- and late-1930s foreign counterparts, the remaining types formed the backbone of the navy's carrier aircraft and land-based aerial arsenal at the outset of hostilities with the Western powers. Both the Kate and the Val were superior in virtually all aspects of performance over their existing British and American counterparts and constituted the attack arm on all of the navy's large fleet carriers. As for the Nell and Betty, these two land-based attack planes were equally proficient weapon platforms for bomb and aerial torpedo payloads; and each possessed a combat range that would only be exceeded by the massive American Boeing B-29.[57]

These two Japanese aircraft types marked a major difference in approach between the Japanese land-based elements and American naval air arms. At the outset of the Indo-Pacific conflict, the United States Navy did not then possess any comparable offensive strike aircraft and would not until the latter half of 1942, when it began to acquire B-24 Liberator bombers in moderate to large numbers. For the majority of the forthcoming war in the Southwest Pacific region, most particularly the Solomons and New Guinea theaters, America's long-range air strike capability was principally assigned to the United States Army Air Corps. Airplanes such as the B-17 Flying Fortress and the B-25 Mitchell were to perform the particularly necessary function of interdicting Japanese sea communications by targeting transport shipping and light naval traffic, aided by the increasing antishipping power of the Royal Australian Air Force (RAAF). In contrast, the Imperial Japanese

Army Air Force would play only a very limited role in antishipping action until the war's final stages, when its aircraft were increasingly committed to the kamikaze offensive in defense of the Japanese Home Islands. Largely equipped with aircraft types designed for ground-support operations, the majority of the army's air-arm strength remained concentrated in China and Burma for the duration of hostilities; it did, however, see service in the Philippines, Malaya, New Guinea, and eventually in defense of Japanese cities against the American B-29 bombing offensive.

In late 1941 the United States Army Air Corps Far East Air Force command received a report from the American military attaché in Tokyo that provided performance details of a new Japanese fighter type. These were dismissed by one officer as a case of the attaché "drinking too much sake," because the Americans (like the British) entertained a fairly low opinion of Japanese aviation as a whole.[58] Given the increasing number of accounts that have addressed various ethnocentric rationales for such Western observations, it is suffice to say here that the underestimation of Japan's aerial capabilities by the British—for it was largely their expertise the Japanese had acquired and exploited—would prove to be a particularly foolish error of judgment. And it became particularly lethal for none more than the unfortunate Allied pilots who would face Japan's aerial capabilities, including the very subject of the attaché's information that had been so casually dismissed.

The Mitsubishi Zeke naval fighter had first flown over China in 1940 and decimated its antiquated opposition. Designed by Horikoshi Jiro, this aircraft presented the greatest single threat to the Allied cause in the Indo-Pacific theater: it had an enormous combat radius of 800 miles, outstanding dog-fighting capabilities, and powerful armament.[59] The presence of this air-craft would permit the Imperial Japanese Navy to establish a wide-ranging umbrella over any chosen area of operations, thereby enabling carrier- and land-based attack planes to strike with impunity and establish absolute air supremacy as required.

Yet this outstanding duralumin machine and the crack pilots who flew it also embodied the inherent weaknesses in Japanese naval aviation that would eventually cost so dearly. Like their colleagues in warship development, the navy's aircraft designers sought every offensive advantage for their charges. Such advantages came at the expense of crucial items such as protective armor, self-sealing fuel tanks, and adequate defensive gunnery for bomb-ers and attack planes. Even a sustained burst of light-caliber machine-gun fire could down a Zeke; and the Betty later became known as the "one-shot lighter" for its propensity to quickly explode when struck by cannon or tracer ammunition.[60] As long as the Japanese retained their superiority in pilots and in aircraft performance, losses could be kept to an acceptable minimum— they had to be, because the acceptable minimum within the Imperial Japanese Navy was far less than elsewhere: the grueling training processes had cost many trainees their lives. No extensive reserves had been prepared; and losses began mounting because of poor work practices of maintenance and delivery crews.[61] And unless ongoing programs for the needed replacement of the Zeke and its compatriots were executed efficiently, the navy's aircrews would eventually be facing a wide suite of vastly superior Allied aircraft types. No such renewal occurred. On 19 June 1944 the navy paid the brutal price: over the Philippine Sea almost the entire Japanese carrier-borne air arm was massacred by the United States Navy's F-6 Hellcat fighters.

The wholesale destruction of the Japanese naval airpower had been delivered by the United States Fifth Fleet—the largest assembly of naval air and surface firepower in the prenuclear age. This unstoppable instrument was the product of an industrial juggernaut Japan could never hope to master. For Fuchida Mitsuo's observations about Japanese irrationality rang true concerning each of the four aspects of the Imperial Japanese Navy that have been examined: instability and conflict within the structure of command and control, a strategy for the seizure and maintenance of an imperial perimeter in the absence of adequate logistical support, the reluctance to abandon the battleship's role as the final tactical arbiter in a great decisive battle, and the provision of air and naval forces entirely engineered for the offensive. Japan's naval ambitions had been placed upon a precipice from the outset. No margin for error existed in the event of any substantial operational setback. Yet at the same instant, the Japanese navy possessed the methods and means, most especially in the form of the Kido Butai, to deliver blows of such magnitude as to annihilate any opposing fleet or squadron, with dramatic consequences for the determination of naval supremacy. Some two years before the disaster of the "Great Marianas Turkey Shoot," Japan's air-naval blitzkrieg would reach its zenith in the Eastern Indian Ocean, compelling the British Eastern Fleet to quit the battlefield in order to avert annihilation.

6

Force Z Revisited

December 1941–March 1942

A s the capital ships *Prince of Wales* and *Repulse* departed the Singapore naval base at 1735 hours on 8 December 1941 many of those who observed their movements from ashore felt a sense of foreboding. As they observed the vessels steaming slowly eastward, Captain O. W. Phillips remarked to a subordinate, "Quos Deus vult perdere, prius dementat"—*those whom the Gods wish to die, they first make mad.*[1] This became an apt description for an ill-conceived expedition that sought to defy a clearly overwhelming hostile air and naval presence. The United States Pacific Fleet's battleline lay shattered within its Pearl Harbor roadstead, the surrounding airfields littered with the scorched and twisted remains of dozens of fighters, bombers, and reconnaissance aircraft. At Clark Field, sixty miles north of Manila, the principal elements of the U.S. Army's Far Eastern Air Force had been bombed to the point of total annihilation. And upon the runways of RAF Malaya Command's vital northern airfields, there too rested the blackened detritus of wrecked and shot-up airplanes, gutter hangers, and charred corpses. All of this bore mute testament to a litany of precision destruction, ruthlessly orchestrated by Japan's formidable naval and army air arms. Yet just as Julius Caesar had strode resolutely to the Senate upon a March day, Admiral Sir Thomas Phillips instructed Force Z to steam northward toward the Gulf of Siam, in spite of the dire warnings of impending peril that had both preceded and accompanied his squadron's departure.

The April 1942 engagement between the British Eastern Fleet and the Japanese Kido Butai followed four months of defeat and retreat for Allied naval forces within the enclosed seas of Southeast Asia. Within this period, the Royal Navy first experienced combat with the Japanese, and did so in a setting far different from the vastness of the Indian Ocean. Just as the Admiralty had been compelled to employ a variety of operational methods against the European Axis fleets, from 8 December 1941 it would be similarly challenged by the developing nature of the war in the Far East. Prior to the surrender of the Netherlands East Indies on 7 March 1942, the small number of British ships in the South China Sea and within the Indonesian archipelago were primarily committed to two tasks, namely defending friendly convoys and attacking enemy convoys. The loss of the *Prince of Wales* and *Repulse* to enemy land-based air attack on 10 December 1941 removed any chance of the British assembling a powerful squadron, similar in formation to the famous Force H of Mediterranean fame, with which to oppose the initial enemy aeroamphibious onslaught. Instead, the remaining British cruisers and destroyers joined their ABDA (American-British-Dutch-Australian) counterparts in fighting an increasingly doomed surface campaign to stop the Japanese invasion groups as they systematically overran the Netherlands East Indies. Revisiting Force Z is necessary for two reasons; first, to reconsider the material significance of the events of 10 December and, second, to explore the chances of British success had there been a different operational environment than what was experienced to the south of Ceylon. In these examinations, a counterfactual analysis is required to address these questions.

Chronology of Far Eastern Events: December 1941–March 1942[2]

1941

7/8 December: Japanese landings at Singora and Patani (Siam) and Kota Bharu (Malaya), Japanese carrier-borne air strike against Pearl Harbor, Japanese land-based air strikes against Singapore, Wake Island, Clark Field, and RAF airfields in northern Malaya; 10 December: Japanese occupy Guam, *Prince of Wales* and *Repulse* sunk by Japanese land-based air strike; 11 December: Japanese landings at Hong Kong, attempted Japanese landing on Wake Island repelled; 16 December: Japanese landings in British Borneo; 22 December:

Japanese landings in the Philippines; 23 December: Japanese occupy Wake Island; 25 December: Hong Kong surrenders.

1942

2 January: Japanese occupy Manila; 10 January: Japanese occupy Kuala Lumpur; 12 January: Japanese landings in the Celebes and Dutch Borneo; 14 January: ABDA Headquarters established in Batavia; 23 January: Japanese occupy Rabaul; 24 January: Battle of the Makassar Strait; 25 January: Japanese landings in northern New Guinea; 26 January: U.S. and Filipino forces retreat to the southern tip of the Bataan peninsula; 28–31 January: Commonwealth forces withdraw from Johore to Singapore Island; 8 February: Japanese landings on Singapore; 14–15 February: Japanese airborne assault on Palembang (Sumatra); 15 February: Singapore surrenders; 19 February: Japanese carrier-borne and land-based air strikes against Darwin; 27 February: Battle of the Java Sea; 28 February: Japanese landings in Java; 7 March: Netherlands East Indies surrender.

Force Z: The Necessity for a Counterfactual Analysis

It is useful to commence with a brief outline of the events after Admiral Phillips' departure from Singapore the evening of 8 December 1941. Prior to Force Z's departure, Phillips had been advised by RAF Malaya Command that no land-based fighter cover would be available and that forward air reconnaissance would not likely be provided. As Force Z was steaming to interdict the Japanese invasion convoys disembarking troops at Singora, Patani, and Kota Bharu, it came under observation by enemy air reconnaissance at dusk on 9 December. Losing the element of surprise, Phillips determined to return to Singapore; however, after receiving a signal that the Japanese had commenced landing activities at Kuantan, his ships altered course to the southwest.[3] On arrival at Kuantan shortly after dawn on 10 December, the British found the invasion report to be false. At 1115 hours Force Z came under attack from land-based aircraft of the Imperial Japanese Navy's Genzan, Mihoro, and Miyauchi air corps. *Prince of Wales* suffered serious damage from two torpedo hits at 1144 that crippled her steering system, propulsion, and electrical power. She was left an easy target for further torpedo strikes. *Repulse* successfully avoided numerous attacks before she too was struck at 1225 by several torpedoes, causing her to quickly roll over and capsize; 796 of her 1,309 officers and crew were subsequently rescued. *Prince of Wales* lingered on until 1320 hours at which time she also foundered; before she sank, destroyers drew close aboard and safely disembarked 1,285 of the 1,612 personnel. However, Phillips elected to go down with his flagship. Of the eighty attacking airplanes, only three were shot down by antiaircraft fire.[4]

The material disposition of Force Z presents a particularly convincing argument against considering the squadron (as it existed) an accurate measure of British naval capabilities. In his January 1942 memorandum concerning the sinking of the two vessels, Admiral Pound admitted that two capital ships and four destroyers did not constitute the Admiralty's existing concept of a balanced fighting force; postwar histories have invariably reached a similar conclusion.[5] Following the outbreak of hostilities with Germany, the Admiralty began to disperse a number of its big ships into squadron-level units, each of these generally consisting of one or more capital ships supported by a single aircraft carrier, half a dozen cruisers, and a screen of up to a dozen destroyers. As Arthur Marder, Russell Grenfell, and others have highlighted, Force Z could have been brought up to strength by adding British and other Allied cruisers and destroyers that were in the vicinity of Singapore, had Phillips delayed his passage north. And the histories have likewise noted the early withdrawal of the carrier *Indomitable*, which had been ordered to Singapore but sustained hull damage in the Caribbean that required repairs.[6] On the basis of these facts, it is clear that Force Z only existed in embryo form as an active squadron, therefore any consideration of its potential effectiveness cannot be adequately undertaken without considering how it might have contended with the Japanese when at its fullest possible strength.

The absence of a practicable operational strategy for Force Z's deployment in the Far East provides a further rationale why its substantive analytical value is limited. Churchill's decision to utilize Phillips' squadron's presence as a "vague menace" to deter Japanese aggression in the Gulf of Siam proved to be an entirely unsound attempt at deterring an amphibious operation that enjoyed the protection of powerful surface and air-screening forces.[7] Within the postwar histories there has been widespread acknowledgment of Churchill's error, and it is clearly evident from the tenor of Pound's memorandum that the Admiralty was fundamentally opposed to Churchill's initiative. Indeed, within *The Grand Alliance* Churchill conceded that Force Z could exercise the vague menace, which he hoped would negatively influence Japanese naval calculations, only by vanishing "among the innumerable islands"

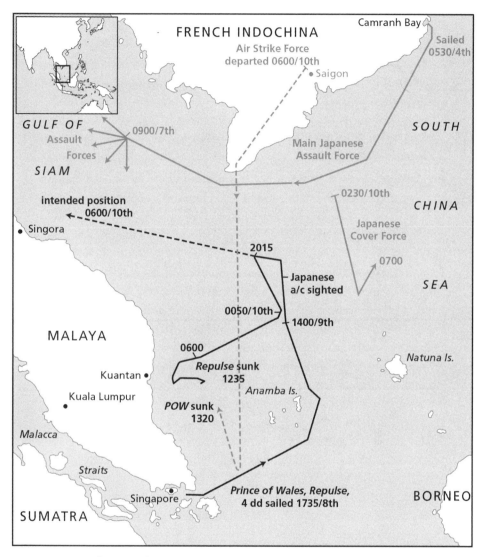

MAP 4. The Loss of HMS *Prince of Wales* and HMS *Repulse*, 10 December 1941

and that, further, no definitive plan had been formulated for its operational use as of 10 December 1941.[8] What is noteworthy about choosing deterrence as the squadron's initial task is that Whitehall had compelled the Admiralty to undertake what was essentially a long-practiced solution for peacetime imperial crises. Attempting to intimidate a nation that possessed one of the most formidable fleets on earth with a display of gunboat diplomacy, a tactic ordinarily employed against smaller and less able opponents, represented a particularly culpable misjudgment on Churchill's part. And to make matters worse, both Whitehall and the Admiralty had supported the appointment of a wholly inexperienced fleet commander to implement the Prime Minister's wishes.

The behavior that Admiral Phillips exhibited in seeking to engage the Japanese with an ill-balanced squadron in the absence of carrier-borne or land-based fighter cover has generated an equivocal interpretation within the postwar accounts. Whereas Phillips' decision to undertake the mission in these circumstances has been rightly lamented, there are historians, such as P. K. Kemp and Arthur Marder, who have argued that the admiral could not have elected to effectively "let the side down" by failing to take action against the Japanese landings.[9] However this line of reasoning should carry little weight when Phillips' actions are compared with the way Admiral Cunningham responded to the Crete crisis: despite the necessity to immediately evacuate thousands of Commonwealth troops, Cunningham refused to risk the deployment of his big ships in a combat setting in which the enemy maintained overwhelming air superiority.[10] Phillips' service background and attitudes toward the air weapon will be seen by the reader as compelling reasons why he was largely unqualified for active command. He possessed no field experience, having been assigned to the Admiralty as Pound's subordinate throughout the opening phase of the war; additionally, he had steadfastly refused to digest any of the lessons airpower had provided during this period. Perhaps the most damning critique of the admiral's abilities will be found within interpretations from both Stephen Roskill and Richard Hough, contending that Phillips had been sent to the Far East to rid the Admiralty of his truculent conservatism, which had consistently alienated his more experienced fighting colleagues.[11]

Within the postwar era, the Force Z disaster has assumed a powerful symbolism, both as the end of an epoch in naval history with the eclipse of the battleship by the airplane and as a sign of Britain's decline and fall as an imperial power. Given that *Prince of Wales* and *Repulse* were the first two capital ships to be sunk at sea by hostile aircraft alone, the symbolism of the disaster is justifiable. There is no doubt that the sinking of these ships represented a particularly galling blow to British national and imperial prestige, most notably as part of the wider circumstances that surrounded the eventual fall of Singapore. However it must also be borne in mind that Force Z came to represent but one more example of the psychological impact that a major naval disaster inevitably generated. Within his account of the pursuit and destruction of the *Bismarck*, Ludovic Kennedy recalled that for the British nation at large, the sinking of the battle cruiser *Hood* in May 1941 "was traumatic, as though Buckingham Palace had been laid flat or the Prime Minister assassinated, so integral a part was she of the fabric of Britain and her Empire."[12] Yet the essential difficulty with adjudging the events off Kuantan as the definitive moment where British naval supremacy was ended, lies in the factors that have been outlined above—that the destruction of Force Z did not reflect the defeat of a reasonably balanced squadron or fleet. Nevertheless, some British naval historians have pursued a counterfactual explanation as to how Admiral Phillips' ships would have fared in opposed combat. These views have ranged from P. K. Kemp's assertion that Force Z (as it existed) could have inflicted another Cape Matapan against Admiral Kondo Nobutake's screening force, to Arthur Marder's interpretation that a strengthened British presence within the Malay Barrier would have been eventually overwhelmed by Japanese naval might.[13] In most instances, however, the volume of analysis has been very limited. Even Malcolm Murfett—whose thoughtful assessment of the differing methods available for a more rigorous naval execution of the Singapore strategy is among the most informative of the available studies—does not address the substance of potential combat outcomes.[14] And it appears that few, if any, authors of the relevant accounts have turned their minds to the subsequent intervention of Nagumo's carriers within the Indonesian archipelago, and the consequences of a clash between the Kido Butai and a Force H–style British opponent in a combat theater where the Japanese possessed land-based naval air superiority. Yet a counterfactual approach can only be credible if the alternative reflects a historically rational disposition of available British and Japanese naval and air assets, and the employment of practicable operational strategies. If these guidelines are followed carefully, it is possible to reconstruct a more robust British naval presence in the South China Sea and the waters of the Indonesian archipelago, and thereby determine whether the Royal Navy and its American, Dutch, and Australian allies possessed any realistic hope of resisting Japan's aeroamphibious conquests in Southeast Asia.

Backhouse-Drax: Composition and Strategy

Following the Munich Conference in September 1938, the strategy for sending a "Main Fleet" to Singapore was replaced with the concept of a "flying-
squadron," as developed by Vice Admiral Roger Backhouse and Admiral
Reginald Drax.[15] Based upon this model, Force Z would have initially consisted of the *Prince of Wales* and *Repulse*, the aircraft carrier *Indomitable*, three
heavy cruisers, four light cruisers, and six destroyers. These dispositions are
based on the reasonable geographic availability of the additional cruisers
and destroyers as of 10 December 1941 and on inclusion of the *Indomitable*,
which had been instructed to join the original squadron but withdrew after
hitting a sandbar shortly into her passage to Singapore. It is assumed in this
instance that for strategic and tactical reasons analyzed shortly, Force Z would
not have contained American or Dutch warships—at least at first.[16] Providing
convoy protection in the Indian Ocean was the most suitable use of older
British ships based at Colombo: the battleship *Revenge*, the aircraft carrier
Hermes, and nine obsolescent light cruisers. When addressing the potential
upgrading of land-based air strength in Malaya and Singapore, however, the
analysis can, at best, point to the reinforcements that arrived in Singapore
from late December onward, including fifty Hurricane fighters and several
understrength light-bomber squadrons. Not even a modest level of assistance from the RAF could be supplied to the Far East until April 1942 due
to competing strategic priorities elsewhere and to the enormous distances
air reinforcements had to be air ferried or conveyed by sea.[17]

The analysis does not assume any significant alteration in the Imperial Japanese Navy's historical dispositions for two reasons. First the vast geographic
range of aeroamphibious operations at the outset of hostilities did not permit
the Japanese to disperse their warships and aircraft until the initial strategic
objectives had been achieved. Second, Japanese planning for a thrust into the
Indonesian archipelago always envisaged landings in Siam, Malaya, and British
Borneo as the means to acquiring forward bases and airfields for a subsequent
advance to be covered by significant elements of the Combined Fleet.[18] Further,
Admiral Yamamoto entrusted the neutralization of the Royal Navy's assets at
Singapore to the 22nd Air Flotilla of the Imperial Japanese Naval Air Force's
Eleventh Koku Kantai (Air Fleet) based in southern Indochina, with rapid
support available from the 21st and 23rd Air Flotillas if required. Tasked with
intercepting any British attempt to interdict the large troop convoys, Admiral
Kondo's Second Fleet consisted of two *Kongo*-class battleships, seven heavy

cruisers, one light cruiser, and fourteen destroyers. Once the small U.S. Asiatic Fleet had been forced to vacate the Philippines, the light carrier *Ryujo* and numerous cruisers and destroyers became available to either reinforce Kondo or to conduct separate operations within the approaches to the Java Sea.[19] Third, from February 1942 the Kido Butai could likewise join the action fresh from its recent rampage in the Pacific.

Given Japan's immediate need to secure advanced bases to facilitate its major thrust into the Netherlands East Indies, the most practicable strategy for the British was to destroy the Malaya-bound convoys. Under such circumstances, the probable outcome would have been the need for the Japanese to regroup and to significantly amend their tightly scheduled timetable; this outcome would provide a vital breathing space for the Allied nations to more effectively organize defenses west of the Philippines. Thus, the degree to which Force Z succeeded in these preemptive operations would likewise determine the fundamental ABDA naval strategy to be used in a wider, subsequent campaign. The best prospects for inflicting significant damage on the Japanese lay in how coordinated attacks were conducted by the flying-squadron and land-based aircraft. As CIC, Far East Command, Air Chief Marshal Sir Robert Brooke-Popham had proposed Operation Matador, a course of action that involved using airpower and ground forces to repel landings in southern Siam. Brooke-Popham devised this strategy knowing that no substantial Royal Navy presence was likely to arrive at Singapore before March 1942 at the earliest.[20] Assuming, however, that the flying squadron became available for deployment, a broader execution of Matador presented the setting for a potential British combined-arms triumph, albeit with the continued need to vastly improve the tenuous interservice relations that prevailed in the Far East.

Brooke-Popham's appointment as CIC Far East in October 1940 had been Whitehall's effort to improve interservice relations, and under his leadership improvements in cooperation between the three services occurred. However, the unfortunate Brooke-Popham possessed perhaps the most ambiguous command instructions for any British staff officer in the entire war: he could exercise no formal authority whatsoever over the Royal Navy, or the Army, or the RAF in forming operational policy. Further, although he was given responsibility for initiating hostilities against the Japanese without prior Cabinet approval, Brooke-Popham's orders forbade him to do so if such action would lead to a violation of Siamese neutrality. As Grenfell subsequently noted, Brooke-Popham had "the supreme political responsibility for provoking a war thrust upon him at a moment of acute international crisis," a manifestly difficult adjudication to be made in circumstances in which the British government did not wish to be cast as the aggressor.[21] Nevertheless, prior to December 1941 he had established a conference system among the future ABDA partners that produced a viable structure for multilateral defense in the Southeast Asian theater. That structure included a proposal for cooperation among British, American, and Dutch naval forces that Admiral Phillips and his American counterpart, Admiral Thomas Hart, USN, discussed on 5 December when Phillips visited Manila. Because the Japanese commenced their southern operations less than seventy-two hours later, there was no practical way to immediately form an integrated Anglo-American naval presence in the South China Sea.[22]

It was equally unrealistic to assemble Dutch warships within a multinational Force Z. As the conduct of the Battle of the Java Sea came to demonstrate, without adequate preparation, operational difficulties could not be overcome by the hasty incorporation of vessels and personnel from a navy that employed a different language and signaling, even if undisturbed by Japanese naval or aerial intervention.[23] In a combined-arms preemptive strike, a homogenous squadron was the only means to achieve the required tactical precision, especially when the enemy deployed a powerful covering fleet and possessed the advantage of land-based air superiority. Indeed the addition of the Netherlands East Indies as an active ally presented the Royal Navy with a much wider problem—that it would eventually be compelled to operate in the expanses of the Indonesian archipelago. Whitehall's original decision in August 1940 to support the Dutch had been based upon the assumption that no practical assistance could be provided beyond using Singapore as a base for the repair and revictualing of Dutch ships.[24] The modest additions to Force Z that the current analysis proposes would have done little to alleviate the ultimate fate of the Indies which, absent a massive injection of Allied naval power, were gravely exposed to invasion because of the need to defend the network of northern entrances to the Java Sea.

When considering the inevitable fall of the Netherlands East Indies, the eventual sacrifice of the ABDA squadron in the Java Sea engagement has been rightly regarded within the histories as a largely fruitless loss of valuable ships in a doomed attempt to delay the final Japanese landings on Java itself. Yet even if the Allied navies could not maintain their command of the archipelago's seas, a delaying strategy executed by an enhanced ABDA presence would not have been entirely devoid of merit. The Japanese landings at Balikpapan on 24 January 1942 and Palembang on 14 February were occasions when the Allied forces involved could have inflicted far greater damage had they been better resourced, given the favorable tactical circumstances in both instances. As Captain Ihara Mitsugo noted in his postwar interrogation, the general level of ABDA resistance was so light that he could make no informed judgment as to how the Japanese navy would have coped with a more capable opponent.[25] However, an additional delay of a week or more in the Japanese timetable provided the potential to enact further resource-denial schemes, namely the destruction of the wellheads and refineries that the Japanese were committed to seizing intact. Had the Allied vessels retired to Ceylon or Australia with this particular task accomplished, Japan would not have enjoyed ready access to the fuel oil it desperately required to augment minimal reserves—a factor the Japanese leadership thoroughly appreciated and feared.[26]

Outcomes: Force Z Returns to Sea

The South China Sea emerged as the stage for the first test of British naval supremacy in the Far East. In summarizing the prospects of the flying-squadron model, Malcolm Murfett posed the fundamental question about its likely effectiveness: "Did it offer something better? On its own the 'flying squadron' represented a highly mobile, rapid-response force, but even with a carrier present it was hardly sufficient to anything other than act on the defensive once it reached the Straits of Johore."[27]

Murfett's commentary will be viewed as correct in his reference to the probability that an enhanced Force Z would have inevitably assumed a defensive posture on arriving at Singapore. However this strategy did not necessarily preclude the squadron from undertaking sorties to intercept Japanese aeroamphibious operations when a defensive British success could be realistically obtained. Force Z in actuality did not possess the required strength to achieve this, although Phillips had correctly believed that, had he been able to break through Admiral Kondo's protective cordon and assault the invasion areas, Japanese transports would have been at his mercy as they disembarked their troops into waiting barges.[28] For the counterfactual squadron to succeed where Phillips failed, three critical outcomes were required: (1) Kondo's Second Fleet had to be neutralized, (2) the three Japanese troop convoys would have to be substantially destroyed, and (3) effective tactics for countering the IJNAF's crack 22nd Air Flotilla had to be devised.

For the purposes of the analysis it is assumed that Admiral Somerville held command over Force Z as he did subsequently with the Eastern Fleet, and the Royal Australian Navy's Commodore John Collins exercised detached command of the squadron's cruiser element. Collins had served with distinction in the Mediterranean and commanded the British China Squadron in December 1941.[29] In the absence of any marked intervention by the 22nd Air Flotilla, chances of the British squadron dominating an engagement against Kondo's fleet were reasonably even. With the presence of the *Indomitable* and the possession of radar there was little to prevent Somerville from engineering a Matapan-style engagement, as Kemp and others have suggested. The most promising tactics to adopt were for *Indomitable*'s Albacore torpedo planes to hit Kondo's force before the two British capital ships joined the fray; meanwhile Collins' cruisers would detach and undertake a high-speed interception of the convoys in accordance with the Admiralty's prevailing Fighting Instructions.[30] Both the *Prince of Wales* and *Repulse* possessed heavier caliber main armaments than the Japanese *Kongo*s and as such they outranged the Japanese as both forces converged. Somerville's big ships would essentially act to "stand-off" Kondo, either preventing his ships from interceding in the subsequent attack by Collins' cruisers against the convoys, or forcing the retirement of the Southern Fleet through inflicting heavy casualties upon it. In either instance the preparatory sinking or crippling of one or more of Kondo's big ships by *Indomitable*'s aircraft presented the most likely basis for this necessary initial British success.

In the absence of a decisive intervention by the Albacores, Force Z faced a particularly stiff fight. In a postwar interview, Kondo recorded his fear that Phillips would execute a similar detaching maneuver to that outlined above, as he believed (incorrectly) that the British squadron had been accompanied by three light cruisers.[31] If the FAA's torpedo planes could not slow the Southern Fleet, the superior speed of the Japanese force made any profitable detachment of the British and Dominion cruisers highly unlikely. Although lacking radar, the Japanese cruisers and destroyers were a menacing proposition, especially at night as they enjoyed the benefit of skilled lookouts and high-quality optics, together with excellent reconnaissance and target-spotting support from the numerous seaplanes that were carried on each of the heavy cruisers. Commodore Collins' dispatch regarding the Java Sea engagement contained reports from several of the senior ABDA participants that repeatedly high-lighted these particular Japanese strengths.[32] And those same cruisers and destroyers were armed with "Long Lance" torpedoes, which would inflict such heavy Allied losses in both the Java Sea and throughout the future night surface battles of the drawn-out Solomons campaign. Regarding the skills of the respective commands, Somerville and Collins held the advantage largely because of their extensive operational experience in the Mediterranean. This was a confrontation that either Force Z or the Southern Fleet could win—the result ultimately hinging upon the inherent human and meteorological variables that had so often determined the course of naval actions.

Yet even if Somerville had been able to sink or expel Kondo's battleships and heavy cruisers while Collins made a clean break for the transports, the destruction of the invasion convoys would have had to commence before Force Z's cruisers arrived on the scene. From the outset of his appointment in the Far East, Brooke-Popham appreciated the vital necessity for launching air strikes against the Japanese as soon as they had penetrated Siamese terri-torial waters.[33] And in the early morning hours of 8 December RAF Malaya Command proceeded to place this plan into operation. Unfortunately, the combination of poor weather, inadequate early warning systems, and fifth-column activity resulted in over half of RAF's bombers being destroyed on the ground as they refueled following their dispersal from Singapore to var-ious airfields in northern Malaya.[34] However, at Kota Bharu, a paltry twelve RAAF Hudson bombers succeeded in defying darkness and torrential rain to inflict heavy casualties upon the Japanese, sinking a large transport and numerous barges packed with troops. The fact that these few aircraft could occasion a level of damage out of all proportion to their numbers firmly demonstrated the feasibility of Brooke-Popham's approach. On this basis a successful large-scale sortie by the RAF possessed the undoubted potential to cause enormous losses among Yamashita's disembarking units. For as Kondo subsequently indicated, the disembarkation of troops, equipment, and stores took up to four days to complete, leaving the convoys dangerously naked to prolonged air attacks and the unwelcome appearance of hostile warships.[35]

Upon three occasions throughout the Japanese offensive in the Indonesian archipelago, Allied warships were ideally positioned to directly assault loi-tering invasion convoys. In two instances the attackers were unable to press home their advantage because of poor tactical coordination and, during the third engagement within the Sunda Strait on 28 February 1942, because of a lack of ammunition, the cruisers *Houston* and *Perth* had not been adequately resupplied with ammunition following the Java Sea disaster the day before.[36] A similar sortie off Siam by a well-organized cruiser force would have most likely brushed aside Vice Admiral Ozawa Jisaburo's small close-escort screen and inevitably inflicted severe losses on the defenseless transports.[37] Achieving a decisive success, however, required the concurrent intervention of Commonwealth ground units advancing from northern Malaya to the invasion areas. If the Siamese airfields at Singora and Patani could not be either occupied or rendered useless by air and naval bombardment, the redeployment of the Japanese army's 3rd Air Division from Indochina would take place with disastrous consequences for the subsequent defense of Malaya. Once the Japanese had established air superiority in the north, the army's fighter and bomber squadrons were able to provide effective support for the army's subsequent ground advances.[38] And that is precisely what occurred during December 1941 and January 1942 as Commonwealth troops were shooed down the peninsula by incessant air raids mounted from these captured airfields.

The operational aspects analyzed above are based on the assumption the Imperial Japanese Navy's 22nd Air Flotilla would have been unable to intervene in a decisive fashion. The flight leader of the Genzan Air Corps, Captain Sonokawa Kameo, clearly outlined the exhaustive level of preparations for sorties against Allied shipping in the South China Sea, noting that the Japanese naval air arm played no active role in operations against Commonwealth ground forces.[39] This was a major departure from the situation the Royal Navy had previously encountered in both the Atlantic and the Mediterranean whereby neither of the opposing Axis air arms were dedicated naval air entities, although the Luftwaffe's *Fliegerkorps X* emerged as a highly proficient antishipping unit. Aside from the fact that the Japanese Nell and Betty bombers were capable of performing air strikes as far south as Singapore Island itself, any attempted interception within a radius of five hundred miles of Saigon brought Force Z under the umbrella of the 22nd Air Flotilla's Zeke fighters.[40] Several British historians, including Geoffrey Till, have contended that alongside available land-based fighter cover, *Indomitable*'s twenty-one fighters were capable of causing headaches for any unescorted Japanese bomber formations; but they have not as readily contemplated the outcome of an encounter in which escorting Zekes were present. Nevertheless, Eric Brown's expert observations are compelling: the participating Hurricanes, Fulmars, and Buffaloes would have been no match for the Zekes in air-to-air combat thanks to the superb flying characteristics of the Japanese machines flown by elite naval aviators.[41]

Herein lay the execution of a concept of air-naval warfare the British had yet to encounter in World War II. In postwar accounts authors have frequently referred to the Force Z disaster by using the term "airpower" in its widest context. Yet there is a subtle distinction, often overlooked: the differentiation between airpower as a whole and naval airpower as an individual entity. Unlike the European nations (but in common with the United States) the Japanese had never come to embrace the ideal of a homogenous national air force. As a result, the Imperial Japanese Navy developed policies and operational doctrines focused on attaining naval supremacy in combination with the Combined Fleet. Indeed as Oi Atsushi has discussed, the heavy prewar investment the navy made in its land-based air assets reflected the need to compensate for the fleet's numerical inferiority in warships.[42] Equipped with long-range bombers and a fighter aircraft that could substantially outrange and outfight its opponents, the navy had achieved the capacity to project a most formidable level of forward air supremacy. Once ensconced on advance airfields, the 22nd Air Flotilla would command Southeast Asian waters from Sumatra to the Philippines, and from Saigon to Darwin. And it would shortly be joined by the 21st and 23rd Air Flotillas, having recently demonstrated their capabilities over land by devastating Clark Field on the opening day of hostilities.[43]

In devising a credible response to this ominous situation, it was extremely hazardous for the Royal Navy to exercise even the upmost circumspection as Admiral Cunningham had advocated in the wake of the Crete fiasco.[44] Once the element of surprise had been lost, the counterfactual Force Z would have been either compelled to retire to Singapore or to risk running the gauntlet of the 22nd Air Flotilla to reach the invasion convoys. By electing to take the first option, Phillips—in reality—might have been able to save his squadron if he had ignored the report concerning Kuantan and proceeded directly to Singapore.[45] Although the best-case scenario did (in Murfett's words) offer something better, it remained highly improbable that the necessary level of sea, air, and ground coordination would be achieved to utterly annihilate Yamashita's disembarking units. The most advantageous result for the British lay in the prospect of dispersing Kondo's Second Fleet and inflicting significant damage on the convoys through a preemptive RAF air strike. However it is difficult to suppose the Japanese would have been entirely prevented from seizing the Siamese airfields and immediately flying in the bulk of their army's 3rd Air Division for subsequent ground-support operations. The poor weather that had aided Phillips in the early stages of his mission also conspired to shield the convoys from accurate aerial reconnaissance; this became a major factor in preventing the RAF from concentrating its bombers in time to prevent the initial disembarkation of enemy troops.[46]

Even supposing the British were able to fully repulse the Japanese landings, the likely future consequences for Somerville's revised squadron and the ongoing defense of Malaya and Singapore were undeniably bleak. Once the fuller resources of the Combined Fleet were inevitably deployed west of the Philippines, the Royal Navy and its Dominion, Dutch, and American allies could only hope to delay the Japanese southward thrust long enough to substantially complete the destruction of the oil facilities and other vital plants and equipment. Although the defenders in Malaya and Singapore would have doubtless been emboldened by a favorable outcome against the Japanese convoys, it is difficult to contemplate anything other than a repeat of the events in Greece, where the initial rebuff by the Italian forces was followed by a successful German invasion. In the absence of the rather unlikely reinforcement of Malaya's fighter defenses by denuding RAF Fighter Command of most of its Spitfire squadrons, the better trained and highly experienced Japanese ground forces, with overwhelming air and naval support, would have eventually prevailed. Further, the defective defensive locations of RAF Malaya Command's airfields in the north of the peninsula, as well as the marked lack of radar and other early-warning methods, clearly favored the advancing enemy forces.[47] The situation that prevailed in the wider expanses of the Indonesian archipelago presented an even more onerous difficulty for the mixed bag of ABDA forces there assembled.

Murfett's concept of the flying squadron becoming in effect a rapid-response force is further enhanced when considering the disposition of Force Z in the aftermath of its opening engagements. Assuming that it somehow emerged more or less unscathed, the squadron would have had a much larger geographic range to cover if the Admiralty had sought to expand its area of operations to include the Netherlands East Indies. Yet this additional burden should be regarded as unremarkable given the precedent set by Force H. In December 1940 Somerville outlined the responsibilities of Force H as they then existed: in addition to controlling the Western Mediterranean against the Italians, the squadron was required to escort convoys to the Eastern Mediterranean, shadow Vichy French warships, hunt for raiders in the Atlantic, potentially conduct offensive operations against the Spanish, and secure the Indian Ocean "in certain other circumstances."[48] Now as Brooke-Popham and Marder have confirmed, the prewar Plenaps[49] accords provided for a multinational response to Japanese aggression, though no specific operational strategy had been contrived. A preemptive British success against the Japanese navy's South China Sea expedition would have allowed for the maintenance of two such rapid-response instruments—Force Z itself and an ABDA collection fielding a minimum of one heavy cruiser, six light cruisers, and a dozen or so destroyers.[50] If effective land-based air support were present, a concentrated, well-organized ABDA force (supplemented by additional British and Australian cruiser reinforcements) constituted a potent threat to the Japanese—in theory at least.

As would have been the case in the Gulf of Siam, the key to any form of Allied success in the Netherlands East Indies did not lie in waging a campaign of drawn out attrition. Instead the most practicable strategy to be pursued was an ABDA surface force attack on the Japanese as they landed at Tarakan and Balikpapan in Dutch Borneo, with the Allied air assets being concentrated on the airfields at Palembang in southern Sumatra. These were high-priority targets for the Japanese because they were among the principal wellheads and refineries in the region.[51] Once the surface force had undertaken its sortie, it would retire to refuel at Surabaya, then destroy the base's oil facilities and decamp to Freemantle or Colombo. At Palembang the RAF and its Allied colleagues could mount an all-out mass air strike against the Japanese invasion shipping, inflicting as much damage as possible before evacuating their airfields and flying to Java. In supposing that Force Z still resided at Singapore, Somerville's squadron may have provided assistance in the waters off Palembang, yet the requirement for his ships to be positioned for a further interception in the South China Sea would have probably precluded its participation east of the Sunda Strait. The ABDA command also possessed at least twenty American and ten Dutch submarines best employed against transport shipping because the Japanese navy's convoy protection methods against submarines were extremely poor, as was the quality of its antisubmarine weaponry.[52]

The outcomes of the actual engagements at Balikpapan (Makassar Strait) on 12 January 1942 and in the estuary of the Musi River to the east of Palembang on 14–15 February, were the most profitable for the Allies throughout the first three months of the Asia-Pacific conflict. At Balikpapan a flotilla of four American destroyers sank four troop transports, whereas RAF bombing and strafing attacks against the Palembang-bound convoy sank or damaged at least six transports and numerous barges, causing very heavy casualties among the transiting troops.[53] With additional resources in each instance, even more substantial loss and damage stood to be inflicted on the Japanese, further frustrating the steady advance of their operational timetables. Yet there also existed compelling reasons why the enhanced ABDA squadron would have little choice but to subsequently withdraw from the theater altogether. Prior to Admiral Karel Doorman's cruiser squadron's final showdown in the Java Sea on 27 February 1942, it had been pursued from one end of the Java Sea to the other in a series of futile attempts to interdict various hostile convoys; inevitably it was frustrated by incessant air attacks from both land-based bombers and the light carrier *Ryujo*.[54] It is unsurprising that Doorman's squadron eventually suffered a crushing defeat; his crews were greatly fatigued by the need to remain on continuous action stations because of the constant round of air attacks. These attacks not only targeted the ships at sea but also continuously disrupted their refueling and revictualing procedures while in port.[55]

On board the heavy cruiser HMS *Exeter*, Petty Officer W. E. Johns witnessed the constant pressure that Japanese land-based airpower applied in the Java Sea: "We were at Tanjong Priok, in Batavia, when orders came and we set sail on 25 February. We steamed in a constant state of first-degree readiness to Sourabaya, arriving off that port in the early afternoon and eventually anchoring at 1600 to a welcome of air raid sirens and Jap bombers. Senior officers had already been rushed ashore for an emergency conference and within three hours we weighed anchor and were at sea again."[56]

Eight days before the Battle of the Java Sea, a further devastating demonstration of Japan's aerial supremacy within the narrow seas took place in the skies over Darwin. On the morning of 19 February 1942, a large formation of aircraft from four of the Kido Butai's aircraft carriers struck shipping and port facilities at Darwin with virtually no warning. Shortly thereafter, elements of the Koku Kantai's 21st and 23rd Air Flotillas repeated the dose, this time revisiting the fate of Clark Field upon the town's RAAF airfield. Although the raids' significance as the first major attacks against Australian soil has gained greater official recognition in recent years, one background aspect of this episode has been barely acknowledged in the histories.[57] For Darwin also enjoyed the dubious honor of becoming the only Allied target struck by a large-scale coordinated attack from the Imperial Japanese Navy's two principal offensive instruments.

The dominant presence of the Japanese navy air arm in the skies over the narrow Southeast Asian seas likewise exposed a principal fallacy in Allied prewar thinking, namely that Japan was, in essence, a second-rate airpower. Sir Robert Brooke-Popham's evaluation of the Japanese being not "air-minded, particularly against determined fighter opposition" was an example of this widespread attitude among senior British and American commanders.[58] This in turn generated a range of fantasies among the Allied forces, such as the Japanese could not fly in the dark because they suffered from visual defects and their planes were constructed from inferior materials. Such illusions were to have often fatal consequences for Allied pilots and aircrew during the initial stages of hostilities. The shattering of these ethnocentric opinions led to a major U-turn in British and American conceptions, with a corresponding decline in Allied morale. In the five months that followed Pearl Harbor, the dismissal of Japanese fighting capabilities became replaced with an increasingly anxious sense among their Western opponents that Japan's armed forces on land, at sea, and in the air might well be invincible. Much of the previous misjudgment of Japanese aerial capabilities in particular can be traced to the almost total official ignorance in British and American command circles of Japan's interwar progress in naval aviation, in spite of both nations having been active participants in the formative stages of the Imperial Japanese Navy's aviation capabilities.[59] Within a matter of days following the carnage at Hawaii, virtually all worthwhile Allied air resistance in Southeast Asia had been obliterated; simultaneously, the comfortable preconceptions of obligatory Western superiority in the skies were revealed to be little more than grossly negligent folly.

The sinking of the *Prince of Wales* and *Repulse* on 10 December 1941 remains to this day one of the great symbolic moments of World War II, not least because it represented a monumentally misconceived failure of British gunboat diplomacy. Aside from the loss of two extremely valuable warships, however, the principal material historical significance of Force Z is the aberrant nature of the disaster off Kuantan. In essence, the circumstances that surrounded this episode were not indicative of the British Admiralty's prior conduct of naval operations in both the Atlantic and the Mediterranean, whereby the concept of the "balance force" governed the vast majority of fleet- and squadron-scale dispositions. Instead, the deployment of Force Z northward on 8 December can be legitimately regarded as the maritime equivalent of the infamous disaster that engulfed the United States 7th Cavalry at the Little Bighorn on 26 June 1876. Similar to George Armstrong Custer, Tom Phillips embarked on an expedition whose chances of success were so outweighed by the overwhelmingly formidable nature of the enemy that awaited him that his actions could only be described as foolish in the extreme. It is difficult to conceive that an experienced fleet commander such as Somerville or Cunningham would have contemplated such an undertaking, especially given the lessons already learned off Norway, Greece, and Crete. But Phillips and Custer alike departed on their respective expeditions with a misplaced belief in invincibility—in Custer's case, his own, and in Phillips' case, that of the modern battleship.

Assembled at something approaching full strength, under competent command, and part of an effectively coordinated offensive action involving ground forces and land-based air support, Force Z was not without prospects in attempting to destroy the various Japanese invasion convoys in the Gulf of Siam. In the absence of Nagumo's carriers, the British could have likewise made profitable use of their integrated fleet tactics to engage and defeat Admiral Kondo's covering battle fleet, with Force Z presumably proficient in the use of radar for night surface actions. That said, the excellence of the Japanese cruiser and destroyer formations in night fighting, particularly with the Long Lance torpedo, and the presence of two *Kongo*-class battleships, would have made Force Z's task immensely difficult unless a decisive level of prior damage had been inflicted by resident aircraft carrier's torpedo bombers. And most significant of all, the British squadron would have to have somehow avoided the attention of the Japanese navy's 22nd Air Flotilla. The presence of Japan's most elite land-based naval air formation represented a potential threat to any Royal Navy vessel within the vicinity of the Singapore naval base and especially to a squadron in transit to or from the Gulf of Siam. With Zeke fighter cover, the 22nd's attack bombers were well capable of neutralizing the counterfactual Force Z. And if the squadron did not arrive in time to prevent the first landings in Siam, the Japanese army's air arm would be quickly on hand to establish air superiority over northern Malaya, impeding RAF operations by striking the local airfields. It must also be recalled that for such an operation to succeed, the level of competence and interservice cooperation exhibited by the British shore-based service commands needed to be much higher than that which prevailed throughout the Malaya-Singapore campaign.

To answer the question posed by Malcolm Murfett, an enhanced Force Z as a flying squadron did indeed offer something better for the immediate defense of Malaya and Singapore.[60] The same could not be said once the Japanese commenced the second phase of their aeroamphibious southward thrust with the invasion of the Netherlands East Indies. Inevitably, Force Z and the ABDA cruiser squadrons would have confronted the full might of the Japanese navy's three principal land-based air flotillas, not to mention eventually encountering four of the Kido Butai's six large carriers. Between them, these fighting instruments of Japan were capable of deploying something in the vicinity of seven hundred aircraft, with approximately four hundred army airplanes available for ground strike and ground support missions if required.[61] To effectively counter this concentration of Japanese airpower, the Allied air forces would have required—at the very least—a thousand first-line land-based aircraft to protect the Netherlands East Indies, an impossible allocation for Britain or the United States to contemplate in the opening stages of the Indo-Pacific conflict. In their absence, the Allied warships were subjected to the sort of constant pressure from the air that neither the Germans nor the Italians could replicate.

Be it through the constant presence of reconnaissance planes buzzing on the horizon or the daily, almost unopposed raids against vital base facilities ashore, and the ABDA squadrons afloat, the Japanese quite literally exhausted their opponents before eventually decimating them. Thus far, their navy had brushed aside its hurriedly organized, ill-prepared cruiser and destroyer opposition in the narrow seas. What loomed further west in the expanse of the Indian Ocean, however, was to be the first real challenge of fleet combat for Japan's rampant naval air conquistadores.

7

Supremacy Surrendered

The Eastern Indian Ocean Showdown

D URING THE COURSE OF THE AFTERNOON ON 8 APRIL 1942, Admiral Sir James Somerville issued one of the most crucial orders in British naval history. Having spent the better part of the previous nine days conducting a fruitless search for a hostile force in waters south of Ceylon, Somerville's Eastern Fleet proceeded to vacate its advanced base at Addu Atoll and withdraw to Bombay. This decision, which had been readily endorsed by the Admiralty later that same day, undoubtedly spared numerous British warships and saved thousands of lives.[1] Yet at the same instant, it also marked the material finality of British naval supremacy. Three hundred years of tradition and reputation were no defense against an opponent whose principal means of waging war at sea was virtually unchallengeable. For the Royal Navy possessed no credible means of repelling the enormous striking power that had been wielded throughout the preceding months by the aircraft carriers of the Imperial Japanese Navy's Kido Butai spearhead. If the prior sinking of the *Prince of Wales* and *Repulse* had inflicted a "direct shock" to Britain's political and military leadership not to mention the British public, the effects upon Britain and the wider British Empire of the destruction of up to five battleships and three aircraft carriers in a single engagement would have been virtually incalculable.[2] So with great—if somewhat late—common sense, Somerville and the Admiralty forfeited a unique opportunity to further

134

engage a fleet that had annihilated its previous targets through stealth as much as through strength. Had the Eastern Fleet persisted in its efforts to engage the Japanese carrier force, the Royal Navy would have stood to suffer a disaster of epic proportions, far surpassing any of its infrequent reverses throughout the previous centuries.

As detailed in chapter one, Japan's Operation C had commenced on 26 March 1942 with the specific intention of neutralizing not only the Royal Navy in the Eastern Indian Ocean but also Allied merchant shipping in the Bay of Bengal. Pursuing the first objective, Vice Admiral Nagumo Chuichi's Kido Butai set course to attack British naval concentrations at Colombo and Trincomalee, on the island of Ceylon. The Royal Navy's Eastern Fleet, however, had advance intelligence of some form of Japanese incursion and had been positioned by its commander, Admiral Sir James Somerville, to ambush the Japanese force. The ambush failed; and after Nagumo's ships were sighted by a British reconnaissance aircraft on the afternoon of 4 April, a large air strike from the Japanese ships attacked Colombo at dawn the next morning. Damage inflicted was minimal; however later the same day, a force of Japanese dive-bombers located and sank the British cruisers *Cornwall* and *Dorsetshire*. Then followed three days of maneuver and fruitless air reconnaissance on both sides; then Nagumo's aircraft struck again on 9 April, this time at Trincomalee. Initial negligible gains were again offset, on this occasion with the sinking of the British carrier *Hermes* and several of her consorts. To the north of the homeward-bound Nagumo, Vice Admiral Ozawa Jisaburo's Second Expeditionary Fleet had successfully executed the second objective by sending twenty-nine merchantmen to the bottom and bringing Allied shipping traffic in the Bay of Bengal to a standstill. Although the Eastern Fleet had been spared a calamitous fate by retiring in the face of such a powerful adversary, the following analysis of the engagement highlights the range of preexisting factors that combined to mark this episode as the definitive moment when the Royal Navy lost its capacity to command the battlefield.

Operational Strategies: Deterrence versus Annihilation

The wartime genesis for the Royal Navy's strategy in the Indian Ocean in the event of armed conflict with Japan can be traced to Whitehall's concession in late July 1940 that a major fleet could no longer be deployed to Singapore.[3]

In point of fact, the so-called Main Fleet option had been mothballed since 1938 when superseded by the Backhouse-Drax flying-squadron model, as explored in chapter six. Just over a year later in August 1941, Winston Churchill and the First Sea Lord, Sir Dudley Pound, debated the means by which British sea communications in the Far East could best be protected against potential Japanese raiding missions in the Indian Ocean. While both agreed that the fundamental principal governing naval operations in the theater would be deterrence of Japanese sorties by the presence of a strong British squadron, they found themselves at odds over both the composition and disposition of such a force. Churchill believed that a small number of the "best ships," including a *King George V*–class battleship and a large aircraft carrier, would exercise "a paralysing effect on Japanese naval action."[4] Pound, whose correspondence with Churchill highlighted Pound's desire to assemble the nucleus for a future Eastern Fleet, opposed the deployment of a *KG-V* battleship, largely because of the ongoing presence of the formidable *Tirpitz* in German waters. Instead, Pound proposed sending both of the Royal Navy's older *Nelson*-class battleships to Trincomalee or Singapore and added the suggestion that both capital ships could be sent to Singapore to increase the strength of a prewar deterrent but would be promptly withdrawn to Trincomalee at the outbreak of hostilities.[5]

Churchill eventually got his way, and from August to November 1941 the various ships initially assigned to Force Z steamed to the Far East, the *KG V*-class *Prince of Wales* as flagship, but no carrier, with *Indomitable*'s withdrawal due to damage.[6] The prior exchange of correspondence between the prime minister and the First Sea Lord highlighted four important factors that were to play crucial roles in the events to follow. The first of these was the practical abandonment of the South China Sea as the primary naval front, emphasized by Churchill's support for what he described as the "triangle Aden-Singapore-Simonstown" strategy, thereby concentrating the Royal Navy's available resources in the Indian Ocean.[7]

Flowing from this, the second factor proved to be the relegation of Singapore as the Admiralty's principal strategic base. Admiral Pound's correspondence to Churchill clearly advocated Trincomalee as an equal option, emphasized by what he regarded as the necessity to immediately withdraw any deterrent force from Singapore in the event of war.[8] The third factor was that whatever British naval force steamed beyond Suez, its main purpose would be to provide deterrence by its very presence, yet likewise be strong enough to destroy any hostile squadrons that disregarded the passive warning. In turn, the fourth factor became firmly established in the minds of Whitehall, the Admiralty, and eventually Somerville himself—the belief that the Japanese would either deploy a small squadron of fast battleships with perhaps a single aircraft carrier, or a cruiser squadron, to interdict British sea communications.[9]

Certainly the Royal Navy would have retained the capacity to counter the Japanese, if the latter's raiding force(s) air component had been limited to the little *Ryujo* or the new light carriers *Zuiho* and *Shoho*. And had the Combined Fleet settled on a purely surface gunnery–oriented force composition, the chosen British operational strategy for the Indian Ocean should be regarded as an appropriate response. Dating from its experiences in World War I, the Royal Navy had enjoyed a number of successes when called upon to track down and destroy German warships engaged in raiding missions. The sinking of the *Graf Spee* and the *Bismarck* demonstrated the ability of the Fleet's hunting groups to successfully undertake this task, with the latter example confirming the value of integrated air-surface operations. However, the inherent dangers in attempting to intercept an enemy force when equipped with outdated warships had been graphically illustrated in November 1914 at Coronel, where two obsolete British armored cruisers were sent to the bottom with all on board lost.[10] And during the pursuit of the *Bismarck* and the cruiser *Prinz Eugen* in May 1941, the much-venerated battle cruiser *Hood* blew up with only three survivors, having sustained hits that penetrated her unmodified deck armor and detonated her magazines. Should the Eastern Fleet be compelled to rely upon the participation of the Admiralty's pre-1930 battleships and battle cruisers, the hazards of obsolescence could not be readily avoided and stood to dramatically escalate if the Japanese chose instead to implement a carrier-centric attack strategy.

By March 1942, however, the Royal Navy's options for a squadron- or fleet-scale disposition in the Indian Ocean were seriously diminished. Aside from the loss of the *Prince of Wales* and *Repulse*, heavy casualties had been likewise sustained in the Mediterranean. The sinking of the *Ark Royal* by a U-boat on 13 November 1941 was followed twelve days later on 25 November by the similar destruction of the battleship *Barham*. Then on the night of 18–19 December 1941, the battleships *Queen Elizabeth* and *Valiant* were crippled at Alexandria by Italy's elite MAS special forces, necessitating lengthy repairs that were not yet complete.[11] These losses left the Admiralty with ten operational battleships and one battle cruiser (*Renown*) to choose from. Of these, the two *Rodney*-class battleships had been plagued by persistent mechanical issues; the *Queen Elizabeth*–class battleship *Warspite* was just returning to service following repairs to heavy damage suffered from the Luftwaffe in the Mediterranean some months before.[12] In terms of aircraft carriers, the obsolescent *Furious* and the four modern *Illustrious*-class ships were the candidates available for deployment beyond Suez. Fortunately for the British, the immediate threat posed in the European theater by the German and Italian naval surface forces was substantially diminished. Although undeniably humiliating for Whitehall and the Admiralty, the successful February 1942 Channel Dash effectively removed the hazard of future German surface-raiding sorties from occupied French ports; the Italians, meanwhile, were still recovering from the severe mauling of their ships at Taranto and Cape Matapan.

So, with both Churchill and the Admiralty unwilling to deploy the Royal Navy's two remaining *KG-V*–class battleships, *King George V* and *Duke of York*, beyond the European theater, the capital ship component of the Eastern Fleet was bereft of Churchill's envisaged "best ships."[13] Instead, Admiral Somerville possessed the *Warspite* as well as the four much-despised R-class vessels, which had been reluctantly slated for convoy protection in the August 1941 evaluations. By contrast, the presence of the modern aircraft carriers *Indomitable* and *Formidable* enthused the prime minister, who had come to believe that "the warfare of aircraft carriers should be developed to the greatest possible extent." Yet as Somerville noted in his subsequent report of proceedings, the Eastern Fleet had emerged as first and foremost a fleet in being.[14] The categorization of this form of strategic formation within the postwar histories has been most frequently associated with a position of weakness on the part of the owning party, be it a matter of momentary operational inferiority or the possession of a numerically inferior fleet as a whole. The pertinent point Somerville made in his classification was the idea of "limit and check" the enemy's advance for as long a timeframe as possible by utilizing either passive, presence-based deterrence or mixing passivity with Admiral Cunningham's upmost circumspection by—if possible—targeting the enemy at its most vulnerable points.[15] When considering, however, the means by which the Royal Navy had thus far confronted its European Axis foes, is it in fact reasonable to suggest that Somerville's actions were actually indicative of common British naval practice?

If Winston Churchill's contention is accepted—that the Admiralty's major strategic challenge resided in its ability to cope with the sheer scale of its global commitments as distinct from the threat of a single belligerent—the aforementioned proposition attracts considerable merit.[16] What the experience of the Royal Navy's campaigns against the Germans and Italians clearly demonstrated is that a single powerful fleet had been inevitably compelled to undertake dispersed operations in a weakened state. In pursuit of the Admiralty's desire to aggressively pursue the German and Italian naval forces wherever and whenever the opportunity arose, circumspection became an absolute necessity when the circumstances required the disposition of available warships upon a minimalist basis. In spite of the advantages that aircraft carriers gave Somerville, Cunningham, and Tovey, their reports and recollections revealed a litany of difficulties including dawdling battleships, the constant lack of sufficient screening vessels, and gossamer-thin land-based air cover.[17] Therefore if the fleet-in-being concept were based upon the need to avoid attrition wherever possible (as Somerville suggested regarding the Eastern Fleet), this element of the definition can be rightly regarded as applying to the majority of operations in both the Atlantic and the Mediterranean.[18] And it remains relevant that the eventual composition of Somerville's force represented the single largest concentration of capital ships and aircraft carriers the Royal Navy came to deploy against an active enemy fleet throughout World War II—a factor regularly overlooked within the postwar accounts.

In this instance the fleet-in-being aspect has most frequently been associated with the condition of the Eastern Fleet's R-class battleships, which comprised the capital ship element of Force B. Described by Churchill and others as little more than floating coffins, there is no disagreement with Somerville's view that these vessels were a significant burden upon the fleet's tactical flexibility, as will be fleshed out in further detail shortly.[19] But if the Eastern Fleet is to be considered an example of the quintessential fleet in being, how does this reflect upon the Admiralty's other fleet- and squadron-scale dispositions in which battleships participated?

These figures reveal that while the R-class vessels were inferior to both *Queen Elizabeth*–class and *Rodney*-class ships in most respects, the speeds of the three classes were sufficiently slow (by 1940s standards) to place all three on the endangered list. As noted in chapter four, the R and *Queen Elizabeth*–classes

Table 4—Comparative Features of Royal Navy Battleships in World War II (pre-1943)

Class	R CLASS	QUEEN ELIZABETH	RODNEY	KING GEORGE V
Length (feet)	624	646	710	745
Displacement (tons)	33,500	33,550	38,000	40,990
Speed (knots)	21	23	23	29.5
Main Armament (inches)	8 x 15	8 x 15	9 x 16	10 x 14
Secondary Armament (inches)	14 x 6	20 x 4.5 dual purpose	12 x 6	16 x 5.25 dual purpose
Antiaircraft Armament	6 x various	14 x various	12 x various	12+ x various

Source: "Dimensions and Particulars of British and Foreign Warships," 216–17; H. Lyon, *The Encyclopaedia of the World's Warships* (Turnout, UK: Leisure Books, 1985).

were equally susceptible to catastrophic damage from torpedo hits, as was clearly illustrated by the fate of the *Royal Oak* and the *Barham*. The point is that without the *King George V*–class, the Admiralty possessed a fleet of battleships lacking the aptitude for fast-moving modern naval warfare. And this meant that outside of the Home Fleet, the Royal Navy's peripheral commands were, as in the past, generally served common fare in terms of their battleship capabilities.[20]

From the outset of hostilities in Europe, the sheer lack of modern battleships possessed by the Admiralty had compelled the British to exercise what amounted to a practical fleet-in-being strategy, both in the Atlantic and elsewhere. Although a significant proportion of its capital ships, cruisers, and destroyers were materially inferior to their German and Italian counterparts, the Royal Navy had limited and checked its opponent fleets through the mixture of deterrence and targeted aggression. Indeed with the exception of the Kriegsmarine's U-boat campaign, the fleet-in-being concept will be appreciated as guiding the fortunes of the three navies concerned. And in so doing, one only needs to reflect upon Whitehall's obsessive paranoia with the activities of the battleship *Tirpitz* to realize that a fleet in being could assume a wide variety of sizes and capabilities. Much of the debate over the eventual composition of Force Z revolved around the presence of this single capital ship, and the decision to deploy the *Prince of Wales* included several recall options for the *King George V*–class battleship should the *Tirpitz* have attempted a breakout into the North Atlantic while Phillips' squadron was in transit to the Far East.[21] In the absence of a Jutland-style slugfest, operational minimalism had become the new reality in the post-Washington era. However, the advent of the Kido Butai meant that just six ships in company possessed the necessary means to deliver overwhelming offensive force through mass aerial strikes by modern dive-bombers and torpedo planes.

A major reason the Operation C raids took on critical significance was the unprecedented nature of the threat posed by the Nagumo-Ozawa sorties. Had the Aden-Singapore-Simonstown concept been primarily designed to cope with an opponent such as the Kriegsmarine, which actively sought to avoid fleet-scale engagements during its surface-raiding missions, this strategy would have been a commonsense operational solution. When dealing with the Japanese, however, the British confronted an opponent with no such scruples when it came to engaging hostile fleets. For their part, the Japanese were pursuing the destruction of the Eastern Fleet in accordance with their "front-and-back" approach—in effect, neutralizing any British naval presence before prosecuting their decisive clash with the aircraft carrier arm of the United States Pacific Fleet.[22] Rather than utilize the presence of Nagumo's carriers in the waters of Southeast Asia as its own fleet in being, the Japanese navy's first preference was to surprise the British fleet, preferably at anchor, and destroy it. If the British sought to actively oppose this attack-minded enemy via ambush at sea, then for the Eastern Fleet's own survival, the combination of preemptive detection and maximum fleet mobility became absolutely paramount. For unlike the situation within the Atlantic theater, whereby the Home Fleet was greatly aided by favorable geography in attempting to intercept breakouts by the Kriegsmarine's warships, no such advantage existed in the Indian Ocean—any standoff blockade of the Malay Barrier inevitably exposed the Eastern Fleet to attack from the Japanese navy's land-based air flotillas.[23]

The Japanese certainly held the upper hand when it came to the choice of available strategies. An expedition into the Indian Ocean proffered numerous entry points, be it the series of narrow straits that separated Sumatra, Java, and the other peripheral islands of the Netherlands East Indies, or the Strait of Malacca separating Sumatra from Malaya. Having exited the Malay Barrier through one of these passages, a Japanese raiding force could utilize the ocean vastness to launch attacks against British sea communications from most points of the compass without the impediment of large land masses.[24] Should such a force seek to surprise the Eastern Fleet's bases at Colombo or Trincomalee, it would do so with complete freedom of maneuver between Sumatra and the Maldives. For the British could not rely upon a network of friendly eyes to give advanced warning of a sortie, as had occurred when the *Bismarck* steamed through the Skagerrak toward the Norwegian fjords. If the Eastern Fleet were to intercept such an expedition, it would be compelled to rely upon long-range reconnaissance provided by RAF Catalina flying boats from Ceylon or upon local air searches from Somerville's carriers south of the island. Yet the British possessed one advantage that remained unknown to the Japanese, namely the secret base at Addu Atoll at the southern tip of the Maldives. Although still incomplete in April 1942, Addu provided the sole means for the Eastern Fleet to flank any Japanese attempt to approach Ceylon from the south or southwest.[25]

As though the geographic advantages the Japanese enjoyed were not enough of a challenge for the Eastern Fleet, the eventual composition of the Japanese navy's Operation C fleets presented the Admiralty with an entirely unique problem. The presence of a light carrier–cum–cruiser force to carry out merchant raiding, together with Nagumo's five fleet carriers, constituted a disposition of warships that neither the Germans nor the Italians were able to assemble. Further, throughout both World War I and World War II, prior to April 1942, the Royal Navy had never been forced to contend with simultaneous coordinated missions by two fleets that were separated by over five hundred miles of ocean. These aspects of the Operation C raids produced a mode of naval warfare that could not only seriously challenge Britain's command of the sea but indeed defeat it. Only the presence of large numbers of long-range, land-based British fighters and strike aircraft, available to simultaneously provide air support in the skies over the approaches to Ceylon and within the Bay of Bengal, could have presented anything like a substantial impediment to the Japanese navy's sorties. Possessing superiority in both airpower and surface gunnery, the Eastern Fleet would have been favored to defeat Ozawa's Second Expeditionary Fleet in a set-piece engagement between the two formations. The presence of Nagumo's carriers, however, tipped the scales firmly against the British, regardless of the physical composition of the fleet or squadron that the Admiralty was able to assemble.

It is readily agreed that annihilation of Somerville's command by the Kido Butai would have generated a major strategic crisis for the Allied powers. Arthur Marder, Eric Grove, and Russell Grenfell, among others, have concluded that severing British sea communications in the Indian Ocean stood to isolate both India and China and simultaneously expose Britain's oil supplies in the Persian Gulf to the direct threat of Japanese naval interdiction.[26] These consequences, which likewise would have included a potentially severe impact upon U.S. capability to provide vital Lend-Lease supplies to the Soviet Union through Iran, were undeniably drastic because the wider Allied presence on the Asian mainland might well have become untenable. Both Marder and Michael Tomlinson have referred to the impact of a major British disaster in the Indian Ocean as being a catalyst for widespread civil unrest within India itself; such unrest would gravely compromise Whitehall's efforts to reach a political settlement with the Indian National Congress in order to maintain India's adherence to the Allied cause.[27] And the histories have additionally speculated that a terminal blow to Churchill's leadership was in the offing, given that the prime minister had already been subjected to a no-confidence motion in the House of Commons following the loss of Singapore and Tobruk. However the prospect of Britain being forced out of the war altogether should be treated with marked caution, absent a similar success from the Kriegsmarine's *guerre de course* in the Atlantic.[28]

Yet there existed an additional possibility, which would be thought by most to be highly fanciful. The idea that the Japanese navy could have mounted a subsequent offensive sortie in the Atlantic cannot be sustained upon then-existing strategic grounds—namely the necessity for Nagumo's and Ozawa's ships to be reincorporated into the Combined Fleet for its sought-after decisive battle with America's Pacific Fleet.[29] However, there can be little doubt that the Japanese certainly possessed the material means to undertake such a feat, as historically improbable as its actual undertaking may have been. If the reader recalls that Admiral Rojestvensky had been able to coax a fleet of predominantly barnacle-encrusted pensioners from the Baltic to the Straits of Tsushima, a similar transoceanic epic was not beyond the possibilities of a modern naval squadron accompanied by its own train of tankers and supply vessels. An expedition of this kind would have also benefited from the support of German raiders, supply ships, and submarines, although actual operational-level cooperation between the respective Axis powers extended little further than isolated joint submarine missions in the Indian Ocean.[30]

And, admittedly, while prospects of a Pearl Harbor–style air strike against Scapa Flow were decidedly unlikely, it is not impossible to suppose that some form of operation utilizing a scaled-down version of the Kido Butai could have wreaked havoc among Allied merchant traffic in the South Atlantic. For, aside from the Kriegsmarine's U-boat flotillas, Nagumo's force provided the Axis with its most potent multihemisphere strike capability against Allied shipping of all kinds.

In April 1940 Winston Churchill had explained that, by attaining what Russell Grenfell subsequently described as "superiority at the decisive point," the Royal Navy would indirectly prevail by projecting its "will" across a theater of operations as a whole.[31] At Jutland in May 1916, the British Grand Fleet achieved just such an outcome through superiority in numbers and firepower, in spite of having suffered the heaviest losses on the battlefield itself. Within the European theater, both prior to April 1942 and thereafter, the Admiralty's employment of what was, in effect, an aggressive fleet-in-being strategy largely succeeded in nullifying the German and Italian surface fleets. Because of the interwar diminution of Britain's fighting strength, its senior service had little alternative but to adopt this approach, especially given that it was already waging what amounted to a global conflict before the Imperial Japanese Navy entered the fray. The general principles of the Aden-Singapore-Simonstown "triangle" strategy differed little from the methods already pursued in both the Atlantic and the Mediterranean, and they stood to produce favorable results if the final combat outcome was likewise to be dictated by the massed gunnery of the British capital ships. Against the Japanese, however, the Royal Navy would be at prohibitive odds to succeed as long as it lacked the aerial resources not only to defend its own ships against Japan's vastly superior air arm, but also to strike against its opponent with decisive effect. Unless the Japanese could be dissuaded from conducting operations in the Indian Ocean by the mere presence of Britain's big ships—and they had not been so dissuaded during the initial stages of their southern advance in December 1941—the character of the clash between such diverse tactical regimes strongly favored Japan's ongoing employment of massed aerial annihilation.

Operational Tactics: Integration versus Concentration

In the year 197 BC, the summit battle of the Second Macedonian War was waged at Cynoscephalae (in the region of Thessaly) between the armies of

Philip V of Macedon, and the Roman general Titus Quinctius Flamininus. This battle was not just the clash of two leading Mediterranean powers but the clash of two paramount tactical dispositions—the Macedonian phalanx versus the Roman cohorts. At Cynoscephalae, the phalanx that had propelled Alexander the Great to military immortality proved to be no match for the more flexible operational unit of what would become the preeminent military state in the ancient world.[32] In May 1940 another such showdown between great powers and their differing battlefield approaches had pitted French deference to the tactics of World War I against Germany's embrace of modern methods based upon the necessity for rapid maneuver. Against the concentrated firepower of the massed German panzer divisions, supported as they were by the overwhelming strength of the Luftwaffe in its favored ground-support role, the dispersed integration of French armor with infantry collapsed within a matter of weeks. Victory had again been achieved through the triumph of the tactical usurper against the established doctrinal order. And in the first days of April 1942, the same scenario stood ready to be played out at sea. Since 1808 the Royal Navy's position as the dominant Great Power fleet had rested principally on the ability of its battle line to shell the opponent into defeat at ranges of ten miles or less. Now it faced an opposed action with an enemy whose striking power was the product of a new generation of thinking, which placed the airplane at the forefront of pre-atomic naval warfare.

At the outset, the British did possess one vital advantage—they knew that the Japanese were coming. Although the Ultra intercepts did not specify the size and composition of the hostile raiding forces. Somerville wasted no time in getting the Eastern Fleet to sea, both to clear Colombo and Trincomalee prior to any potential Japanese air strikes and to set an ambush for the Japanese ships.[33] The fleet was further favored by the relatively close proximity of Addu Atoll to the west, allowing for refueling without need to return to Colombo. Also at Somerville's disposal were two land-based RAF reconnaissance squadrons equipped with long-range Catalina flying boats. Yet in the absence of firm intelligence as to the makeup of the opposing fleet, the admiral's decision to attempt to engage the Japanese, initially through a moonlight attack by carrier-borne Albacore torpedo planes, was by any measure an extremely risky undertaking. There would be no benefit from the presence of Ceylon's recently revamped land-based fighter cover—it was out of range to the north. A first sighting by the Japanese, acknowledged by

Somerville in his subsequent Report of Proceedings as the principal barrier to the success of his plan, and the Eastern Fleet would rapidly find itself in very serious trouble.[34] For the British, the 30–31 March interception attempt missed its mark; but there were evident signs, during the attempt and after, that the material condition of Somerville's battleships in particular would act to restrain the flexibility of his command, or indeed destroy it.

Even before a shot had been fired, the ills of the 1930s were apparent within the Eastern Fleet. As noted in chapters two and three, the Admiralty had failed to undertake major maintenance overhauls for the majority of the British capital ship arm during the prior decade, and this included the four Rs. The consequences for Somerville's command were profound. The abject slowness of the vessels meant that Force A, which contained the two modern carriers and the reconditioned *Queen Elizabeth*–class battleship, *Warspite*, would have to literally lure the enemy into the vicinity of Force B, an eventuality Somerville planned for in the disposition of his forces.[35] Further, during daylight hours especially, Force A would be compelled to operate within close proximity to Force B in order to provide at least some fighter protection. With virtually no effective antiaircraft armament between them, the Rs were helpless. By maneuvering in this fashion, Force A likewise compromised its own ability to quickly close to interception range by nightfall and to do so without being spotted by Japanese shipboard reconnaissance aircraft.[36] And if speed (or lack thereof) were not enough of an impediment, the lack of endurance among the Rs and the light cruisers in Force B imposed an even further operational restraint. Having sprung an empty trap, Somerville had no alternative but to steam to Addu and refuel. Aside from their prodigious consumption of fuel oil, the old battleships did not possess sufficient onboard water supplies for both mechanical and drinking purposes—a major drawback when operating in equatorial conditions.[37]

Little wonder that Somerville vented his frustration with a "Damm and blast" in correspondence with his wife after the 4 April late-afternoon sighting of a portion of Nagumo's battleship screen by an RAF Catalina, piloted by Squadron Leader L. J. Birchall—the first sighting of the Kido Butai in the war thus far.[38] With the refueling of Force B still under way, the Eastern Fleet had been caught completely out of position as the Japanese prepared to attack Colombo at dawn the next morning. On Easter Sunday, 5 April 1942, the ghosts of Pearl Harbor and Force Z descended separately upon the Indian Ocean. Although few targets were to be had at Colombo, a ferocious air battle overhead pitted Japan's Zekes against the most formidable defending fighter force they had yet encountered. Jousting with the mixed force of Hurricanes and Fulmars that confronted them, the Japanese fighters won the melee by a better than two-to-one margin, losing a single Zeke and six Vals in the process. Although the Hurricane had achieved fame as an interceptor in temperate northern climates, its flying performance suffered through having to provide additional filtration for the aircraft's in-line engine, which otherwise would have experienced mechanical difficulties when operating in tropical or desert conditions.[39] By contrast, the unfortunate Fulmars, the monoplane heir to the Royal Navy's interwar infatuation with the fighter-reconnaissance concept, were easily downed by the Zekes. This presented further confirmation—if any were needed—that the fundamental reasoning behind the fighter-reconnaissance concept was fatally flawed in airspace dominated by modern single-seaters.[40]

On 10 December 1941 it had taken the eighty-something twin-engine attack planes of the Japanese navy's 22nd Air Flotilla just under two hours to sink the *Prince of Wales* and *Repulse*. In the mid-afternoon of 5 April 1942, it took a similar number of dive-bombers from Nagumo's carriers just fifteen minutes to sink the *Cornwall* and *Dorsetshire*. With no more than the human brain and a simple ringed bombsight, the Japanese aviators inflicted a level of accuracy upon the doomed cruisers that still rivals microchip-guided weaponry performance today. Expertly flown, the Type 99 Vals succeeded in exposing two brutal truths about the respective strengths of the Japanese and British carrier-borne air arms: First was the demonstration of what lay in store for the remainder of the Eastern Fleet if these elite aircrews chanced to encounter it. Two of the fastest and most maneuverable of Somerville's ships had been sent to the bottom—and sent there without Nagumo having to fly off his torpedo-armed Type 97 Kates. And second, since December 1941 another self-inflicted wound from the 1930s had eventually deprived the FAA of even a limited dive-bombing capability: the FAA's remaining Blackburn Skuas were removed from shipboard service. The British Air Staff's stubborn reticence to invest in the dive-bombing doctrine, and the low priority afforded to the production of the Skua in the late 1930s, left the FAA a very poor second behind its Japanese adversary in terms of the tactical flexibility of its available carrier-borne striking power.[41]

With the refueling of Force B completed on 5 April, Somerville now maneuvered the Eastern Fleet to launch another interception attempt against the Japanese; Force A and Force B would engage the enemy at dawn the next day.[42] If the first attempted ambush on 30–31 March had been highly risky, Somerville's tactics on this occasion were undoubtedly reckless. Although he still did not know the full composition of the opposing force, the admiral was certainly aware that Colombo had received a heavy air attack, and that the absence of signals from his two cruisers strongly indicated they had been attacked and probably sunk by a large formation of aircraft that appeared briefly on *Indomitable*'s radar on the afternoon of 5 April.[43] Further signals from Colombo later that same day confirmed enemy aircraft carriers operating in his area. Subsequently, Admiral Algernon Willis, Somerville's second in command, questioned his superior's decision to seek battle on both occasions against such a superior force, concluding that only the necessity to refuel at Addu on 3–4 April saved the Eastern Fleet from disaster.[44] With Nagumo again a no-show on the morning of 6 April, Somerville's ships were again compelled to set course for Addu for refueling. Twice now the British fleet had dodged a bullet; and Somerville, in spite of his prior combat experience and mounting respect for the power of naval aviation, had clearly exercised a degree of rashness similar to that which had cost Tom Phillips his life four months before.

Incredibly, Somerville was favored by the inability of Nagumo's reconnaissance to locate the main body of the Eastern Fleet from 4–7 April; at different points in time, Somerville's ships were approximately seventy to eighty miles shy of the Kido Butai.[45] Failure of the Japanese scout planes to locate the main British force, especially in light of the brilliant performance of the Japanese navy's air reconnaissance in the Java Sea, represented an uncharacteristic lapse for a navy that had set, and would continue to set, high standards in this particular field.[46] Indeed the events of 4–9 April served as a classic example in action at sea of the "fog of war" and as a reminder that without effective reconnaissance, material superiority could not readily dictate the terms of the battle. The Japanese were to find this out in a most painful fashion at Midway just two months later when the inferior American carrier contingent succeeded in surprising and sinking four of Nagumo's carriers. This reminder is all the more timely when considering the central themes of this volume. The history of naval warfare is littered with countless examples of how the intangibles of the battlefield such as fleet-command interpretation of enemy dispositions—both known and unknown—or natural phenomena (i.e., weather) could lead to an outcome other than that forecast. Even with

Converted from an incomplete battle cruiser in the mid-1920s and further modified a decade later, the Japanese aircraft carrier *Akagi*, in company with her compatriot *Kaga* and the American vessels *Lexington* and *Saratoga*, was one of the four largest aircraft carriers to be constructed during the interwar period. *U.S. Naval Institute photo archive*

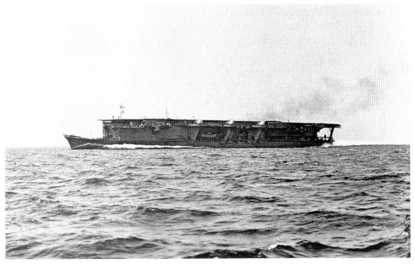

A classic flush-deck aircraft carrier, the *Ryujo*'s bridge can be observed just under the forward edge of her flight deck. The ship underwent a major refit after her initial sea trials in the early 1930s revealed the ship's instability in a heavy swell due to top-heavy configuration. *U.S. Naval Institute photo archive*

The Japanese aircraft carrier *Shokaku* and her sister *Zuikaku* were the two most technically advanced members of the Imperial Japanese Navy aircraft carrier fleet at the outbreak of hostilities between Japan and the Allied nations in December 1941. *Shokaku* participated in every major carrier engagement except Midway before she was torpedoed and sunk by the American submarine *Cavalla* on 10 June 1944 at the Battle of the Philippine Sea. *U.S. Naval Institute photo archive*

Zuikaku combined excellent seaworthiness with high speed and heavy defensive armament. Her battle record was equaled only by the highly decorated U.S. carrier *Enterprise*. Both *Shokaku*-class ships proved to be formidable opponents for the British and Americans alike. *U.S. Naval Institute photo archive*

The smallest of the Kido Butai's six fleet carriers at 15,900 tons, *Soryu* embarked more than sixty aircraft but lacked adequate armor protection, especially for her flight deck, which made the ship particularly vulnerable to dive-bombing attacks. *U.S. Naval Institute photo archive*

Slightly larger than *Soryu*, *Hiryu* sported her bridge island on the port side, reportedly so that formation aircraft landings with *Soryu* could be conducted with greater efficiency. This resulted in a number of fatal crashes during evaluation. Like her smaller sister, she possessed a very high speed but was poorly shielded against bomb damage. *U.S. Naval Institute photo archive*

HMS *Formidable* was a critical participant at the Battle of Cape Matapan on 28 March 1941. Her Albacore torpedo planes scored crippling hits on the Italian battleship *Vittorio Veneto* and the heavy cruiser *Pola*, enabling British battleships to close upon and destroy the *Pola* and two other enemy heavy cruisers. Despite her heavy armor, the *Formidable* would have been extremely vulnerable to a concentrated Japanese carrier-borne attack due to her lack of modern fighter aircraft. *U.S. Naval Institute photo archive*

One of the four *Illustrious*-class aircraft carriers built for the Royal Navy, HMS *Indomitable* benefited from heavy armor protection for both her flight deck and hull. The downside of this concentration on defensive protection was the lack of available hanger space and a correspondingly small air group. *Naval History and Heritage Command*

The first British carrier specifically designed as such, HMS *Hermes* played an important role during the evolution of British naval aviation in the 1920s. By 1939, however, she was too slow and too lightly armed to participate in a fast-moving fleet engagement and was mostly assigned to convoy protection duties. *U.S. Naval Institute photo archive*

Vice Admiral Nagumo Chuichi commanded the Kido Butai in its initial odyssey across two oceans from December 1941 until April 1942. Although regarded by many postwar historians and observers as indecisive (primarily for failing to order a third strike at Pearl Harbor), Nagumo was responsible for preserving the Imperial Japanese Navy's principal first-strike weapon during the early stages of the war. *U.S. Naval Institute photo archive*

Widely acknowledged as the Imperial Japanese Navy's most accomplished tactician, Vice Admiral Ozawa Jisaburo commanded the Second Expeditionary Fleet in the Bay of Bengal during Operation C. He is perhaps best remembered for outwitting Halsey at Leyte Gulf, despite being in command of only a sacrificial decoy carrier force, bereft of its trained air groups that had been annihilated at the Battle of the Philippine Sea. *U.S. Naval Institute photo archive*

One of Britain's most experienced fighting admirals, Admiral Sir James Somerville enjoyed considerable success in the Mediterranean and during the May 1941 pursuit of the German battleship *Bismarck*. However, he was unprepared for the extent of Japanese naval air power when assigned to command the Eastern Fleet, and his subsequent actions placed the fleet in a precarious position until he withdrew from the area after being accurately appraised of the enemy's dispositions. *Imperial War Museums*

Vice Admiral Sir Algernon Willis, Somerville's second-in-command of the Eastern Fleet, subsequently criticized as unduly reckless his commander's decision to intercept the Kido Butai. *Imperial War Museums*

One of the most remarkable combat aircraft ever conceived, the Japanese Mitsubishi Type 0 Zeke naval fighter combined excellent performance and long-range ability to make it the perfect foundation of the Imperial Japanese Navy's long-range air umbrella. It easily bested the RAF Hurricanes it encountered over Ceylon in April 1942. Although outclassed later in the war, when flown by a skilled pilot it still represented a tricky proposition for superior Allied fighters. *U.S. Naval Institute photo archive*

The Japanese Aichi Type 99 Val dive-bomber, although carrying a lighter payload than Germany's infamous Ju-87 Stuka, proved to be as much of a lethal antishipping weapon against the Eastern Fleet in the Indian Ocean as it was against the Americans in the Pacific during the first two years of the war. Vals also proved to be highly efficient in the kamikaze role during the Okinawa campaign. *U.S. Naval Institute photo archive*

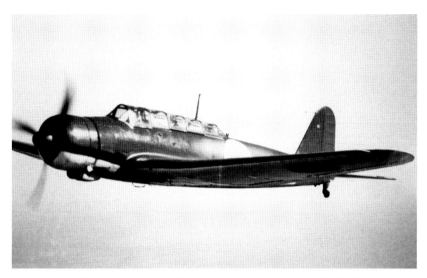

The Japanese Nakajima Type 97 Kate attack bomber, the world's leading torpedo strike aircraft until the introduction of the Grumman TBF Avenger, was primarily responsible for devastating Battleship Row at Pearl Harbor. It proved equally effective at the battles of the Coral Sea and Midway and the carrier engagements during the course of the Solomon Islands campaign. It was not, however, employed offensively by Nagumo against the Royal Navy during the course of Operation C, with the Vals inflicting all of the destruction at sea. *U.S. Naval Institute photo archive*

Though a fast and well-armed heavy cruiser, HMS *Cornwall* and her companion heavy cruiser *Dorsetshire* were overwhelmed and sunk by Nagumo's Vals in less than twenty minutes on 5 April 1942, albeit in the absence of any British fighter cover. *Imperial War Museums*

HMS *Hermes* is shown here on operations prior to the Operation C raid, with a single squadron of Fairey Swordfish torpedo bombers on the aft section of the flight deck. *Imperial War Museums*

With an enclosed cockpit and modern fuselage, the British Fairey Albacore torpedo bomber nevertheless represented a retrograde step for the Fleet Air Arm; the aircraft retained a biplane configuration and was helpless against modern fighter aircraft. *Imperial War Museums*

Another example of the Fleet Air Arm's fighter-reconnaissance mindset, the Fairey Fulmar naval fighter reconnaissance was a capable bomber destroyer but was heavily outclassed when pitted against single-seat Axis fighters. *Imperial War Museums*

The British Blackburn Skua naval fighter–dive-bomber epitomized the Fleet Air Arm's obsession with multirole aircraft in the 1930s. Withdrawn from carrier service in 1941, the Skua's absence left the Royal Navy without a specific dive-bombing capability, thereby severely compromising the FAA's capacity to carry out multidimensional air strikes. *U.S. Naval Institute photo archive*

The British Hawker Sea Hurricane fighter, a shipboard conversion of the famous Battle of Britain participant, could usually handle its European Axis fighter opposition; however, the Zeke proved to be another proposition entirely. *Imperial War Museums*

In what was one of the Royal Navy's worst disasters of World War II, the HMS *Prince of Wales* and HMS *Repulse* were sunk after coming under attack off Malaya, 10 December 1941. The sinking of the two British capital ships helped confirm the superiority of the airplane on the naval stage. *Imperial War Museums*

This picture of the sinking of the Japanese carrier *Hiryu* at Midway, 5 June 1942, shows the forward elevator deck blown out of the elevator well. *Hiryu* survived the initial destruction inflicted upon the Kido Butai by U.S. Navy SBD dive-bombers the previous day, only to be targeted and sunk after her own aircraft had inflicted mortal blows upon the American carrier *Yorktown*. *U.S. Naval Institute photo archive*

The Japanese carrier *Zuikaku*, the last surviving member of the Kido Butai, is shown under attack at Cape Engano on 25 October 1944. *Zuikaku* was employed at Leyte Gulf as part of Vice Admiral Ozawa's carrier decoy force, having lost most of her air group in the Battle of the Philippine Sea. She eventually succumbed to repeated American carrier air strikes and sank on the afternoon of 25 October. *U.S. Naval Institute photo archive*

the best available evidence, it is impossible to predict—with 100 percent certainty—that a major clash between Somerville and Nagumo would have produced a crushing Japanese triumph. Yet with the evidence at hand in this instance, the percentile margin between probability and certainty was as thin as could be reasonably expected.

Having reentered Addu on the morning of April 8, Somerville's thinking fell squarely upon the side of probability. When formulating his tactical approach for 30–31 March, he had based his calculations of the geographic position from where the Japanese carriers would likely launch air attacks against Ceylon, upon his estimate that the Japanese aircraft were similar in performance to the FAA's Albacores.[47] Two days after issuing the order to retire from the area, Somerville corresponded with a fellow senior officer, offering a different perspective: "These Jap bombers certainly are the devil and we have to revise all our ideas. You see we have never been up against carrier aircraft before. . . . It's a damned unpleasant lesson we have to learn. My poor Albacores, Swordfish and Fulmars are useless against the Japs unless we can catch them at night."[48]

These remarks encapsulated why Somerville's decision to forgo further opportunities for battle as of 8 April could not be rationally contradicted. His observation also represented something of a road-to-Damascus moment on his part when it came to his views of Japanese fighting capabilities. As experienced a commander as he was, Somerville had nevertheless harbored prior doubts as to the abilities of Nagumo's pilots, especially when it came to night flying, apparently unaware that the Japanese flyers did possess experience in that combat environment.[49] By stating that the existing British concepts of carrier aviation would have to be completely reconsidered, he conceded—in so many words—that both the Royal Navy and its FAA could not wage war against a first-line carrier power until it possessed both the aircraft and tactics to do so.

If any further proof was required of the parlous situation for the Eastern Fleet, it was to be found in the vicinity of Trincomalee just after dawn on 9 April. Having failed to detect Somerville's main force to the southwest, Nagumo proceeded to execute the second of his preplanned air strikes. The progress of this episode mirrored almost exactly the circumstances of 5 April, with a raid against land targets inflicting minimal-to-modest damage, another air battle mastered by the Japanese, and the subsequent sinking of the carrier *Hermes*, her two escorts, and two fleet auxiliaries. Captain A. I. S. Crockett, a marine gunnery officer on board *Hermes*, said of the attack by the same contingent of Vals that had sunk *Cornwall* and *Dorsetshire* on 5 April, that it was "carried out perfectly, relentlessly, and quite fearlessly.... The aircraft ... peeled off in threes, coming straight down on the ship out of the sun on the starboard side."[50] Like the majority of her compatriots in Force B, the twenty-something *Hermes* had not undergone a major interwar refurbishment. Her low speed meant she could not launch her Swordfish torpedo planes without a substantial headwind.[51] She possessed no fighters and fewer than a dozen antiaircraft guns for her own defense. On any measure, *Hermes* was totally unsuited for any form of operation except convoy support or as a training vessel. Her fate yet again personified the warning from Tsushima thirty-seven years before: the majority deployment of obsolete warships within a fighting fleet against a powerful modern opponent should be avoided at all costs.

The Kido Butai's mission had come to an end. Admiral Nagumo's charges had mauled the Eastern Fleet but not destroyed it; and the Japanese had been subjected to the indignity of a surprise raid on 9 April by an RAF Blenheim squadron that had caught them totally unawares, though with no damage inflicted. Among other Western historians, Stephen Roskill, Arthur Hezlet, and Arthur Marder have duly noted Nagumo's failure to crush the Eastern Fleet, with Marder assessing the Japanese admiral's abilities as "B-class" at best.[52] Fuchida Mitsuo's assessment of Nagumo and many of his senior colleagues is even more pointed. In a particularly blunt assessment Fuchida considered Nagumo to be an indecisive commander, in his view a major failing within the Imperial Japanese Navy's officer corps as a whole.[53] Much of the criticism directed at Nagumo has focused upon his apparent blunder in failing to order a third air strike at Pearl Harbor. Yet as Marder has recorded in his summation of the Operation C raids, "Although Nagumo did not annihilate the Eastern Fleet, he ensured, at trifling cost, that there would be no British counter-attacks on the Malay Barrier for two years." By driving off the Royal Navy in this fashion, the Japanese were, as they had planned, in a sound position to concentrate nearly their full naval weight in fulfilling Admiral Yamamoto's desire to confront and defeat the remainder of the United States Pacific Fleet.[54] Meanwhile away to the north in the Bay of Bengal, another form of Japanese naval operation had most certainly accomplished its desired objectives.

The disaster that befell the Arctic convoy PQ-17 in early July 1942 has been remembered as one of the worst episodes of its type, with twenty-three merchant ships sunk by a combination of the Kriegsmarine's surface warships, U-boats, and the Luftwaffe's Norway-based bombers.[55] By contrast, too little memory is to be found today of the destruction of a greater number of ships by the Imperial Japanese Navy's Southern Expeditionary Fleet. Yet Ozawa's force succeeded in utilizing convoy-raiding tactics every bit as lethal as those employed by the Germans, with the addition of Okumiya Masatake's air group on board *Ryujo* for good measure. Twenty-nine merchant ships had been sunk, Allied merchant shipping in the area brought to a standstill, and the Burmese coastline secured for the Japanese Army's ground advance.[56] Ozawa had fruitfully employed every resource at his disposal—surface gun-fire, surface and submarine torpedo attacks, and air strikes—to pulverise the defenseless enemy merchant ships. That attack proved to be the last of its kind mounted by the Japanese in the Indo-Pacific theater. The irony of Ozawa's success was that he commanded a formation the British were prepared for. If Operation C had been limited to Ozawa's sortie alone, the British would have been well placed to conduct a successful operation against the enemy formation, in line with their preexisting strategic expectations of Japanese activities in the Indian Ocean.[57] The essential weakness in British planning, however, was no allowance ever having been made for the westward deploy-ment of the Japanese fleet's most powerful strike weapon.

In the tactical sphere, concentration had mastered integration, though not in the form of a wholesale massacre. Thankfully for the Eastern Fleet, Somerville and the Admiralty had come to their collective senses in the nick of time, though not before two ill-advised attempts by Somerville to replicate the triumph of Cape Matapan. Commodore Ralph Edwards, the admiral's chief of staff, bluntly stated the Japanese fleet "would polish us off in a matter of minutes. Our carrier force was two to their five, but our carrier force is equipped with aircraft, all of whom, with very few exceptions, are completely outclassed."[58] The restrictions imposed by his aged big ships upon the Eastern Fleet's tactical flexibility were evident from the outset. Only the extraordinary failure of the Japanese reconnaissance aircraft to locate the fleet saved the British from total catastrophe. Yet enough was observed of Nagumo's avia-tors, and their superior quality aircraft, to conclude that for the remainder of Somerville's command, the immediate future was pretty bleak. However one postwar British naval historian in particular observed light at the end of the tunnel. Both he, and a number of his colleagues, remained convinced the Japanese had achieved success against the archetypal fleet in being, but it was hardly a worthy contest among equals. Had a fighting fleet been present instead, with two or three additional aircraft carriers rather than the Rs, and some additional shore-based torpedo-bomber squadrons in support, Somerville could have challenged Nagumo "with confidence."[59] The author who published this summation was Stephen Roskill.

Challenging Nagumo with Confidence?
The Roskill Opinion

Stephen Roskill has been justifiably regarded as one of the foremost postwar practitioners in the field of naval history. His multivolume work, *The War at Sea 1939–1945*, placed him alongside Samuel Eliot Morison in producing one of the great narrative accounts of the twentieth century. A member of the British Naval Staff from 1939 until 1941, he saw subsequent active service as the executive officer on board the New Zealand cruiser *Leander* until 1944. Roskill was awarded the Distinguished Service Cross for his role in preventing the sinking of *Leander* after she had been hit by a torpedo during a night engagement with the Japanese in the Solomons on 13 July 1943. Postwar, he became the Royal Navy's official historian from 1946 until 1960 and thereafter held a number of prominent academic positions in Britain and the United States.[60] His critique of the April 1942 engagement is important as he provides a best-case interpretation of a clash between Somerville and Nagumo. In the absence of this particular line of inquiry, the question of British supremacy on the naval battlefield remained unaddressed. Yet in testing Roskill's opinion against the evidence we have explored thus far, a central problem emerges. In making his assessment, the author did not provide specific parameters for the full disposition of his revised Eastern Fleet, nor for the respective tactical doctrines to be executed. In proceeding through this issue, the same general principles for assembling a counterfactual analysis shall be applied as they were in chapter six.

As Roskill did not directly specify which form of tactical regime Somerville would utilize, we will assemble two counterfactual scenarios—the integrated scenario and the concentrated scenario. In the integrated scenario, it is assumed that the British again employed their by now "standard" integrated fleet model.[61] Accordingly, Somerville's Force A retained its original configuration, while Willis' Force B now consisted of the aircraft carriers *Illustrious* and *Victorious*, the battleships *Nelson* and *Rodney*, and the battle cruiser *Renown*, with the original cruiser and destroyer screen remaining in place. In the concentrated scenario, it is assumed that the British opt for their own Kido Butai–style spearhead. The Eastern Fleet in this scenario therefore consists of the four *Illustrious*-class carriers, the two *KG-V*–class battleships *King George V* and *Duke of York*, and the battle cruiser *Renown*, with a combination of the most modern cruisers and destroyers from the former Force A and Force B to form the screening force. Although all the listed vessels were available at various times within March–May 1942, it must be recalled that both Churchill and the Admiralty would have been very unlikely to commit both of their most modern battleships to the Far East with the *Tirpitz* still a threat to the Russian convoys.[62] Ashore, Admiral Layton received an extra dozen Catalinas and three squadrons of twin-engine Bristol Beaufort torpedo bombers, as Roskill specified. From the Japanese perspective it is assumed that Nagumo's fleet retained its original form, however it should be noted again that the Kido Butai was not at full strength, the aircraft carrier *Kaga* having returned to Japan.

On the basis of all the relevant evidence examined thus far, the integrated scenario model remained the most likely to be adopted, as the battleship still remained central to the Admiralty's preferred fleet combat mode. With the addition of the two fleet carriers in Force B, Somerville would have possessed an approximate total of 180 aircraft, consisting of roughly 60 fighters and 120 torpedo bombers, which were the same type as those in the original engagement. The increased size of Somerville's fighter air component, backed as it was by surface-to-air radar—one of the very few advantages the British actually possessed—permitted him to mount a far more effective fighter cover over his ships in daylight.[63] The possibility of an effective night sortie by the fleet's torpedo bombers also improved significantly, however there were serious practical difficulties in executing this operation. Although the FAA had achieved a great triumph at Taranto in November 1940 with a night-time air strike, the targets were immobile at their moorings. At Cape Matapan, the decisive air-launched torpedo hits on the Italian battleship *Vittorio Veneto* and the heavy cruiser *Pola* were made before total darkness had fallen.[64] Attempting a nighttime strike on numerous carriers and battleships maneuvering at high speed, under very heavy enemy antiaircraft fire, and contending with defending Zekes presented a particularly daunting task for a likely unescorted force of very slow-flying biplanes. Still, the chances of the FAA Albacores and Swordfish pressing home an effective, radar-guided attack—and surviving the experience—were considerably higher than the alternative, namely being shot down piecemeal by Nagumo's marauding fighters in daylight.[65]

Yet as much as the integrated scenario Eastern Fleet represented an improvement over the real thing, a number of the same basic weaknesses remained. First, with the Royal Navy still committed to the ideal of an ultimate surface gunnery interception, Admiral Somerville would continue to be hampered by slow capital ships, in this case, the *Rodney* and *Nelson*. Aside from the two *KG-Vs* and the *Renown*, all the other available British capital ships were members of this category. As in the case of the Rs, the Eastern Fleet would find itself exposed to interception for a longer period should Somerville have determined to close for a night action.[66] Second, the British carriers continued to be inadequately equipped with single-seat fighter aircraft. It was not possible for Somerville to simultaneously provide for an effective combat air patrol *and* an effective fighter escort for his Albacores and Swordfish. And third, the Eastern Fleet possessed no dive-bombers. By contrast, the British faced the prospect of being attacked not only by swarms of Vals but also by large numbers of Kates in the type of coordinated attack that would serve the Japanese well during the 1942 carrier battles against the Americans in the Pacific. And although the FAA's increased fighter strength would have created much stiffer resistance if primarily retained overhead Somerville's command, it is difficult to contemplate the British gaining the upper hand against much greater numbers of superior Zeke fighters and their elite pilots. Even allowing for the inevitable ebb and flow of the fog of war, the Eastern Fleet, largely because of inherent frailties, remained at long odds to prevail using integrated fleet tactics.

In expressing his opinion, Stephen Roskill did not consider the prospect of a total commitment by the Admiralty to in effect replicate a Jutland-scale decisive battle in the Far East, such an outcome being all but strategically impossible (examined in chapter eight). His chosen changes to Somerville's fleet disposition, however, did leave open the prospect of a carrier-centric spearhead clash, had the British elected to alter their tactical approach as the best-case means to challenge Japan's most formidable fighting fleet. This scenario undoubtedly provided the Eastern Fleet with its best opportunity to engage Nagumo with some confidence, especially in terms of battlefield maneuver. At last without the need to adjust tactics to accommodate slower vessels, and with his fast capital ships committed to an escort role, Somerville would have been able to far better exploit the vast ocean space south of Ceylon in an attempt to surprise the Japanese. In doing so, the British would have been in a much more favorable position to strike Nagumo while avoiding wholesale detection themselves—Somerville's prerequisite for a battlefield success.[67] Nevertheless, the Eastern Fleet remained in possession of the inferior naval air arm for the reasons explained previously, and in the absence of tactical surprise, the FAA's torpedo-bomber squadrons would have had to run the Zeke gauntlet in order to press home their attacks. Additionally, the Japanese aircraft benefited from longer range than their British counterparts—they could be launched to attack Somerville's ships before the British could close the range sufficiently to fly off their own air strikes.[68]

Roskill's additions to Admiral Layton's land-based air support were likewise indicative of the reality of the period, with no prospect of a very large-scale reinforcement by RAF Bomber or RAF Coastal Command. Regardless of whether Admiral Somerville would have utilized an integrated or spearhead tactical regime at sea, the availability of an effective land-based antishipping capacity was a critical component in a more robust British response. As Somerville himself pointed out, the use of FAA torpedo-bomber squadrons deployed on Ceylon did not provide the punch required because of the need for long-range aircraft.[69] The Bristol Beaufort was, in April 1942, one of the RAF's principal torpedo-bombing options, and it had achieved previous successes in both the Atlantic and Mediterranean theaters. If the Beauforts were able to achieve the same level of surprise as the Blenheims had on 9 April, the chances of crippling or sinking one or more of the Japanese carriers were definitely heightened. Minus surprise however, the RAF's light bombers were sitting ducks for the Zekes, especially given the absence of long-range British fighter escorts. The aircraft types capable of penetrating Japanese airspace and evading active interception in their strike attempts, such as the Bristol Beaufighter and de Havilland Mosquito fighter bombers, were not yet in service in sufficient numbers.[70] Somerville, however, would have been considerably aided by extra Catalina flying boats, which would have given him the capacity to far more accurately assess the strength of the enemy fleet and to accordingly strengthen his ability to attack Nagumo at the moment of best opportunity, should he have chosen to do so.

Although the Roskill opinion imagined an alternative situation in which the Royal Navy benefited by the unlikely simultaneous presence of almost all of its operational aircraft carriers, it does provide a legitimate viewpoint as to Admiral Somerville's chances of success with an improved Eastern Fleet. And further to Stephen Roskill's credit, he did not envisage the FAA rearmed with modern American aircraft, as it would not be properly reequipped as such for another two years. There can be little doubt that the addition of the *Illustrious* and *Victorious* to the ranks of the Eastern Fleet would have strengthened Somerville's hand; by riding their share of luck, the British may well have secured a staggering victory against the odds. Two months later, on 4 June 1942 at Midway, the chance sighting of a Japanese destroyer through dense cloud led Lieutenant Commander Wade McClusky's SDB dive-bomber squadron to Nagumo's carriers; it was at precisely the moment the ships were at their most vulnerable—their decks full of aircraft and refueling/rearming activities in progress in the hangars below.[71] Unfortunately, the revitalized Eastern Fleet was still a hostage to the inherent flaws of its carrier-borne aviation. Through the power and size of its Zeke fighter component, the Kido Butai still held the decisive advantage in establishing air superiority over the battlefield. And with this superiority, Nagumo's bomber elements were more than capable of inflicting mortal blows on even the most modern British warships. Given these factors in particular, Somerville may well have challenged Nagumo with confidence, but would have likely presided over the aerial ruination of British sea power by Nagumo's aviators.

On 10 April 1942, Captain Hiraide Hideo, spokesman for Japanese IGHQ, broadcast the following message on Japanese radio: "Britain was proud of its naval tradition of 'annihilating the enemy on sight,' but today, this seems to have changed to the slogan 'run on sight of the enemy.' The British Navy, which once ruled the seven seas, is not the same navy that the once mighty Britannia had. It is a pity that the British public still pins its last ray of hope on such a weak fleet."[72]

Gratuitous propaganda aside, the heart of Hideo's message is hard to argue with. From September 1939 the understrength Royal Navy had still been able to dominate opposed fleet combat, at least until April 1942. In this battle, however limited the physical exchanges may have been, the end of the Royal Navy's lengthy reign as the world's most powerful fighting fleet was finally at hand. Arthur Marder said of the engagement that Somerville, like Admiral Jellicoe at Jutland before him, could have lost the war for Britain in an afternoon, given the drastic strategic consequences of such a defeat.[73] The retirement of the Eastern Fleet to Bombay and later East Africa, avoided the imposition of that outcome, but at the same instant confirmed the sheer inequality of British tactics and aerial firepower in a combat environment in which destruction of the enemy was assigned to the airplane alone. Not unlike the outcomes at Cynoscephalae and the Ardennes, the modern tactical structure succeeded in toppling its predecessor and, in doing so, heralded a new and devastating stage in the narrative of naval conflict in World War II.

8

From Juno to Ten-Ichi

The Status of the Forgotten Decisive Battle

I N THE AFTERMATH OF THE GERMAN BATTLESHIP *BISMARCK*'S destruction on 27 May 1941, the then-captain Russell Grenfell made the following observations as to how and why that ship had been eventually cornered and sunk by the pursuing British forces:

> Without a Coastal Command flight, the *Bismarck* would not have been sighted in the Norwegian fiord. Without a Fleet Air Arm flight, her departure would not have been discovered. Without cruisers in the Denmark Strait, she would not have been sighted on her way through that passage. Without heavy ships to engage her next morning, she would not have been hit and her course brought round to where the *Victorious'* aircraft could torpedo her. Without Coastal Command aircraft, she might not have been resighted after being lost. Without the aircraft from the *Ark Royal*, she would have not been decisively slowed-up. Without the destroyers it would have been difficult to keep track of her during the night. And without the battleships, she would probably not have been sunk.[1]

Grenfell's incisive assessment did more than encompass one of the most famous naval episodes in the course of World War II; it likewise provided a broad blueprint for the operations by which the Royal Navy sustained its supremacy as a fighting fleet for the two and a half years of conflict prior to April 1942. Yet as outlined at the outset of this work, the engagement that resulted in the eclipse of Britain's command of the naval battlefield remains in memory a relatively minor tussle, especially when contrasted with the great naval air showdowns that followed in the Pacific. A reconsideration of the relative status of Operation C becomes necessary, particularly in view of the events and circumstances explored in previous chapters. This exercise involves contrasting the Ceylon confrontation with other fleet- and squadron-scale opposed actions in which either, or both, of the protagonists deployed aircraft carriers within their combat formations. These actions range from the sinking of the British carrier *Glorious* in the latter stages of the Kriegsmarine's Operation Juno off Norway on 8 April 1940 to Operation Ten-Ichi, the forlorn Okinawa-bound suicide mission undertaken by the Japanese super-battleship *Yamato* on 6–7 April 1945.[2] Beginning with background strategies, Operation C is contrasted with its contemporaries by examining a range of mutual factors including the operational disposition of warships and aircraft, the exercise of combat command, the execution of battle tactics, and the specific evolving role of wartime carrier-borne naval aviation.

In each of the three largest fleet naval battles in the 1939–45 conflict, the actions by relevant aggressors at Midway (2–6 June 1942), the Philippine Sea (19–21 June 1944), and Leyte Gulf (23–26 October 1944) were contrived with broad strategic objectives in mind. The Japanese at Midway were seeking to expand their eastern defensive island perimeter and simultaneously to control the Central Pacific through the destruction of the United States Pacific Fleet's carrier arm.[3] By capturing the Mariana Islands and liberating the Philippines, the Americans sought to ensure the final defeat of Japan itself. With the Marianas taken, virtually all Japanese cities were to fall under the thrall of American B-29 raids, while the recapture of Luzon, following initial landings at Leyte, in particular would sever Japan's critical lifeline to her principal sources of fuel oil in the Indonesian archipelago. Conversely at Midway, the Americans were planning to ambush and destroy Admiral Nagumo's carrier spearhead; for their part, the Japanese sought to fight what they regarded as their Kantai Kessen in the Philippine Sea and eventually at Leyte as well.[4] Yet the primary strategic motivations underpinning the Operation C sorties were no less compelling. By clearing the Royal Navy from the Eastern Indian Ocean and thereby protecting the left flank of the Imperial Japanese Army's Burmese campaign, the southwestern portion of Japan's expanded empire would be secure, including all the vital wellheads and refineries that had been captured in her initial southward offensive. As for the British, Admiral Somerville's Eastern Fleet was deployed for combat in the mistaken belief that it would be preventing a small but powerful Japanese raiding force from interdicting the vulnerable Far Eastern sea-lanes, just as the Admiralty had sought to prevent *Bismarck* from inflicting similar mayhem in the Atlantic.[5]

The strategic consequences that flowed from these naval actions were equally profound. Losing four of its six most powerful aircraft carriers at Midway cost the Imperial Japanese Navy dearly: the effective neutralization of its most dangerous fighting instrument. The loss of the Marianas, following as it did the massacre of Japanese naval aviation at the Philippine Sea, resulted in Japan's cities being eventually reduced to cinders, one by one. And defeat at Leyte Gulf ensured that the remnants of the Japanese navy, along with the remainder of its nation's military machine, were condemned to an idle fate through the final severing of fuel supplies, already severely depleted by attacks from American submarines. By contrast, the Operation C raids did ensure that relative peace and quiet were maintained in the vital resource areas of the Indonesian archipelago for at least two years; although from 1943 onward this advantage was undoubtedly weakened by the steadily growing impact of American submarine warfare. Yet with Japanese leadership unwilling to immediately exploit the withdrawal of the Eastern Fleet, an even bigger opportunity was lost.[6] Had the Japanese navy maintained a powerful presence in the Indian Ocean, a potentially disastrous outcome for Allied grand strategy, it would have generated serious ramifications over a much wider geographic area, as illustrated in chapter seven. As at Midway, where a Japanese victory would have ensured mastery over the Pacific—at least until the United States was materially able to stage a counteroffensive—the Allied cause in the Far East would have faced a similar crisis if India had been occupied or the major Western supply links to China had been cut altogether.

When considering the question of operational dispositions, Operation C was certainly not in the same category as Midway, the Philippine Sea, or Leyte Gulf in terms of the total number of warships and carrier-borne aircraft deployed in those actions. More than 130 warships and approximately 500 aircraft were committed in the Midway-Aleutians action, and the Philippine Sea and Leyte involved more than 150 and 230 warships, respectively, with over 1,000 airplanes in each instance.[7] The majority of the other actions of interest contained an average of between 50 and 65 warships; actions in the Pacific included 200 to 300 aircraft per battle. With 63 ships present, overall participation in the Indian Ocean mirrored that of the battles of Eastern Solomons (24 August 1942) and Santa Cruz (26 October 1942) but utilized more vessels than either Cape Matapan or the Coral Sea (40 and 50 ships, respectively).[8] Operation C mustered approximately 440 airplanes, the largest number deployed outside of the three biggest actions. It is likewise noteworthy that the Ceylon engagement was attended by 5 of the Kido Butai's 6 large carriers, the largest such disposition (for an opposed fleet combat) of the war. In comparison, the British deployed half of their most modern fleet carriers and over half of their available capital ships. Based upon these numbers, it is plain this battle lacked little in comparison with the other engagements fought; both sides had committed a significant portion of their respective carrier and battleship arms, and Japan had committed two-thirds of its carrier-borne aircraft then in service.[9]

In the majority of the carrier operations in question, the leading commanders possessed prior combat experience, particularly Admiral Somerville. Somerville, however, faced the most onerous of tasks when it came to the perennial military problem of striking a balance between risk and reward. Unlike his Japanese and American counterparts, the British commander was committed to a tactical regime that could not be implemented over lengthy distances. In order for his integrated fleet tactics to succeed, Somerville had to close the combat range to something in the vicinity of ten to twenty miles so that his battleship arm could bring Admiral Nagumo's ships under effective fire. This meant that the maximum distance at which he could launch air strikes against the Japanese would be considerably less than in a carrier-versus-carrier duel. Similar to Admiral Cunningham at Cape Matapan, and to Somerville's own experience in battle at Calabria (9 July 1940), the mobility of his fleet was again hampered by the slow speed of his battleships.[10] In the carrier engagements that followed in the Pacific, neither the Japanese nor the Americans were subject to such an impediment. On the occasions where arguably excessive risks were taken, such as Admiral Spruance's launching a late afternoon air strike in the Philippine Sea (at the point of extreme range for his aircraft) or Admiral William "Bill" Halsey's decision to pursue Admiral Ozawa's decoy force at Leyte, these risks arose primarily from the peculiar progression of these engagements.[11]

Given the material limitations to tactical flexibility, Somerville was particularly reliant on the quality of his available intelligence, through both codebreaking and battlefield reconnaissance. Codebreaking material available from Bletchley Park's Ultra decoders provided vital basic information about Japanese naval intentions in the Indian Ocean but fell short of the level of detail extracted by U.S. Navy commander Rochefort and his staff prior to the Coral Sea and Midway actions.[12] When considering the acquisition of intelligence on the battlefield itself, the conduct of aerial reconnaissance in the Indian Ocean was comparable with other similar actions, including the likelihood of critical error, further expanded upon later. Like the Americans and Japanese, the British were favored with the presence of long-range flying boats. Shorter-range reconnaissance missions were flown off the decks of Somerville's carriers. A specific advantage for the Eastern Fleet lay in the use of airborne radar by the British snoopers—a technology advance the Americans would not fully embrace until 1943 and the Japanese would never adequately acquire. It was, however, the Imperial Japanese Navy that possessed the most effective shipboard reconnaissance capability of the three powers, especially through the proliferation of floatplanes on board their heavy cruisers and battleships. Also, the Japanese alone invested heavily in high-performance reconnaissance-specific aircraft types, including models such as the Navy Type 17 ("Myrt"), a late-war carrier airplane that proved to be virtually invulnerable to interception by the latest model American fighters.[13] Submarines were likewise crucial sources for battlefield information; however their contribution in this role during the Operation C sorties was, besides Ozawa's commerce raiding activities, nonexistent.

When it came to the issue of tactical deployment of aircraft carriers for battle, the methods favored by the three carrier powers were markedly different. Of the three, the British were most inclined toward single-carrier deployment in fleet and squadron dispositions, as well as smaller-scale operations. These choices proved extremely costly early in the war—the loss of *Glorious* to surface attack followed the sinking of *Courageous* by a U-boat in September 1939; in both instances, each carrier was escorted by only a handful of destroyers.[14] Both *Ark Royal* and *Victorious* participated in the pursuit of the *Bismarck*, with *Ark Royal* part of Force H and *Victorious* serving with the Home Fleet. In opposing Operation C, the Eastern Fleet became the first Royal Navy fleet or squadron to deploy three carriers in battle under the same overall command. In assembling their carriers for action, the Japanese usually favored a demarcation in formation between their navy's light and heavy carriers. In the Philippine Sea, Ozawa's carriers were divided into three groups, with the three light carriers positioned at the spear tip of the Kido Butai. Light carriers were also deployed in this manner as decoys. *Ryujo* served the role in the Eastern Solomons action, whereas Ozawa's entire carrier force was tasked with this function at Leyte.[15] In contrast, the Americans attempted wherever possible to muster their carriers into battle groups of two or more; and by the time of the Philippine Sea, the 5th Fleet's offensive carrier arm was subdivided into task groups containing two heavy carriers and two light carriers each.

The same contrasts existed in the types of aircraft on board the aircraft carriers of the three combatants. From the outset of hostilities, the Americans pursued a policy of equipping their carriers with functional, rugged designs powered by large, reliable engines. Two of the best-known examples of these were the Grumman near twins—the F6 Hellcat fighter and the TBF Avenger torpedo bomber—the latter replacing the hapless Douglas Devastator after the Devastator's disastrous performance at Midway.[16] For their part, Japanese designers produced a more aesthetically pleasing line of carrier aircraft, the majority of which lacked the armored protection and self-sealing apparatus to cope with the later-model American fighters. Engine design proved to be a major snag for the Japanese navy, a primary factor in Mitsubishi's inability to replace the Zeke with its successor, the Model 22 *Reppu* ("Sam"). The Zekes and their mostly inexperienced pilots were left to be slaughtered by the Hellcats over the Philippine Sea.[17] Yet of the three carrier powers, it was the pre-1943/1944 British aircraft contingent that most exhibited the gulf between fleet support and fleet spearhead. The FAA aircraft on the *Indomitable* and *Formidable* at Ceylon—biplane torpedo bombers, fighter reconnaissance (Fulmar), a lash-up land-based fighter (Sea Hurricane), and an imported American carrier fighter (F4 Wildcat/Martlet)—were, with the exception of the Martlet and the Sea Hurricane, products of a system designed to support, rather than assume, the leading combat role. Of this group, the Sea Hurricane and the Martlet most noticeably confirmed the lack of British interwar effort to develop a modern single-seat carrier fighter; the absence of a purpose-designed dive-bomber was likewise apparent.

Compared with their Japanese opposites, the Eastern Fleet's pilots and aircrew were relatively inexperienced, an advantage the Japanese also held over their American opponents until at least March 1943. However, the Americans proved to be fast learners. Through innovations such as the "Thatch Weave," the American Wildcats were able to exert gradual equality with the Zekes and eventually began to inflict punishing losses on both the Zekes and the bomber elements the Zekes were assigned to protect.[18] The truly mortal blow inflicted on Japanese naval aviation emerged in March 1943 when Admiral Yamamoto reassigned the vast majority of his carrier-borne aircraft to land bases to carry out a series of large raids against targets in the Solomons and Papua. These attacks against amphibious transport anchorages achieved little and came at a dreadful cost to the navy's pilots and aircrews; by the conclusion of the naval element of the Solomons campaign in October 1943, combat attrition left but a handful of Japan's best naval aviators.[19] Unlike the Americans and British, the Japanese lacked a well-trained reserve. From 1944, their training programs descended into growing chaos, as the ace naval pilot, Commander Sakai Saburo, later recalled:

> I found it hard to believe, when I saw the new trainees staggering along the runway, bumping their way into the air. The Navy was frantic for pilots, and the school was expanded almost every month, with correspondingly lower entrance requirements. Men who could never have dreamed even of getting near a fighter plane before the war were now thrown into battle. Everything was urgent! We were told to rush the men through, to forget the finer points, just to teach them how to fly and shoot. . . . It was a hopeless task. Our facilities were too meagre, the demand too great, the students too many.[20]

Given the sharp decline in Japanese aviator skills following the Solomons campaign, it was not surprising the Japanese navy flyers were decimated in the "Great Marianas Turkey Shoot" of June 1944. Vice Admiral Ozawa's two major air strikes at the Philippine Sea lost 42 out of 69 aircraft and 98 out of 128 aircraft, respectively. No major damage was inflicted on the ships of the American 5th Fleet.[21] In assessing the contrasting frequency, size, damage inflicted, and losses taken of and from strikes in the carrier actions considered here, Operation C sat at the lower end of the scale with four major raids—the same number that took place at Santa Cruz. The largest number of carrier air strikes (per action) took place in the Coral Sea, Midway, the Philippine Sea, and Leyte Gulf. Three of Admiral Nagumo's strikes in the Indian Ocean involved eighty or more aircraft, of similar size to those executed in the Pacific battles. Casualties sustained by the attacking forces ranged from a handful of airplanes in the Indian Ocean, to the extreme losses suffered by Ozawa's squadrons; casualties in the order of twenty to forty aircraft per side, per strike were not uncommon, especially during the early Pacific actions.[22] Of particular note was the relatively minimal number of ships sunk in any given air strike; the loss of the carriers *Akagi*, *Kaga*, and *Soryu* at Midway stood as the highest number of large ships (cruiser size and larger) sent to the bottom in a single raid. In this respect, Operation C ranked in the upper echelons, the *Cornwall* and *Dorsetshire* having been sunk in the 5 April strike by Nagumo's dive-bombers.

Aside from the hazards of defending fighters and antiaircraft fire, the fog of war became a universal frustration for those seeking to inflict a knockout punch. If Operation C has been remembered less because of the lack of combat between the principal elements of the Eastern Fleet and the Kido Butai, it was not alone in experiencing the errors and ill fortune that constantly arose on the battlefield. At Coral Sea in particular, inaccurate reconnaissance became a major contributor to the ebb and flow of battle. Both primary carrier forces were, at one point just seventy miles apart, and several Japanese aircraft attempted dusk landings on American carriers by mistake![23] In the subsequent Pacific actions, mistakes in identification, along with often unfavorable weather—which was certainly in evidence at Coral Sea—led to air strikes against incorrect targets or strikes into skies above empty ocean; hence, at times, a high attrition rate on either side. Add to such errors the impact of command decisions, many based on faulty reconnaissance, and the effects could be devastating. The fate of Nagumo's carriers at Midway became an object lesson. Likewise, warships were liable on occasion to air attacks from friendly fire; one of the best examples was an unsuccessful strike by a squadron of Swordfish from *Ark Royal* against the light cruiser *Sheffield*—the squadron believed they were attempting to torpedo the *Bismarck*.[24] When the impact of the fog of war is considered, it was distinctly possible that any of the aforementioned carrier actions could have taken place in circumstances where no weighty clash of arms was destined to occur.

When land-based airpower became embroiled in naval action involving aircraft carriers, its non-reconnaissance impact prior to June 1944 was slight. Of the earlier battles, only Midway saw the defenders commit over thirty land-based aircraft to strikes against sighted enemy naval forces.[25] Ceylon and Midway witnessed the only substantial air battle overhead when subjected to an incoming raid; on both occasions the defending Allied fighters were roughly handled. The level of damage land-based airpower inflicted in these engagements did not match the results obtained in other forms of air-naval operations, where four capital ships—*Prince of Wales, Repulse, Roma,* and *Tirpitz* were each sunk by land-based air attack. In the 25 October 1944 engagement off Samar,[26] however, a new form of aerial warfare made its terrifying entrance: the first squadron-level kamikaze attacks were thrown against American escort carriers, with the USS *St. Lo* sunk and several others heavily damaged.[27] Japanese conventional land-based air activity at both Leyte and the Philippine Sea proved to be heavy, but also extremely costly, with American fighters inflicting a level of carnage similar to that inflicted on Vice Admiral Ozawa's carrier-borne flyers. Undoubtedly one of the most profitable uses of land-based aircraft during carrier operations came on the afternoon of 18 April 1942, nine days after the sinking of the *Hermes*: Tokyo and other Japanese cities were bombed by a force of U.S. Army Air Corps B-25 bombers under Colonel James "Jimmy" Doolittle's command, after takeoff from the carrier *Hornet* some seven hundred miles east of Japan. The psychological effects of the attack were far greater than the physical damage inflicted, and resulted in rapidly accelerated Japanese planning for the proposed Midway-Aleutians operation, as opposition within the navy staff to Yamamoto's chosen strategy rapidly crumbled away.[28]

Although eventually superseded by the aircraft carrier as the new capital ship, the battleship was still able to command the limelight in the last actions of the Indo-Pacific conflict. During the opening period of the war, both battleships and battle cruisers retained much of their relevance as offensive weaponry in the Atlantic and Mediterranean theaters. In Operation C, the British continued their integrated practices, while the Japanese employed their four fast battleships as escorts for Nagumo's carriers. This became standard Japanese practice until Leyte, where Vice Admiral Kurita's battleship force undertook the major assault role against the American beachhead. After losing the super-battleship *Musashi* on 24 October 1944 in the Sibuyan Sea to swarming attacks from hundreds of aircraft from Admiral Halsey's Third

Fleet carriers, the following morning Kurita's ships fell upon the exposed American rear at Samar. Kurita was dissuaded from inflicting wholesale destruction by waspish resistance from a handful of destroyers, together with aircraft flying from the American escort carriers; he withdrew after losing three of his heavy cruisers.[29] For all of the carrier-based Pacific actions American battleships participated in, they, like their Japanese counterparts, served as close carrier escorts, with ever-increasing antiaircraft protection on board. Their antiaircraft presence was to prove particularly effective in several clashes, although it could not prevent the kamikazes from inflicting extremely heavy loss and damage to American shipping off Okinawa from April to July 1945.[30] The Japanese, however, experienced the full cycle of fortune when they, as the nation that had introduced the carrier spearhead in such devastating fashion at Pearl Harbor, conducted their final offensive naval operation with the super-battleship *Yamato*, a small escort force, and with no air cover whatsoever in sight.

The clash between the Eastern Fleet and the Kido Butai deserves to be placed in the same company as the other great naval actions of the 1939–45 war at sea. From the strategic perspective, the objectives that led the Imperial Japanese Navy to undertake Operation C—and the consequences for both Japan and Britain—were at least as important as those that surrounded Midway, the Philippine Sea, and Leyte Gulf. And in terms of operations, the Ceylon episode paralleled—indeed exceeded—other carrier-centric battles in some aspects but did not match its counterparts in others, and generated its own unique operational character in doing so. The conflict between two distinctly differing tactical doctrines and two different ways of seeing, especially when it came to the role of carrier-borne naval aviation, became the first, and last, of its kind. And though it is certainly true that the absence of large-scale combat between the two fleets did not compare with the outcomes from most of its counterparts, aspects of the battle's conduct served to mute this particular contrast. When Nagumo's Vals plastered *Cornwall* and *Dorsetshire* in just fifteen minutes on 5 April 1942, the Japanese threw down the proverbial aerial gauntlet. In declining to pick it up, Somerville acknowledged defeat through the preservation of his fleet. Yet without recourse to general battle and the likely annihilation of his ships, the British commander likewise confirmed the relegation of the Royal Navy to the status of a second-tier combatant in the evolving war between the flat tops. From the Japanese perspective, Operation C proved to be the noontide for the navy's aerial spearhead—the last hurrah before the Pacific and the eventual systematic destruction of the Japanese fleet and its carrier-borne air arm.

9

Beyond Singapore

Operation C and the "Two Ocean Dilemma"

THE FALL OF SINGAPORE ON 15 FEBRUARY 1942 HAS BEEN described by A. J. P. Taylor, among others, as the greatest capitulation in British military history.[1] To this day, Singapore remains the historiographical centerpiece of the collapse of British imperial defense in the Far East during the initial Japanese onslaught—a concrete symbol of Whitehall's determination to pursue victory in Europe, even at the expense of seriously denuding British defenses east of Suez. Winston Churchill made no apology for this policy when he explained that if "the Malay peninsula had been starved for the sake of Libya and Russia, no one is more responsible than I, and I would do exactly the same again."[2] Thirty years before, Frederick Eggleston, an Australian diplomat and intellectual, had warned such a fate could befall the British Empire at sea if Britain were forced to confront a German-Japanese alliance, describing this scenario as Britain's "two ocean dilemma."[3] Within the relevant post-1945 historiography, Eggleston's forecast has come to assume broader dimensions and differing labels, emphasizing the lack of British military commitment as a whole in the Far East. The concept of the two-ocean dilemma is today accepted as a bedrock interpretation as to why significant portions of the British Empire in the region were so quickly overrun during the first six months of the Indo-Pacific conflict. As the Australian historian David Day said of

Singapore, Britain "relied upon the symbolism of Singapore as a statement of British power and resolve, while declining to reinforce this linchpin of the Empire with sufficient forces to ensure its inviolability."[4]

Beyond Singapore, however, loomed Operation C and, through its execution, an avenue for further expanding our current understanding of Eggleston's fundamental problem for British sea power in World War II. Initially an assessment is required as to whether the two-ocean dilemma theory reflected the reality of British naval dispositions and operations against the three Axis powers. Central to the issue was the varied nature of the war the British were fighting at sea, and the differing frequency of various forms of warfare the Royal Navy found itself involved in prior to April 1942. From there, the assessment proceeds to a specific case study of what Winston Churchill described in his histories as "Australasian Anxieties."[5] Of all of the Dominion nation-states, Australia found herself the most firmly impaled on the horns of Eggleston's dilemma: her northern coastline lay directly in the path of the rampant Japanese following the fall of the Netherlands East Indies in March 1942. By relating the lessons arising from Operation C to the threat posed by Japanese naval operations in Australian coastal waters, it is possible to both evaluate the effectiveness of a British response and to determine whether Australia could have been brought to her knees in the absence of a Japanese invasion. Addressing these issues does not involve any challenge to the existing historical significance bestowed on the fall of Singapore, but rather it seeks to portray the events in the Indian Ocean as an equally important element of any discussion surrounding the perils of British imperial defense in the Far East.

In his 1912 essay, Frederick Eggleston believed that the catalyst for a British two-ocean dilemma would arise through naval rivalry between Britain and Germany and that a subsequent German-Japanese alliance would force White-hall into a posture of national defense. In this event, Eggleston surmised, the Royal Navy had no alternative but to concentrate its resources in the Atlantic to meet the German threat, and the British squadrons in the Far East and the Pacific were to be recalled as a consequence. As an Australian, he identified the major strategic problem for his country, namely the control of imperial defense policy from London. "Can any nation," Eggleston wondered, "depend for its defense upon a foreign policy conducted by statesmen responsible to another nation?"[6] This conundrum still rang true in September 1939, by which time the naval threat to the British Empire was assuming an even more awkward position than Eggleston had anticipated. By July 1940, the Royal Navy was already required to meet separate challenges from the German and Italian fleets, and the geographical extent of the naval war had expanded beyond the Atlantic and the Mediterranean, albeit thus far in the form of individual raiding sorties by German warships, merchant raiders, and submarines. Yet in a cablegram to Australian prime minister Robert Menzies on 23 December 1940, Churchill advised his counterpart that while it would be foolish to throw away current British naval successes in the Mediterranean, this theater would be sacrificed in order to confront the Japanese if Australia was "seriously threatened" by invasion.[7]

With this background outlined, we return to 31 March 1942 and the Eastern Fleet over two hundred miles south of Ceylon, waiting in ambush for the anticipated arrival of a Japanese naval force. In the prior period dating from 1 December 1941, the British had deployed to the Far East a total of one modern (*Prince of Wales*) and five World War I–vintage battleships, a battle cruiser, two modern (and one obsolete) aircraft carriers, three heavy cruisers, five light cruisers, and eighteen destroyers. In practical terms, the disposition of capital ships and aircraft carriers was approximately the same as the combined 1941 strength of the Mediterranean Fleet and Force H and not dissimilar from the number of big ships in regular service with the Home Fleet throughout the same year.[8] Given the geographical breadth of the Royal Navy's commitments, as well as the heavy loss of capital ships and carriers prior to December 1941, the deployment of this number of vessels to a supposedly secondary theater of operations would appear, at first glance, to be a firm repudiation of the two-ocean dilemma concept in its strictly naval context. This, however, was not necessarily the case. As we have already observed, and shall dissect further, Eggleston's assessment existed as a geographic fact even before the entry of Japan into the conflict, but it would be the peculiar ebb and flow of the naval war as a whole that determined how the Royal Navy dealt with the problem. And it should not be overlooked that the Imperial Japanese Navy, by sending its carrier spearhead to the Indian Ocean, was likewise confronting its own two-ocean dilemma—the need to remove the British threat in the west before its second great showdown with the Americans to the east.

Stephen Roskill's reference to the Admiralty's need for flexibility in the concentration of British naval power illustrated the only practicable means by which Britain could manage the two-ocean dilemma until American support became available in bulk.[9] The nature of the war the British were fighting at sea prior to December 1941 undoubtedly assisted in this regard. Eggleston's suggestion, when referring to the danger of a German-Japanese naval alliance, was based upon the presumed presence of large surface battle fleets, such as those being developed by the British and the Germans in 1912.[10] Given the particular era of his authorship, he understandably did not consider the future impact of either submarine warfare or airpower. With no large German battle fleet present throughout World War II, the majority of Atlantic naval operations were convoy related, with a somewhat lower requirement for the mass presence of British capital ships and aircraft carriers at Scapa Flow than would have otherwise been the case. In the Mediterranean, while the Admiralty was opposing a powerful and modern Italian fleet, the Italian policy of fleet in being aided the Royal Navy by permitting the British to muster small but highly effective squadron and fleet dispositions, each possessing sufficient strength to act as aggressive fleets in being themselves. And in the Indian Ocean where roving German merchant raiders were plying their trade, most of the Admiralty's burden fell upon individual heavy cruisers to hunt down and destroy those solitary predators.[11] Under these circumstances, the Royal Navy possessed the flexibility to concentrate its big ships if required, but only if, at that particular moment the ebb and flow of the naval situation permitted the British to do so.

What the Royal Navy did accomplish in this regard was to markedly reduce the frequency of surface engagements against the Germans and Italians by June 1941, and it do so by successfully exercising Grenfell's superiority at the decisive point.[12] The losses suffered by the Italians at Taranto and Cape Matapan drastically reduced the presence of the Italian fleet at sea. And as Grand Admiral Eric Raeder recalled, Hitler forbad any further naval activity in the Atlantic by his big ships following the loss of the *Bismarck*.[13] Unlike the battle in the Atlantic between Allied convoys and the U-boats, waged on a month-to-month basis, the reduction of the threat posed by the European Axis surface naval forces permitted both Churchill and the Admiralty to seriously consider basing a fleet in the Far East and permitted the Admiralty to formulate a timescale in which this could occur. What became clear from the Admiralty's deliberations in August 1941, however, was that little prospect existed for sending a large force to Singapore during the remainder of 1941 and that an Eastern Fleet could be assembled, at the earliest, only by April or May 1942.[14] Much of the delayed availability of the required battleships and aircraft carriers arose from the need for overhauls, refits, and damage repair, as well as the subsequent loss in action of some of the contemplated vessels, such as the carrier *Ark Royal*. The other difficulty was procuring cruiser and destroyer screens, especially given the demands of the convoy war, a conundrum further compounded by significant losses in British cruisers and destroyers to Luftwaffe air attack in the Mediterranean, particularly during the evacuation of Crete.[15]

Based on the presence of the Eastern Fleet in the Indian Ocean alone, there is apparent evidence to conclude that the Admiralty was capable of circumventing Eggleston's interpretation when the opportunity arose. When the relative effectiveness of the force deployed is considered, however, the pendulum swings back. As a fighting formation, the Eastern Fleet was clearly formed along the lines of prior successful experience in the European theater; against a German or Italian opponent, the fleet would have likely performed in a manner similar to the Admiralty's existing European dispositions. And if Admiral Somerville had intercepted a Japanese raiding force that matched the Admiralty's expectations in size and composition, the chances for success would have been favorable. Instead, Somerville unknowingly attempted to pick a fight with the one Axis fleet that was fully capable of destroying any battle formation the Royal Navy attempted to deploy against it. Likewise, the utilization of the Eastern Fleet as a fleet-in-being deterrent by its presence alone (bearing in mind Somerville's desire to avoid the attrition of his ships), was no more effective than Force Z had been in attempting to avoid war in the first place. Unlike the Germans and the Italians, the Imperial Japanese Navy was, far from being dissuaded by the presence of British capital ships and aircraft carriers, of a mind to engage and obliterate the enemy vessels en masse.[16] Therefore, without the disposition of a fleet that could meet, on equal terms, the naval air firepower at Japan's disposal, it is difficult to contemplate the Royal Navy being able to overcome Eggleston's dilemma, with potentially dire consequences for his own nation.

After the establishment of white settlement in 1788, Australia resided at the geographic peripheries of the British Empire, and with this isolation came a growing regard for the perils—real and imagined—that arose from the ambitions of European great powers in the Pacific. The French, Russians, and Germans were all regarded by the six Australian colonies as potential threats at varying stages during the nineteenth century, with hostile naval raids on Sydney and other large coastal centers being the chief cause for alarm. Following the outbreak of the Crimean War in 1854, these concerns further accelerated, with the Australian republican activist John Dunmore Lang doubting publicly whether the Royal Navy would be in a position to intercede if the continent became subject to foreign attack.[17] In 1871 British observer Colonel Godfrey Mundy made the following comments regarding Australian attitudes toward the defense of Sydney in particular:

> During the past two years the colonial public print has indulged in repeated and most unwise discussions on the subject of the [Sydney] harbour defences, and the helpless state and hoarded wealth of the great southern emporium—entering on details singularly useful and instructive to any national enemy mediating a foray, and indeed suggestive of such an understanding to any tolerably powerful pirate unpreoccupied [sic] by the happy idea. Sydney, twaddling over the hundreds of thousands in her bank vaults and the facility with which she might be laid under by an enterprising foe, always reminds me of a fussy old hen cackling an unintentional but not lest tempting, invitation to the roving fox.[18]

Fears over invasion too, never dwelt far below the surface in Australian minds. With Japan being increasingly viewed as a threat since the 1894–95 Sino-Japanese War, a growing sense of alarm over Australia's security marked her first decade as a nation following Federation in 1900–01. Never consulted over the signing of the 1902 Anglo-Japanese Alliance, and opposed to its extension three years later, Australia's leaders maintained their distrust of Japanese ambitions throughout the course of World War I.[19] Speculation over Japanese intentions toward Australia likewise occupied the minds of Australian public commentators. In a 1909 essay titled "The Australian Crisis," its author, C. H. Kirmess, speculated as to how the Royal Navy would combat a fictional impending Japanese invasion of the Northern Territory:

> The naval resources at the command of the [British] Imperial authorities offered, therefore, material enough for a combination equal to the task of blowing the Japanese fleet out of the water.

That meant that twelve or thirteen of the largest and most modern battleships and cruisers, at least twelve older first-class battleships, as many older first-class armoured cruisers, and a cloud of mosquito craft would have to be despatched to the other side of the globe, 13,000 miles away. The proposition was impossible of execution, simply because the portion of the British Navy remaining in home waters, after the departure of such a fleet to the Far East, would not have been strong enough to guarantee the safety of the heart of the Empire.[20]

Kirmess' concerns over the potential strength of the Japanese fleet in 1912 were certainly justified in 1914 when a report, tabled in the Australian Senate several months prior to hostilities, revealed that the Imperial Japanese Navy very considerably outnumbered the combined British, Australian, and New Zealand capital ship presence in the Pacific. The report had been tabled in response to efforts by the Admiralty to utilize the nascent Australian and New Zealand navies in the North Sea, a request that the Australian government had declined in March of the same year.[21] Although the Australian decision was eventually reversed following the final destruction of Von Spee's German Pacific Squadron in December 1914, Whitehall and Canberra remained at odds over Japan. Nevertheless, Australian prime minister W. M. "Billy" Hughes reminded his colleagues at the 1921 Imperial Conference that Australia relied upon the security of the Royal Navy rather than the authority of the League of Nations.[22] The following year, however, on 29 June 1922, naval officer and Australian parliamentarian Walter M. Marks warned of a new dimension to the Japanese threat in a speech to the House of Representatives: "If Japan should be considered the potential enemy of Australia, as certain sections of our press would have us believe ... then there is nothing to prevent her ... from sending the *Akagi* or the *Hosho*, or both, accompanied by her battleflagship *Nagato*, to Australia, and if she does, who is going to stop her from hauling down our flag? These aeroplanes could fly over Sydney Heads from 100 miles away and Australia would be taken. . . . The Japanese are not inferior to the Australians or British—they can fly all right."[23]

Marks' prediction was again echoed in November 1935, this time by the former Australian intelligence specialist Edmund Piesse. During the early 1930s, divergent views among Australia's military leadership regarding defense funding priorities had led to a splitting of ideas along service lines. The "invasionist" supporters in the army and the air force sought greater funding for national defense, with some, including then-colonel J. D. Lavarack, a future Army chief of staff, arguing the British would be unable to comply with their commitments under the Singapore strategy to send a fleet as repeatedly promised. The "imperialists," those who supported the Singapore strategy and favored the idea that the Japanese would undertake raids against the Australian mainland but would not invade, represented the Royal Australian Navy and leading figures in the conservative coalition government.[24] Although in sympathy with the invasionist camp, Piesse believed that the Japanese would likewise indulge in raids by surface warships as well as engineer a surface blockade. In his published assessment titled "Japan and the Defence of Australia," Piesse made two particularly pertinent observations. First, he outlined the comparative strengths of the British and Japanese fleets as they existed in 1935, with specific reference to the disadvantages the British battle fleet suffered in terms of speed, armament, and age. And second, he, like Marks, speculated about the power of the Japanese carrier-borne air arm being deployed on a large scale, stating that modern carriers "could bring within easy flying distance enough aircraft to endanger our main cities."[25] On 11 December 1941, four days after the power of the Kido Butai had fallen upon Hawaii, the Australian chiefs of staff advised the government about the five major threats Australia faced from Japanese military action, with an "attack by carrier-borne aircraft" topping the list.[26]

This threat was realized on 19 February 1942: approximately 180 aircraft from four of Nagumo's carriers struck Darwin, sinking five transports and three small warships and causing heavy damage to port facilities. The attack shocked the Australian nation, and Prime Minister Curtin made pointed reference to it in 22 February correspondence, part of an ongoing argument with Churchill over the redeployment of the Australian 6th and 7th Divisions from the Middle East.[27] With the fall of the Netherlands East Indies less than a month later, northern Australia lay completely exposed, and shortly thereafter, Operation C was undertaken. The time and location of the operation had specific relevance to Australia's defense. In March 1942 the Australian chiefs of staff believed Darwin could be invaded as early as April 1942 by up to two Japanese divisions, and in March 1942 the Japanese planners themselves had recommended an invasion limited to Darwin as a possible "future option."[28] If the Japanese had decided to launch such an assault immediately following the capture of the Indies, the relatively close proximity of Darwin would have meant that troopships and escorts recently involved in the capture of Java, Ambon, and Timor would be readily available. Darwin's capture would also have benefited the Japanese by effectively closing all Allied access between the Indian and Pacific Oceans via waters north of Australia. From the defensive perspective, as of April 1942—had the Japanese navy undertaken such an offensive—the Eastern Fleet would have been the only substantial British or American fleet geographically capable of intervening. Further, the composition of Admiral Somerville's command would likely have been similar to his command that attempted to engage Nagumo once the Kido Butai commenced operations in the Indian Ocean.

Within his fictional account of a Japanese invasion, C. H. Kirmess was undoubtedly correct in assuming the Royal Navy in 1912 possessed the requisite firepower to blow the Imperial Japanese Navy out of the water, if it could have been deployed to the Far East in sufficient force. In mid-1942 the Royal Navy's chances of successfully repelling a Japanese amphibious operation against a northwestern Australian target were parlous at best. In the absence of the Kido Butai, the Eastern Fleet would have most probably had to contend with significant elements of the Japanese navy's land-based Eleventh Koku Kantai, which would have likely controlled the sea approaches by operating from airfields recently captured in the Celebes and Timor. And even minus Nagumo's carriers, the likelihood of a powerful surface covering force being present and potentially including one or more light carriers was very high. Given, however, that the Japanese had planned to destroy the bulk of British sea power by April 1942, the presence of Nagumo's carriers could be taken as reasonably certain—unless the Americans undertook a major concurrent naval diversion in the Central Pacific. And given what was demonstrated in the actual engagement between both fleets, a crushing Japanese victory, courtesy of Nagumo's elite pilots and aircrew, also loomed large in Australian waters. Yet to this day, the issue of whether the Royal Navy—if deployed on a fleet scale—could have defeated its Japanese opponent on the battlefield, as distinct from the British fleet's capacity to turn up in the first place, remains virtually unexplored within the relevant Australian historiography. And as Australian historian Peter Stanley remarked, Australian postwar historiographical emphasis upon the American intervention in the South-West Pacific Area theater has come to obscure the importance of naval operations in the Indian Ocean theater—most especially in the case of Operation C.[29]

Aside from offering a window into the likely prospects of the British successfully repulsing, at sea, an attempted Japanese assault against northern Australia, Operation C featured a means of naval execution that would have posed a dire threat to Australia's continued participation in the Allied war effort. The combination of the Kido Butai, returned to full strength with the addition of the absent large carrier *Kaga*, and the Second Expeditionary Fleet conducting similarly concurrent missions along the southeast Australian coastline, presented the setting for a cavalcade of devastation. There is available evidence that a similar mission format had been contemplated by Fuchida Mitsuo and Genda Minoru, the two senior aerial planners of the attack on Pearl Harbor, who discussed the possibility of future air attacks against Sydney, while in transit to Midway.[30] Assuming for the moment that such a sortie *had* taken place (with the United States Pacific Fleet's carrier arm presumably neutralized beforehand) within the first six months of 1942, southeastern Australia lay all but helpless before it. No modern fighter aircraft guarded the airspace over Newcastle, Sydney, and Port Kembla; there were insufficient patrol aircraft to provide reconnaissance and to guard the shipping lanes in the Tasman Sea.[31] Convoys and coastal shipping enjoyed limited, if any, convoy escort; in the period June–July 1942, Japanese submarines attacked over twenty merchant ships in the waters off the New South Wales coast, sinking nine of them. And if one act personified the desperation of the Australian authorities at the time, it was the equipping of tiny Tiger Moth biplane trainers with bomb racks, so as to supplement the RAAF's already very meager antishipping capabilities.[32]

Based upon the outcome of its operations in the Bay of Bengal, there was no reason to suppose Vice Admiral Ozawa's Second Expeditionary Fleet would not have inflicted similar, or indeed much greater, destruction in the Tasman Sea. Ozawa's force was ideally composed to both interdict eastern Australia's overseas shipping routes and thoroughly neutralize the nation's vital coastal shipping assets. Likewise, the employment of the light carrier *Ryujo* and her accompanying heavy cruisers, supplied with tanker support, presented the ideal opportunity to target secondary coastal centers with air attacks and surface bombardments. As for primary targets such as Newcastle, Sydney, and Port Kembla, the Kido Butai possessed sufficient firepower to cripple critical port facilities, coastal defenses, war industries, civil and military transport hubs, and other important utilities and infrastructure assets—virtually all of which were in range of carrier-launched air strikes. The combination of heavy raids, and bombardment from Nagumo's fast battleship escorts, was more than capable of knocking out large targets such as the steelworks in Newcastle and Port Kembla. Given that a single Japanese seaplane had been able to fly across Sydney on 17 February and 30 May 1942 without any reaction from the defenses whatsoever, the chances of the Japanese flyers replicating the surprise they had achieved at Pearl Harbor were very high indeed.[33] Even Canberra, Australia's capital city, and the location of the nation's Federal Parliament, came under the thrall of Nagumo's Kates and Vals, with their ever-present massed Zeke escort to repel whatever inadequate aerial resistance awaited them.

Given the desperately understrength state of Australian air defenses in early to mid-1942, there can be little doubt that an Operation C–style military assault against Australia's southeast was well placed to crush that nation's most important defense and transportation infrastructure. By doing so, the Japanese navy would have largely succeeded in isolating the continent in accordance with Tokyo's Plan FS, without having to extend its operations through the New Hebrides, New Caledonia, and the Fiji Islands.[34] In 1933 the Australian minister for defense, George Pearce, had emphasized the importance of the southeast in Australia's capacity to safeguard her national interests in any future war. With the vast majority of the nation's population and industry concentrated in this region, this was an entirely commonsense attitude to take. However, his view assisted in sowing the future seeds for a bitter dispute over what became known as the "Brisbane Line" following the outbreak of war with Japan; at that time members of Curtin's government and the military clashed over where Australia's land defenses should be primarily deployed to resist a Japanese invasion.[35] In terms of the likelihood of a major hostile invasion of Australia's east coast, a topic that has generated considerable controversy within Australian historiography, this analysis makes no definitive judgment upon the respective arguments advanced. What it does suggest, however, is that a naval operation similar to that in the Indian Ocean did provide the Japanese with the potential to decisively cripple Australia's ability to wage war. Whether such an outcome would have ultimately compelled the Australian government to seek a political settlement with Japan in the absence of an invasion, remains to this day a matter for considerable conjecture.

In 1912 Frederick Eggleston portrayed a future in which British sea power was unable to cope with a war against a German-Japanese alliance, thereby abandoning the Far East to its fate in order to defend Great Britain itself. When considering the global disposition of the Royal Navy in the first three years of World War II, the deployment of the Eastern Fleet to the Indian Ocean in March 1942 rebutted the two-ocean dilemma. The varying nature and frequency of combat at sea and the capacity of the British Admiralty to be flexible in the mustering of its resources did provide the opportunity for the Royal Navy to steam to the east of Suez in strength. Yet the two-ocean dilemma was as much a measure of effectiveness as it was of numerical size. As the outcomes at Trafalgar and Tsushima demonstrated, a smaller effective force was capable of routing a larger, but less effective, opponent. In April 1942 the Royal Navy, which had showed itself capable of dealing with its European opposition since September 1939, confronted an enemy employing both tactics and weapons that rendered any British formation inadequate in fighting a carrier-versus-carrier engagement—the apex of battle in the modern naval age. And given this situation, the Eastern Fleet did not possess the wherewithal in battle to prevent a potential Japanese assault against northern Australia Additionally, the structure of Japan's Operation C, the utilization of independent raiding forces, including the concentration of the Japanese navy's big carriers, posed a mortal threat to the ability of Britain's most loyal Dominion ally to remain an active part of the overall Allied war effort. The events off Ceylon in April 1942 were indicative of a dilemma in which operational effectiveness served as the ultimate determinant.

Conclusion

A S THE MIKADO'S REPRESENTATIVES SIGNED THE instruments of Japan's surrender on board the battleship USS *Missouri* in Tokyo Bay on 2 September 1945, the United States Navy stood alone and unchallenged in its command of the sea. From early 1944 the Americans had successfully contrived the means to deliver overwhelming levels of lethal force both above and below the waves. Whether in naval combat or in support for amphibious operations, no other fleet or land-based air arm could match the United States for size and firepower. Victory over the Imperial Japanese Navy became assured once American naval production reached full steam and the new *Essex*-class fleet carriers were introduced in mid-1943; a series of gifted commanders were then able to wage a wide-ranging campaign in the Central Pacific to destroy Japan's Combined Fleet and devastate its land-based air support. In the process, the Japanese naval air arm found itself completely ill-equipped to counter the United States Navy's powerful new aerial acquisition, the F6 Hellcat fighter. It had been specifically designed to defeat the Japanese Zeke and did so handsomely.[1] Beneath this umbrella the United States Pacific Fleet overcame its pre-1943 deficiencies and terrorized its way to the doorstep of metropolitan Japan, reducing the Combined Fleet to an immobile ruin in the process. At the same instant, the destruction of Japan's capacity to wage war had been likewise accelerated by the systematic extermination of its merchant marine through the prolific exploits of America's unrestricted submarine warfare campaign.

For the Royal Navy the disposition of the British Pacific Fleet, as a virtual satellite of the United States Navy's Third/Fifth Fleet throughout the Okinawa campaign and subsequent air operations against the Japanese home islands, confirmed its status as a subordinate maritime power. Less than two weeks after the April 1942 events off Ceylon, the Admiralty had acknowledged the need for the prioritization of aircraft carrier construction within its construction program, with the First Lord noting that "the course of the war has demonstrated convincingly the large part that aircraft, properly trained, equipped and directed, can play in the conduct of the war at sea."[2] The composition of the rejuvenated Eastern Fleet, which returned in strength to Ceylon in January 1944, reflected the primacy of the carrier-borne air weapon in the Admiralty's thinking; and when the Pacific Fleet arrived off Okinawa in March 1945 its spearhead consisted of four fleet carriers with two fast battleship escorts. At this late hour, however, British naval supremacy had become a distant memory. Overcoming enormous odds, the initially ill-prepared Royal Navy demonstrated its mettle in the eventual defeat of its German and Italian opponents, yet it was unable to master the requirements for competing in the new age of opposed aircraft-carrier combat against Japan. All too late the British were compelled to recognize that a Fleet Air Arm, primarily designed as a fleet-support instrument, was unable to challenge an opponent that, first and foremost, pursued the destruction of its enemy through massed carrier-borne air strikes.

The decision by Admiral Sir James Somerville on 8 April 1942 to withdraw the Eastern Fleet from battle marked the moment the Royal Navy surrendered its supremacy in fleet combat—the device through which it had maintained Britain's command of the seas from the days of Trafalgar. Such an outcome was the inevitable culmination of the two decades in which British sea power had been unable to adapt to the realities of a naval world governed by treaty and fiscal restraint. Whereas Britain had pioneered use of the air weapon at sea in the latter stages of World War I, the interwar evolution of its naval airpower became a necessary subsidy for an aging battle fleet, instead of a new and powerful offensive force in its own right. In the process, both the Admiralty and the RAF largely disavowed the means and methods for successfully competing in the forthcoming aircraft carrier era, most particularly through shunning single-seat fighters and failing to establish a genuine multidimensional striking capability. While these weaknesses could be endured when ranged against lesser opponents, they could not be hidden once the Royal Navy encountered an enemy that valued the naval airplane as the primary instrument in the destruction of its foes. The Zekes, Vals, and Kates that flew from the decks of Japan's carriers were the product of an alternative developmental stream, devoted as it was to all-out attack. And while this devotion to the offensive would eventually be the undoing of the Imperial Japanese Navy, its methods and aerial resources were, quite simply, too advanced for an opponent that, as of April 1942, remained hostage to the necessity of combining the present and the past in order to prevail upon the battlefield.

When the Eastern Fleet met the Kido Butai off Ceylon, the outcome was no mere skirmish. The British had assembled their biggest formation yet for an opposed fleet combat, whereas the Japanese committed five of their six largest carriers. For eight days the respective forces sought each other out, and on the occasions when contact was made by the Japanese, Admiral Nagumo's flyers demonstrated their lethal skill in rapidly sinking the unfortunate British ships that had drawn their attention. Somerville's attempts to give battle betrayed the frailties of the interwar period, as he attempted to compensate for the basic inadequacies of his battle line, most particularly its lack of mobility and endurance. These circumstances highlighted the major weakness of the Royal Navy's global agenda—not deploying ships where required, but rather deploying a force against a method of warfare for which the Admiralty possessed no effective response. Additionally, the clash between the two fleets took place under the wider umbrella of Japan's Operation C, a preplanned initiative designed to drive the Royal Navy from the vicinity of the Japanese Empire's newly acquired western borders. In performing this sortie, the Japanese largely succeeded in their task; and through the conduct of their independent formations, they served warning to vulnerable nations such as Australia, already reeling from the loss of "Fortress Singapore," as to the potential devastation its eastern seaboard would have faced in the event of a similar mission. If the narrative of the Singapore strategy, including the Force Z disaster and the fall of Singapore itself on 15 February 1942, served as the crucible for Britain's initial military collapse in the Far East, Operation C stood as the brutal reality facing any attempt on Whitehall's part to fulfill its long-standing assurances by defending the region through naval means.

In 1982, some forty years later, the waters surrounding the Falkland Islands witnessed what remains to this day the last engagement between nations possessing aircraft carriers. Carrier-borne jets, helicopters, satellite reconnaissance, and guided missiles replaced the piston-engine aircraft and free-fall munitions that determined the outcome off Ceylon in April 1942. The British eventually won the struggle against their Argentine opponents, but not before suffering an aerial pummeling similar to that experienced by Somerville's command. Yet again, the ghosts of the past had arisen, recalling those climactic days in the Indian Ocean, where over a century of British supremacy in naval combat was consigned to history—the ultimate price for an aging fleet steaming into battle beneath neglected skies.

NOTES

Introduction

1. M. Tomlinson, *The Most Dangerous Moment* (London: William Kimber, 1976), 14; E. Grove, *The Royal Navy Since 1815: A New Short History* (New York: Palgrave Macmillan, 2005), 197.
2. D. Macintyre, *The Battle for the Pacific* (London: Angus & Robertson, 1966), 51.
3. P. S. Dull, *A Battle History of the Imperial Japanese Navy: 1941–1945* (Annapolis, MD: Naval Institute Press, 1975), 104.
4. J. Terraine, *White Heat: The New Warfare 1914–18* (London: Book Club Associates, 1982): 75–76; R. Parkinson, *The Late Victorian Navy—The Pre-Dreadnought Era and the Origins of the First World War* (Wool-bridge, UK: The Boydell Press, 2008), 8.
5. Parkinson, *The Late Victorian Navy*, 37.
6. J. Beeler, "Steam, Strategy and Schurman: Imperial Defence in the Post-Crimean Era, 1856–1905," in K. Neilson and G. Kennedy (eds.) *Far Flung Lines: Studies in Imperial Defence in Honour of Donald McKenzie Schurman* (London: Frank Cass, 1996), 36.
7. Capt. A. T. Mahan, USN, *Naval Strategy—Compared and Contrasted with the Principles and Practices of Military Operations on Land* (London: Sampson Low Marston, 1911), 209–21.
8. Beeler, "Steam, Strategy and Schurman," 32.
9. Mahan, *Naval Strategy*, 221.
10. Parkinson, *The Late Victorian Navy*, 8.
11. C. Cantrill, "UK Expenditure 1880–1914," http://www.ukpublicspend ing.co.uk.
12. Parkinson, *The Late Victorian Navy*, 92.
13. *The Battleships* (DVD), Australian Broadcasting Corporation, 2002.
14. R. Hillsborough, *Samurai Revolution: The Dawn of Modern Japan Seen through the Eyes of the Shogun's Last Samurai* (Tokyo: Tuttle Publishing, 2014), 218, 400; A. J. Marder, *Old Friends, New Enemies: The Royal Navy and the Imperial Japanese Navy*, vol. 1, *Strategic Illusions, 1936–1941* (Oxford: Clarendon Press, 1981), 3–5.

15. O. Warner, *Great Sea Battles* (London: Spring Books, 1963), 244–45.

16. Ibid., 246–48.

17. Port Arthur had fallen to the Japanese on 2 January 1905 while the 2nd Pacific Squadron was still en route to Tsushima.

18. Terraine, *White Heat*, 50, 76.

19. N. Lambert, "Economy or Empire? The Fleet Unit Concept and the Quest for Collective Security in the Pacific," in Neilson and Kennedy, *Far Flung Lines*, 61–67; N. Meaney, *A History of Australian Defence and Foreign Policy*, vol. 1,: *The Search for Security in the Pacific* (Sydney: Sydney University Press, 1976), 186.

20. Warner, *Great Sea Battles*, 255–59.

21. Meaney, *The Search for Security*, 230.

22. M. Carlton, *First Victory 1914: HMAS Sydney's Hunt for the German Raider Emden* (North Sydney: William Heinemann, 2013), 227–28.

23. *The Battleships* (DVD).

24. Parkinson, *The Late Victorian Navy*, 29.

25. Terraine, *White Heat*, 53–55.

26. Ibid., 192.

27. H. Montgomery Hyde, *British Air Policy between the Wars 1918–1939* (London: William Heinemann, 1976), 25–27.

28. Beatty, "Speech at Lord Mayor's Banquet 9.11.1923," Doc. 131 [BTY/11/8/230] in B. Ranft (ed.), *The Beatty Papers: Selections from the Private and Official Correspondence of Admiral of the Fleet Earl Beatty*, vol. 2, *1916–1927* (Aldershot, UK: Scolar Press for the Navy Records Society, 1995), 260.

29. P. Kennedy, *The Rise and Fall of British Naval Mastery* (London: Macmillan Press Limited, 1983), 304.

Chapter 1. The Battle

1. M. Okumiya, J. Horikoshi, and M. Caidin, *Zero! The Story of Japan's Air War in the Pacific 1941–45* (New York: Ballentine Books, 1973), 91.

2. M. Fuchida and M. Okumiya, *Midway: The Battle that Doomed Japan* (Annapolis, MD: Naval Institute Press, 1992), 65.

3. M. Stille, *Imperial Japanese Navy Aircraft Carriers 1921–45* (Oxford: Osprey Publishing, 2005), 11–17.

4. N. Barber, *Sinister Twilight: The Fall of Singapore* (Glasgow: Collins, 1976), 253.

5. B. Collier, *Japanese Aircraft of World War II* (New York: Mayflower Books, 1979), 58, 97, 116.

6. Okumiya, Horikoshi, and Caidin, *Zero!,* 91–92.

7. R. Grenfell, *Main Fleet to Singapore: An Account of Naval Actions of the Last War* (Singapore: Oxford University Press, 1987), 164.

8. J. Greene, *War at Sea: Pearl Harbor to Midway* (New York: Gallery Books, 1988), 117.

9. A. J. P. Taylor, *The Second World War: An Illustrated History* (London: Penguin, 1976), 62.

10. J. Somerville, "Report of Proceedings of Eastern Fleet from 29th March to 13th April 1942," Office of the British Naval Commander-in-Chief, Eastern Fleet 18th April 1942, Number 4. S/4682: paragraph 27. http://www.naval-history.net/xDKWD-EF1942-Introduction.ht

11. W. S. Churchill, *The Second World War*, vol. 4, *The Hinge of Fate* (London: Cassel, 1951), 156; J. Somerville, "To His Wife," 4.4.1942, Document (Doc.) 232 in M. Simpson (ed.), *The Somerville Papers: Selections from the Private and Official Correspondence of Admiral of the Fleet Sir James Somerville, G.C.B., C.B.E., D.S.O./edited by Michael Simpson with the assistance of John Somerville* (Aldershot, UK: Scolar Press for the Navy Records Society, 1995), 399.

12. Somerville, "Report of Proceedings," paragraph 27.

13. Greene, *War at Sea*, 119.

14. E. M. Brown, *Duels in the Sky: World War II Naval Aircraft in Combat* (Annapolis, MD: Naval Institute Press, 1988), 80.

15. "To Pound," 2.3.1942: Doc. 216, *The Somerville Papers*, 389.

16. E. M. Brown, *Duels in the Sky*, 213.

17. Both the Swordfish and the Albacore were designed to carry bombs instead of torpedoes; however, these types were equipped with torpedoes in virtually every opposed action involving British carriers and enemy warships.

18. Somerville, "Report of Proceedings," paragraphs 5–7.

19. R. Hough, *The Longest Battle: The War at Sea 1939–45* (London: Cassell, 2003), 222–25.

20. C. Forbes and D. Pound, *The Fighting Instructions 1939* (C.B. 4027) ADM 239/261, http://www.admirals.org.uk/records/adm/adm239.

21. Churchill, *The Hinge of Fate*, 155–56; Somerville, "Report of Proceedings," paragraph 24.

22. Somerville, "Report of Proceedings," paragraph 23.

23. "To His Wife," 4.4.1942: Doc. 232, *The Somerville Papers*, 399.

24. Somerville, "Report of Proceedings," paragraph 30.

25. Ibid., paragraph 31.

26. Fuchida and Okumiya, *Midway*, 66.

27. Chiefs-of-Staff Weekly Review (hereinafter COSWR) (No. 136) of the Naval, Military and Air Situation from 0700 April 2nd to 0700 April 9th, 1942, The National Archives (hereinafter TNA) United Kingdom (hereinafter UK) CAB/66/27/6-0001, 2–3. http://www.thenationalarchives. gov.uk/. The figures relating to the number of aircraft shot down in the course of the Colombo raid have varied widely within wartime and postwar accounts. The majority of recent (post-1990) British, Japanese, and American sources cite the above figures as the correct tally.

28. Okumiya, Horikoshi, and Caidin, *Zero!*, 92; Somerville, "Report of Proceedings," paragraph 36.

29. Okumiya, Horikoshi, and Caidin, *Zero!*, 92; Fuchida and Okumiya, *Midway*, 68; Churchill, *The Hinge of Fate*, 160; E. Brown, *Duels in the Sky*, 100; A. J. Marder, M. Jacobsen, and J. Horsfield, *Old Friends, New Enemies: The Royal Navy and the Imperial Japanese Navy*, vol. 2, *The Pacific War, 1942–1945* (Oxford: Clarendon Press, 1990), 131.

30. Somerville, "Report of Proceedings," paragraph 40.

31. Dull, *Imperial Japanese Navy*, 108–9.

32. Somerville, "Report of Proceedings," paragraph 52.

33. Dull, *Imperial Japanese Navy*, 110.

34. Marder, Jacobsen, and Horsfield, *The Pacific War 1942–1945*, 136.

35. A. Wavell, *Despatch: Operations in Eastern Theatre, Based on India, from March 1942 to December 31, 1942*, LDNGZT Issue 37728, 18.9.1946 (print), 4664–665.

36. Somerville, "Report of Proceedings," paragraph 53–57.

37. Churchill, *The Hinge of Fate*, 160.

38. COSWR No. 136, 2.4.1942–9.4.1942, CAB/66/27/6-0001, 2–3.

39. D. Gillison, *Royal Australian Air Force 1939–1942* (Adelaide, Australia: The Griffin Press, 1962), 499–500; Okumiya, Horikoshi, and Caidin, *Zero!*, 93.

40. COSWR No. 136, 2.4.1942–9.4.1942, CAB/66/27/6-0001, 2–3; E. Brown, *Duels in the Sky*, 100.

41. Okumiya, Horikoshi, and Caidin, *Zero!*, 94.

42. Marder, *Strategic Illusions 1936–1941*, 136–37.

43. Greene, *War at Sea*, 117.

Chapter 2. Scylla and Charybdis

1. "Report of the Committee on National Expenditure," Cabinet Conclusions 17.2.1922, TNA (UK), CAB/23/29-0011, 2.

2. "Navy Estimates," Memorandum, Chancellor of the Exchequer 7.2.1925, TNA (UK), CAB/24/171-0072, 2.

3. Montgomery Hyde, *British Air Policy 1918–1939*, 442.

4. W. D. Weir, "Memorandum on the Future of the Air Force," 3.1.1919, TNA (UK), CAB/24/72-0092, 1–2; "Sir Hugh Trenchard to Beatty," 22.11.1919 [AIR 8/17/2A] Doc. 33 in Ranft (ed.), *The Beatty Papers*, vol. 2, *1916–1927*, 82–85.

5. "War with America," Evidence by Rear-Admiral Herbert Richmond to the Bonar Law Capital Ship Inquiry, 5 January 1921, Doc. 442 in G. Till, E. Grove, and J. Sumida (eds.), "Part VII 1900–60: General Introduction," in J. B. Hattendorf and A. W. H. Pearsall (eds.), *British Naval Documents 1204–1960* (Aldershot, UK: Scolar Press, 1993), 769–72.

6. R. F. MacKay, *Balfour: Intellectual Statesman* (Oxford: Oxford University Press, 1985), 330.

7. "The Washington Treaty, 1922" (Articles I–IX), Doc. 443 in Hattendorf and Pearsal (eds.), *British Naval Documents 1204–1960*, 772–77; N. H. Gibbs, *Grand Strategy*, vol. 1, *Rearmament Policy* (London: H.M.S.O. 1976), 19.

8. W. S. Churchill, "Report of Committee to Examine Part 1 (Defence Departments) of the Report of the Geddes Committee on National Expenditure," Memorandum 4.2.1922, TNA (UK), CAB/24/132-0091.

9. "Development of Singapore Naval Base," Memorandum, Imperial Defence Committee (IDC) 16.6.1921, TNA (UK), CAB/23/26.

10. "Relations between the Navy and the Air Force," Memorandum, First Sea Lord [FSL] 6.2.1922, TNA (UK), CAB/24/132-100; "Air Defence—The Part of the Air Force in the Future of Imperial Defence," Cabinet Conclusions 15.3.1922, TNA (UK), CAB/23/29-0018; "The Relations of the Navy and the Air Force," Cabinet Conclusions 31.7.1923, TNA (UK), CAB/23/46-0015; "Report of a Sub-Committee on National and Imperial Defence," 15.11.1923, TNA (UK), CAB/24/162-0061.

11. G. Till, A*irpower and the Royal Navy 1914–1945—A Historical Survey* (London: Jane's Publishing, 1979), 65–66; Lord Birkenhead, "Report on

Cruisers," 14.12.1927, Naval Programme Committee, 14.12.1927, TNA (UK), CAB/24/190-0005.

12. W. Bridgeman, "Navy Estimates 1929," 6.12.1928, Memorandum by First Lord of the Admiralty, TNA (UK), CAB24/199-0034; P. Snowdon, "Memorandum by Treasury on Financial Aspects of the Naval Conference," 16.12.1929, TNA (UK), CAB/24/209-0012.

13. W. W. Fisher and G. C. Upcott, "Navy Estimates 1930," 13.12.29, Joint Reply by Admiralty-Treasury on Navy Estimates, TNA (UK), CAB/24/209-0014, 5.

14. S. Baldwin, "Imperial Defence Policy" 16.7.1934, Interim Report by the Ministerial Committee on Disarmament Dealing with Air Defence," TNA (UK), CAB/24/250-0018; S. Baldwin, "Statement Relating to Defence," 3.3.1936, P.M. Statement to House of Commons, TNA (UK), CAB/24/260-0029, 3–4.

15. T. Inskip, "Progress in Defence Requirements," 1.2.1937, Memorandum by the Minister for the Co-Ordination of Defence, TNA (UK), CAB/24/267-0041; T. Inskip, "Comparison of the Strength of Great Britain with that of Certain Other Nations as at January 1938," 3.12.1937, Report by the Chiefs-of-Staff Sub-Committee, TNA (UK), CAB/24/273-0021.

16. "*Libelle of Englyshe Polycye* (*ca* 1436)," Doc. 4, Hattendorf and Pearsall (eds.), *British Naval Documents 1204–1960*, 12.

17. P. Snowdon, Memorandum 16.12.1929, CAB/24/209-0012.

18. W. D. Weir, Memorandum 3.1.1919, CAB/24/72-0092.

19. D. Reynolds, *Britannia Overruled—British Policy and World Power in the 20th Century* (London: Longman 2000), 99, 114; Taylor, *The Second World War*, 19.

20. W. Churchill, "Navy Estimates 1925–1926," 29.1.1925, TNA (UK), CAB/24/171-0039, 2–3.

21. M. Hankey, "The Part of the Air Force in the Future of Imperial Defence," 8.3.1922, TNA (UK), CAB/23/29-0016, 9–14.

22. Beatty, "To His Wife," 22.1.1925, Doc. 150 [BTY/17/69/76–79] in Ranft, *The Beatty Papers*, vol. 2, *1916–1927*, 277.

23. J. Ferris, "The Last Decade of British Maritime Supremacy 1919–1929," in Nelson and Kennedy, *Far Flung Lines*, 162.

24. "Dimensions and Particulars of British and Foreign Warships," in C. N. Robinson (ed.), *Brassey's Naval Annual 1936* (hereinafter BSY 1936) (London: William Clowes, 1936), 194–198.

25. Reynolds, *Britannia Overruled*, 99, 114.

26. Gibbs, *Rearmament Policy*, 14.

27. Beatty, "To His Wife," 20.2.1922, Doc 108. [BTY/17/59/29–32] in Ranft, *The Beatty Papers*, vol. 2, *1916–1927*, 208; Memorandum 8.3.1922, CAB/23/29-0016, 10–14; "Air Defence—The Part of the Air Force in the Future of Imperial Defence," 15.3.1922, TNA (UK), CAB/23/29-0018, 1–4.

28. Marder, *Strategic Illusions, 1936–1941*, 8; J. Ferris, "Student & Master: The United Kingdom, Japan, Airpower, and the Fall of Singapore, 1920–1941," in B. Farrell and S. Hunter (eds.), *Sixty Years On: The Fall of Singapore Revisited* (Singapore: Eastern Universities Press, 2003), 98–99.

29. Memorandum 29.1.1925, CAB/24/171-0039, 6.

30. M. Murfett, "Reflections on an Enduring Theme: The "Singapore Strategy" at Sixty," in B. Farrell and S. Hunter (eds.), *Sixty Years On*, 5.

31. "Plans Division Naval Staff," 4.1.1921, Doc. 67 [BTY/8/1/7–8] in Ranft, *The Beatty Papers*, vol. 2, *1916–1927*, 139.

32. C. N. Robinson, "Naval Forces of the British Empire" in C. N. Robinson and H. M. Ross (eds.), *Brassey's Naval Annual 1930* (BSY 1930) (London: W. M. Clowes, 1930), 15.

33. Memorandum 16.6.1921, CAB/23/26.

34. C. Bell, " 'How Are We Going to Make War' ": Admiral Sir Herbert Richmond and British Far-Eastern War Plans," *Journal of Strategic Studies* 20: 123–41 in A. Lambert (ed.), *Naval History: 1850–Present*, vol. 2 (Aldershot, UK: Ashgate Publishing, 2003), 31–39; Ferris, "The Last Decade of British Maritime Supremacy," 140; Grenfell, *Main Fleet*, 45, 51.

35. P. K. Kemp, *Key to Victory: The Triumph of British Sea Power in World War II* (Boston: Little, Brown, 1957), 16–18; Kennedy, *Rise and Fall*, 274; Grenfell, *Main Fleet*, 6.

36. W. Bridgeman, "Navy Estimates" 5.2.1925, Memorandum by the First Lord of the Admiralty, TNA (UK), CAB/24/171-0068, 21–22.

37. "The Relations of the Navy and the Air Force," 31.7.1923, CAB/23/46-0015.

38. Memorandum 4.2.1922, CAB/24/132-0091, 4.

39. C. Bowyer, *History of the RAF* (London: Bison Books, 1977), 63.

40. A. Boyle, *Trenchard* (London: Collins, 1962), 524–25; E. C. Shepherd, *The Air Force of Today* (Glasgow: Blackie & Son, 1939), 29; Till, *Airpower and the Royal Navy*, 31.

41. A. Hezlet, *Aircraft and Seapower* (London: Cox & Wyman, 1970), 119, 130.

42. P.M. Statement 3.3.1936, CAB/24/260-0029, 3–4.

43. Memorandum 1.2.1937, CAB/24/267-0041, 4.

44. Interim Report 16.7.1934, CAB/24/250-0018, 1; Reynolds, *Britannia Overruled*, 116.

45. Memorandum 1.2.1937, CAB/24/267-0041, 7–11; Montgomery Hyde, *British Air* Policy, 491; Till, *Airpower and the Royal Navy*, 96.

46. Joint Reply 13.12.1929, CAB/24/209-0014, 1–5.

47. C. Andrew, *The Defence of the Realm: The Authorised History of MI5* (London: Penguin Books, 2009), 162–63; P. Williamson, *National Crisis and National Government: British Politics, the Economy and Empire 1926–1932* (Cambridge: Cambridge University Press, 1992), 402, 423.

48. Memorandum 4.2.1922, CAB/24/132-0091, 6; Gibbs, *Rearmament Policy*, 79.

49. Memorandum 6.12.1928, CAB24/199-0034, 1–3; Memorandum 16.12 .1929, CAB/24/209-0012,1–5; Joint Reply 13.12.1929, CAB/24/209-0014, 1–5.

50. Memorandum 1.2.1937, CAB/24/267-0041, 3–4; Kennedy, *Rise and Fall*, 292–94.

51. "List of British and Foreign Ships," BSY 1941, 216–56.

52. Report 14.12.1927, CAB/24/190-0005, 5; Memorandum 16.12.1929, CAB/24/209-0012, 2–3.

53. "The Building of the *Ark Royal*, 1934," Doc. 505, in Hattendorf and Pearsall (eds.), *British Naval Documents 1204–1960*, 943.

54. Volage [*pseud.*], "British Naval Air Progress," BSY 1936, 116; Albatross [*pseud.*], "Foreign Fleet Air Arms," BSY 1936, 129–30; H. G. Thursfield, "British Naval Air Progress," in H. G. Thursfield (ed.), *Brassey's Naval Annual 1937* (BSY 1937) (London: W. M. Clowes, 1937), 140; Till, *Airpower and the Royal Navy*, 75; Hezlet, *Aircraft and Seapower*, 126–27.

55. Memorandum 6.2.1922, CAB/24/132-0100, 2; Memorandum 4.2.1922, CAB/24/132-0091, 3; Memorandum 8.3.1922, CAB/23/29-0016, 1–2.

56. L. S. Casey, *Naval Aircraft* (London: Phoebus, 1977), 18; P. L. Holmes, "Marine Aviation," BSY 1930, 118–20; The Editor of "Flight," "Marine Aviation" in C. M. Robinson and H. M. Ross (eds.), *Brassey's Naval Annual 1933* (BSY 1933) (London: W. M. Clowes, 1933), 202.

57. Collier, *Japanese Aircraft*, 96.

58. T. Inskip, "The Navy and Its Relation to the Fleet Air Arm and Shore-Based Aircraft," Memorandum 21.7.1937, TNA (UK), CAB/24/270-0044, 7–9; T. Inskip, "The Navy and Its Relation to the Fleet Air Arm and Shore-Based Aircraft," Supplementary Memorandum 26.7.1937, TNA (UK), CAB/24/270-0045, 1–3; Thursfield, "British Naval Air Progress" (BSY 1937), 133–36; H. G. Thursfield, "British Naval Air Progress," in H. G. Thursfield (ed.), *Brassey's Naval Annual 1938* (hereinafter BSY 1938) (London: W. M. Clowes, 1938), 137–40; Boyle, *Trenchard*, 548–49.

59. H. G. Thursfield, "British Naval Air Progress" in H. G. Thursfield (ed.), *Brassey's Naval Annual 1939* (hereinafter BSY 1939) (London: W. M. Clowes, 1939), 170–71; Interim Report 16.7.1934, CAB/24/250-0018, 1–3; Viscount Swindon, "Pledges Given as Regards Parity with the German Air Force," 22.1.37, Memorandum by the Secretary of State for Air, TNA (UK), CAB/24/267-0028, 1–2; Viscount Swindon, "Further Expansion of the First-Line Strength of the Royal Air Force: Parity with the German Air Force," 27.1.1937, Memorandum by the Secretary of State for Air, TNA (UK), CAB/23/87-0006, 1–2.

60. D. Richards, *RAF Bomber Command in the Second World War: The Hardest Victory* (London: Classic Penguin, 2001), 126.

61. Ibid., 8.

62. Shepherd, *The Air Force of Today*, 182.

63. Viscount Swindon, "Plan for Further Expansion of First-Line Strength of the Royal Air Force," 14.1.1937, Memorandum by the Secretary of State for Air, TNA (UK), CAB/24/267-0019, 1–2; I. Kershaw, *Making Friends with Hitler: Lord Londonderry and Britain's Road to War* (London: Allen Lane, 2004), 108, 152; Montgomery Hyde, *British Air Policy*, 490; Taylor, *The Second World War*, 29.

64. M. Hankey, "The Singapore Base—Defence and Development of the Naval Base," 2.8.1926, Minutes of the Committee for Imperial Defence, TNA (UK), CAB/23/53; M. Hankey, "The Singapore Base—Defence and Development of the Naval Base," 14.7.1927, Minutes of the Committee for Imperial Defence, TNA (UK), CAB/24/188; M. Hankey, "The Singapore Base—Defence and Development of the Naval Base" 13.12.28, Minutes of the Committee for Imperial Defence, TNA (UK), CAB/24/199.

65. D. Richards and H. St. George Saunders, *Royal Air Force 1939–1945*, vol. 2, *The Fight Avails* (London: H.M.S.O., 1975), 7–8; S. Ward, "Security:

Defending Australia's Empire," in D. M. Schreuder and S. Ward (eds.), *Australia's Empire* (Oxford: Oxford University Press, 2008), 248.

66. "Defence Policy and Requirements—Singapore Defences," 19.7.1935, Memorandum by the Committee for Imperial Defence, TNA (UK), CAB/24/256; "Malaya—Period before Relief," Minutes of the Committee for Imperial Defence 4.3.1938, Doc. 110 in J. Robertson and J. McCarthy, *Australian War Strategy 1939–1945—A Documentary History* (St. Lucia: University of QLD Press, 1985), 140–42.

67. Till, *Airpower and the Royal Navy*, 201.

Chapter 3. In the Outhouse

1. Till, *Airpower and the Royal Navy*, 47.
2. Beatty, "Speech at Lord Mayor's Banquet 9.11.1923," Doc. 131, *The Beatty Papers*, 259–60.
3. Casey, *Naval Aircraft*, 18.
4. Ibid., 12, 40.
5. Hezlet, *Aircraft and Seapower*, 27, 53; A. Preston, *Aircraft Carriers* (London: Bison Books, 1979), 13, 17–19; Till, *Airpower and the Royal Navy*, 60–63.
6. H. G. Williams, "Aircraft Carriers," in A. Richardson and A. Hurd (eds.), *Brassey's Naval and Shipping Annual 1924* (hereinafter BSY 1924) (London: W. M. Clowes, 1924), 110–13.
7. Hezlet, *Aircraft and Seapower*, 114; Williams, "Aircraft Carriers," BSY 1924, 112.
8. Preston, *Aircraft Carriers*, 41; Till, *Airpower and the Royal Navy*, 68; C. N. Robinson, "Naval Forces of the British Empire," in A. Richardson and A. Hurd (eds.), *Brassey's Naval Annual 1926* (London: W. M. Clowes, 1926), 12; E. Altham, "Foreign Navies," in A. Richardson and A. Hurd (eds.) *Brassey's Naval Annual 1928* (London: W. M. Clowes, 1928), 31.
9. Preston, *Aircraft Carriers*, 31; Till, *Airpower and the Royal Navy*, 43; Casey, *Naval Aircraft*, 50.
10. "The Navy and Its Fleet Air Arm," in A. Richardson and A. Hurd (eds.), *Brassey's Naval and Shipping Annual 1925* (hereinafter BSY 1925) (London: W. M. Clowes, 1925), 90.
11. Gibbs, *Grand Strategy*, vol. 1, *Rearmament Policy*, 364.
12. Kennedy, *Rise and Fall*, 281; Shepherd, *The Air Force of Today*, 91.

13. "The Navy and Its Fleet Air Arm," BSY 1925, 93; Robinson, "Naval Forces of the British Empire," BSY 1930, 25.

14. Memorandum 6.2.1922, CAB/24/132-0100, 5–8; Gibbs, *Grand Strategy*, vol. 1, *Rearmament Policy*, 363–64.

15. Casey, *Naval Aircraft*, 18; The Editor of "Flight," "Marine Aviation," BSY 1933, 202–3; The Editor of "Flight," "Marine Aviation," in C. M. Robinson and H. M. Ross (eds.), *Brassey's Naval Annual 1934* (hereinafter BSY 1934) (London: W. M. Clowes, 1934), 206; Lord Londonderry, "The Royal Air Force Programme for 1934," Memorandum 22.3.1934, TNA (UK), CAB/24/247-0057, 1–2; M. Hankey, "Royal Air Force Programme for 1934," Memorandum 28.2.1934, TNA (UK), CAB/23/78-0007, 9.

16. E. Altham, "Foreign Navies," BSY 1933, 35; E. Altham, "Foreign Navies," in C. M. Robinson and H. M. Ross (eds.), *Brassey's Naval Annual 1935* (hereinafter BSY 1935) (London: W. M. Clowes, 1935), 35–36; Till, *Airpower and the Royal Navy*, 69.

17. The Editor of "Flight," "Marine Aviation," BSY 1933, 202; Hezlet, *Aircraft and Seapower*, 117.

18. The Editor of "Flight," "Marine Aviation," BSY 1935, 160; Till, *Airpower and the Royal Navy*, 147.

19. O. Stewart, "Aeroplanes Operating at Sea," in H. G. Thursfield (ed.), *Brassey's Naval Annual 1940* (hereinafter BSY 1940) (London: W. M. Clowes, 1940), 131.

20. E. Brown, *Duels in the Sky*, 9–11; Casey, *Naval Aircraft*, 45–47.

21. Stewart, "Aeroplanes Operating at Sea," BSY 1940, 132–33; E. Brown, *Duels in the Sky*, 7; Shepherd, *The Air Force of Today*, 195.

22. Volage [*pseud.*], "British Naval Air Progress," BSY 1936, 114; Wings [*pseud.*], "The Fleet Air Arm—A Middle View," BSY 1937, 192; E. Colston-Shepherd, "Naval Aircraft Production," BSY 1938, 166; Hezlet, *Aircraft and Seapower*, 126; Till, *Airpower and the Royal Navy*, 99.

23. Zetes [*pseud.*], "The Meaning of Air Strength to a Fleet," BSY 1936, 149; L. Bridgeman, "Naval Aircraft Production," BSY 1936, 175; Montgomery Hyde, *British Air Policy*, 490; Preston, *Aircraft Carriers*, 54; Till, *Airpower and the Royal Navy*, 100–101.

24. Till, *Airpower and the Royal Navy*, 99.

25. E. Brown, *Duels in the Sky*, 22, 32–33; Gibbs, *Grand Strategy*, vol. 1, *Rearmament Policy*, 369.

26. "The Relations of the Navy and the Air Force," 31.7.1923, CAB/23/46-0015.

27. E. Brown, *Duels in the Sky*, 145–47; *Jane's Fighting Aircraft of World War II* (London: Random House, 2001), 108, 119, 121.

28. Phoenix [*pseud.*], "The Fleet Air Arm," in C. N. Robinson and H. M. Ross (eds.), *Brassey's Naval Annual 1931* (London: W. M. Clowes, 1931), 150; Albatross [*pseud.*], "Foreign Fleet Air Arms" in C. N. Robinson and H. M. Ross (eds.), *Brassey's Naval Annual 1932* (hereinafter BSY 1932) (London: W. M. Clowes, 1932), 103; Observer [*pseud.*], "Expansion of Naval Air Forces," BSY 1938, 191; Till, *Airpower and the Royal Navy*, 72.

29. Wings [*pseud.*], "The Fleet Air Arm—A Middle View," BSY 1937, 193; Colston-Shepherd, "Naval Aircraft Production," BSY 1938, 166; Thursfield, "British Naval Air Progress," BSY 1938, 145; Thursfield, "British Naval Air Progress," BSY 1939, 175.

30. Kennedy, *Rise and Fall*, 288; Observer [*pseud.*], "Expansion of Naval Air Forces," BSY 1938, 196.

31. Forbes and D. Pound, *The Fighting Instructions*.

32. W. S. Churchill, "Churchill-Beatty Correspondence on Royal Navy-RAF Relations," 17.3.1922, Doc. 67, *The Beatty Papers*, 211.

33. "Approach, Contact and Action," Clause(s) 274–78, Section VI, *The Fighting Instructions*, 46–68.

34. "Functions of Fleet Aircraft" Doc. 506, *British Naval Documents 1204–1960*, 948–49.

35. "General Instructions," Clause 480: Section X, *The Fighting Instructions*, 82–85.

36. "Types of aircraft available for reconnaissance," Clause(s) 144–46: Sec. III, *The Fighting Instructions*, 29–34; Zetes [*pseud.*], "The Meaning of Air Strength to a Fleet," BSY 1936, 145.

37. Albatross [*pseud.*], "Foreign Fleet Air Arms," BSY 1936, 129, 134; F. O. Ruge, "The New German Navy," BSY 1937, 95; P. Vincent-Brechignac, "French Naval Air Service," BSY 1937, 165, 168; L. Sansonetti, "The Royal Italian Navy," BSY 1938, 82.

38. "Approach, Contact & Action," Clause(s) 273–74: Sec. VI, *The Fighting Instructions*, 46–68; Volage [*pseud.*], "British Naval Air Progress," BSY 1936, 106–8; Securus [*pseud.*], "Influence of Air Power upon the Control of Sea Communications," BSY 1938, 184–86; Hezlet, *Aircraft and Sea Power*, 123–24; Till, *Airpower and the Royal Navy*, 146.

39. H. G. Thursfield, "Naval Events of 1937," BSY 1938, 15–16; H. G. Thurs-field, "Naval Manoeuvres of 1934," BSY 1935, 85–94; Till, *Airpower and the Royal Navy*, 143–45.

40. Hezlet, *Aircraft and Sea Power*, 116; Thursfield, "Naval Manoeuvres of 1934," BSY 1935, 92; Albatross [*pseud.*], "Foreign Fleet Air Arms," BSY 1936, 129; Colston-Shepherd, "Naval Aircraft Production," BSY 1938, 166.

41. Casey, *Naval Aircraft*, 40.

42. Thursfield, "British Naval Air Progress," BSY 1938, 145–46; Till, *Airpower and the Royal Navy*, 142–43.

43. Hough, *The Longest Battle*, 213.

44. Observer [*pseud.*], "Expansion of Naval Air Forces," BSY 1938, 191; Brown, *Duels in the Sky*, 8–9.

45. Volage [*pseud.*], "British Naval Air Progress," BSY 1936, 108. Based upon the contents of their respective articles, it is clear that the likes of Securus, Volage, and other anonymous correspondents were serving Royal Navy officers.

46. Observer [*pseud.*], "Expansion of Naval Air Forces," BSY 1938, 196; Hezlet, *Aircraft and Sea Power*, 124–26; "Instructions for Aircraft Carriers and Attached Vessels," Clause(s) 267–72: Sec. VI, *The Fighting Instructions*, 46–68.

47. Till, *Airpower and the Royal Navy*, 76; Preston, *Aircraft Carriers*, 61.

48. Cabinet Conclusions 31.7.1923, CAB/23/46-0015, 2; Memorandum 21.7.1937, CAB/24/270-0044, 1–4; Montgomery Hyde, *British Air Policy*, 159.

49. Memorandum 1.2.1937, CAB/24/267-0041, 7–9; Zetes [pseud.], "The Meaning of Air Strength to a Fleet," BSY 1936, 143–44; Hezlet, *Aircraft and Sea Power*, 130.

50. A more extensive examination of Japanese and American fleet tactics is undertaken in chapter five.

51. H. Rosinski, "Mahan and the Present War," BSY 1941, 203.

52. Report 3.12.1937, CAB/24/273-0021, 3–4; H. Rosinsky, "German Theories of Sea Warfare," BSY 1940, 97–100; G. Bennett, *Naval Battles of World War Two* (Barnsley, UK: Pen & Sword, 2003): 68.

53. Kemp, *Key to Victory*, 29; Kennedy, *Rise and Fall*, 295; Till, *Airpower and the Royal Navy*, 167.

54. W. Baumbach, *Broken Swastika: The Defeat of the Luftwaffe* (Maidstone, UK: George Mann, 1974), 84; E. Raeder, *My Life* (Annapolis,

MD: Naval Institute Press, 1960), 233–38; H. G. Thursfield, "Foreign Fleet Air Arms," BSY 1939, 187–88; W. Murray, *Luftwaffe* (London: George Allen & Unwin, 1985), 6–7; Bennett, *Naval Battles of World War Two*, 33; Hezlet, *Aircraft and Sea Power*, 131; C. Bekker, *Hitler's Naval War* (London: MacDonald & Jane's, 1974), 95, 165.

55. Ruge, "The New German Navy," BSY 1937, 86; S. Roskill, *The War at Sea, 1939–1945*, vol. 2, *The Defensive* (London: H.M.S.O., 1954), 52, 57–59.

56. E. Altham, "Foreign Navies," BSY 1938, 38–41; Roskill, *The Defensive*, 61; R. O'Neill, *Suicide Squads: The Men and Machines of World War Two Special Operations* (London: Salamander, 1999), 67–68.

57. W. Baumbach, *Broken Swastika*, 132.

58. "Comparison of the Strength of Great Britain with that of Certain Other Nations as at January 1938," CAB/24/273-0021, 25; B. Gunston, *German, Italian and Japanese Fighters of World War II* (London: Lansdowne Press, 1980), 84–85.

59. Sansonetti, "The Royal Italian Navy," BSY 1938, 82; E. Altham, "Foreign Navies," BSY 1939, 41; R. Mallett, "The Italian Naval High Command and the Mediterranean Crisis, January–October 1935," *Journal of Strategic Studies*, 22 (1999), 77–102 in Lambert (ed.), *Naval History 1850–Present*, 167–68.

60. Altham, "Foreign Navies," BSY 1938, 32–34; Brechignac, "French Naval Air Service," BSY 1937, 168.

61. Report 3.12.1937, CAB/24/273-0021, 9; Vigilance [*pseud.*] "Foreign Fleet Air Arms," BSY 1937, 161–62; Altham, "Foreign Navies," BSY 1939, 36–37.

62. S. Odgers, *The Royal Australian Navy: An Illustrated History* (Hornsby, Australia: Child & Henry, 1982), 77–78; J. Schull, *Far Distant Ships: An Official Account of Canadian Naval Operations in World War II* (Ottawa: King's Printer, 1952), 430–35.

63. Odgers, *The Royal Australian Navy*, 75.

64. Germany was not a party to the Washington Treaty. German interwar naval limitations had been imposed under the 1919 Treaty of Versailles.

Chapter 4. Broad Oceans, Narrow Seas

1. Richards, *RAF Bomber Command*, 20–22.

2. Rosinski, "Mahan and the Present War," BSY 1941, 204.

3. W. S. Churchill, *The Second World War*, vol. 1, *The Gathering Storm* (London: Cassell, 1948), 475.

4. E. M. Cherpak, *Register of the Herbert Rosinsky Papers* (Newport, RI: Naval Historical Collection, 1988) http://www.usnwc.edu/Academics/ Library/RightsideLinks/Naval.

5. Rosinski, "Mahan and the Present War," BSY 1941, 192–94.

6. A. T. Mahan, *Naval Strategy*, 214; Rosinski, "Mahan and the Present War," BSY 1941, 195.

7. Ibid., 197.

8. Ibid., 203; A. Oi, "The Japanese Navy in 1941," in D. M. Goldstein and K. V. Dillon (eds.), *The Pacific War Papers: Japanese Documents of World War II* (Dulles, VA: Potomac Books, 2004), 6.

9. Rosinski, "Mahan and the Present War," BSY 1941, 204.

10. C. Salmaggi and A. Pallavisini, *2194 Days of War—An Illustrated Chronology of the Second World War* (London: Windward, 1977), 17–230. The supplied chronology is provided as a date reference guide only; it is not included as an abridged narrative of the events in question.

11. Rosinski, "Mahan and the Present War," BSY 1941, 204; Churchill, *The Gathering Storm*, 323.

12. Roskill, *The Defensive*, 7.

13. Rosinski, "Mahan and the Present War," BSY 1941, 205.

14. J. Tovey, Despatch 27.5.1941: *Sinking of the German Battleship Bismarck*, LDNGZT Issue 38098, 14.10.1947: 485390, http://www.london. gazette.co.uk/issues/38098/supplements; A. Cunningham, Despatch 11.11.1941: *Battle of Matapan*, LDNGZT Issue 38031, 29.7.1947: 3593, http://www.london.gazette.co.uk/issues/38031/supplements; A. Cunningham, "Operation HATS, 29 August–5 September 1940," Doc. 90 in M. Simpson (ed.), *The Cunningham Papers: Selections from the Private and Official Correspondence of Admiral of the Fleet Viscount Cunningham of Hydenhope,* vol. 1, *The Mediterranean Fleet, 1939–1942* (Aldershot, UK: Ashgate—Navy Records Society, 1999), 141.

15. K. Doenitz, *The World at War: Episode Ten*—"Wolfpack: U-Boats in the Atlantic 1939–1944," interview with BBC Television 1973, DVD recording; A. Speer, *Inside the Third Reich: Memoirs by Albert Speer* (New York: Bonanza Books, 1982), 197–201; W. Baumbach, *Broken Swastika*, 84; J. Cornwall, *Hitler's Scientists—Science, War and the Devil's Pact* (London: Penguin Books, 2003), 271; Raeder, *My Life*, 235–37.

16. S. Roskill, *Churchill and the Admirals* (London: Collins, 1977), 247–60; A. Marder, " 'Winston Is Back': Churchill at the Admiralty 1939–40," *English Historical Review* 5: 1–60 in Lambert (ed.), *Naval History 1850–Present*: 187–267.

17. Taylor, *The Second World War*, 22–23; Roskill, *Churchill and the Admirals*, 116.

18. Somerville, "To the Admiralty," 6.12.1940, Doc. 108, *The Somerville Papers*, 207; "From Admiral of the Fleet the Earl of Cork and Orrey," Doc.110, *The Somerville Papers*, 209; A. Cunningham, "To Pound," 22.9.1940, Doc. 98, *The Cunningham Papers*, 151–52.

19. Tovey, Despatch 27.5.1941, LDNGZT Issue 38098, 14.10.1947, 4853; A. Cunningham, Despatch 9.7.1940, *Report of an Action with the Italian Fleet off Calabria,* LDNGZT Issue 38273, 27.4.1948, 26, 44, http://www.london.gazette.co.uk/issues/38273/supplements.

20. J. Somerville, "Somerville's Observations on the Action off Cape Spartiveno, Doc. 117, *The Somerville Papers*, 215; C. Forbes, Despatch 17.7.1940: *Norway Campaign*, LDNGZT Issue 38011, 8.7.1947: 3170, http://www.london.gazette.co.uk/issues/38011/supplements; J. Somerville, "Report of Proceedings, 7–11 November 1940," Doc. 94, *The Somerville Papers*, 179; A. Cunningham, Despatch 4.8.1941: *The Battle of Crete*, LDNGZT Issue 38296, 21.5.1948, 3103, http://www.london.gazette.co.uk/issues/38296/supplements.

21. Rosinski, "Mahan and the Present War," BSY 1941, 205.

22. Cunningham, Despatch 11.11.1941, LDNGZT, 3592; Cunningham, Despatch 9.7.1940, LDNGZT, 2643; "Somerville's Observations on the Action off Cape Spartiveno," Doc. 117, *The Somerville Papers*, 213; Churchill, *The Gathering Storm*, 367.

23. Rosinski, "Mahan and the Present War," BSY 1941, 206.

24. H. G. Thursfield, "A Naval Chronicle," BSY 1940, 51; O. Stewart, "Air Operations and the War at Sea," BSY 1941, 102; D. Macintyre, *The Battle of the Atlantic* (London: Severn House, 1975), 30; D. Brown, *Carrier Operations of World War II*, vol. 1, *The Royal Navy* (London: Ian Allen, 1974), 13, 18.

25. "The Protection of Trade, 1937," Doc. 447, Hattendorf and Pearsall (eds.) *British Naval Documents 1204–1960*, 781.

26. Cunningham, Despatch 9.7.1940, LDNGZT, 2644; Cunningham, Despatch 4.8.1941, LDNGZT, 3119; J. Tovey, Despatch 20.5.1942, *Convoys*

to North Russia 1942, LDNGZT Issue 39041, 13.10.1950, 5141, http://www.london.gazette.co.uk/issues/39041/supplements.

27. Baumbach, *Broken Swastika*, 132.

28. B. Ramsey, Despatch 18.6.1940: *The Evacuation of the Allied Armies from Dunkirk and Neighbouring Beaches*, LDNGZT Issue 38017, 17.6.1947, 5141, http://www.london.gazette.co.uk/issues/38017/supplements.

29. J. Tovey, Despatch 12.9.1941: *The Carrier Borne Aircraft Attack on Kirkness and Petsamo*, LDNGZT Issue 38300, 25.5.1948, 3169, http://www.london.gazette.co.uk/issues/38300/supplements; "Report on Operations MC2 and MC3, 16–24 December 1940," Doc. 128, *The Cunningham Papers*, 212; Hezlet, *Aircraft and Sea Power*, 145; Kemp, *Key to Victory*, 67; Till, *Airpower and the Royal Navy*, 177.

30. W. S. Churchill, *The Second World War*, vol. 2, *Their Finest Hour* (London, Cassell, 1949), 519, 534.

31. Rosinski, "Mahan and the Present War," BSY 1941: 206.

32. Cunningham, Despatch, LDNGZT 11.11.1941: 3592.

33. Baumbach, *Broken Swastika*, 101.

34. Raeder, *My Life*, 350; Bekker, *Hitler's Naval War*, 258; Hezlet, *Aircraft and Sea Power*, 185.

35. "The Mediterranean, 1935," Doc. 446 in Hattendorf and Pearsall (eds.), *British Naval Documents 1204–1960*: 780; Cunningham, "To Pound," 23.5.1941, Doc. 220, *The Cunningham Papers*, vol. 1: 410.

36. Hough, *The Longest Battle*, 225–27.

37. E. Brown, *Duels in the Sky*, 17–18, 35–37.

38. Churchill, *Their Finest Hour*, 528.

39. Rosinski, "Mahan and the Present War," BSY 1941, 207.

40. H. G. Thursfield, "A Naval Chronicle" in H. G. Thursfield (ed.), *Brassey's Naval Annual 1942* (hereinafter BSY 1942) (London: W. M. Clowes, 1942), 7, 30; Churchill, *The Grand Alliance*, 464; Roskill, *The Defensive*, 538.

41. A. Cunningham, Despatch 19.3.1941: *Operation EXCESS*, LDNGZT Issue 38377, 10.8.1948, 4511, http://www.london.gazette.co.uk/issues/38377/supplements; Tovey, Despatch 20.5.1942, LDNGZT, 5141; Doenitz, "Wolfpack" (DVD); Kennedy, *Rise and Fall*, 303; Bekker, *Hitler's Naval War*, 235–36.

42. Doc. 447, Hattendorf and Pearsall (eds.), *British Naval Documents 1204–1960*, 786.

43. W. S. Churchill, *The Second World War*, vol. 3, *The Grand Alliance* (London: Cassell, 1950), 724; Thursfield, "A Naval Chronicle," BSY 1942, 40, 51; Bennett, *Naval Battles of World War Two*, 71; Hezlet, *Aircraft and Sea Power*, 183–85.

44. Churchill, *The Grand Alliance*, 104–5; Raeder, *My Life*, 362; Tovey, Despatch: LDNGZT 27.5.1941, 4848.

45. Tovey, Despatch: LDNGZT 20.5.1942, 5140–143; Raeder, *My Life*, 285; L. Kennedy, *Pursuit: The Sinking of the Bismarck* (London: Cassell, 1974), 33; Hezlet, *Aircraft and Sea Power*, 191; Roskill, *The Defensive*, 368.

46. Cunningham, Despatch 9.7.1940, LDNGZT, 2644; "Somerville's Observations on the Action off Cape Spartiveno," Doc. 117, *The Somerville Papers*, 213–15.

47. Cunningham, Despatch 11.11.1941, LDNGZT, 3591–3593; J. Somerville, "To His Wife 28.11.1940," Doc. 102, *The Somerville Papers*: 200–202; H. Harwood, Despatch 2.6.1942: *The Battle of Sirte of 22nd March 1942*, LDNGZT Issue 38073, 16.9.1947, 4371–373, http://www.london.gazette.co.uk/issues/38073/supplements.

48. A. Willis, Despatch 8.12.1941, 29.12.1941: *Actions against Raiders*, LDNGZT Issue 38349, 9.7.1948, 4009–12, http://www.london.gazette.co.uk/issues/38073/supplements; Churchill, *The Grand Alliance*, 463.

49. Churchill, *Their Finest Hour*, 525; Odgers, *The Royal Australian Navy*, 88–94; Roskill, *The Defensive*, 277–80.

50. Rosinski, "Mahan and the Present War," BSY 1941, 203.

51. Cunningham, "War Diary March 1941," Doc. 163, *The Cunningham Papers*, 307; Cunningham, "To Pound 28.12.1941," Doc. 301, *The Cunningham Papers*; Mallett, "The Italian Naval High Command," 167–68, in Lambert (ed.), *Naval History 1850–Present*; O'Neill, *Suicide Squads*, 175.

52. Tovey, Despatch, LDNGZT 19.2.1941, 3169–177; Thursfield, "A Naval Chronicle," BSY 1941, 16–17; Thursfield, "A Naval Chronicle," BSY 1942, 27.

53. A. Cunningham, Despatch 8.6.1941: *Report of an Action against an Italian Convoy on the Night of the 15th/16th April 1941*, LDNGZT Issue 38237, 11.5.1948, 2913–914, http://www.london.gazette.co.uk/issues/38073/supplements; "British Submarines at War, Part 1, 1939–1942," *Campaign Summaries of World War 2*, http://www.navalhistory.net/ww2CampaignsBritishSubs.htr/; Thursfield, "A Naval Chronicle," BSY 1942, 14, 34.

54. Rosinski, "Mahan and the Present War," BSY 1941, 207–8.

55. Kennedy, *Rise and Fall*, 306–25.

56. Baumbach, *Broken Swastika*, 90; Tovey, Despatch: LDNGZT 20.5.1942, 5141–143.

57. Rosinski, "Mahan and the Present War," BSY 1941, 207; Taylor, *The Second World War*, 65; A. Tusa and J. Tusa, *The Nuremberg Trial* (London: Macmillan London, 1983), 193.

58. "The Protection of Trade, 1937," Doc. 447, Hattendorf and Pearsall (eds.), *British Naval Documents 1204–1960*, 783.

59. Richards, *RAF Bomber Command*, 290.

60. Ibid., 163–64; Bennett, *Naval Battles of World War Two*, 44–45.

61. Hough, *The Longest Battle*, 269.

62. Taylor, *The Second World War*, 129–30.

63. Richards, *RAF Bomber Command*, 252–53.

64. Churchill, *The Grand Alliance*, 572–78.

Chapter 5. Niitaka Yama Nobore!

1. Rosinski, "Mahan and the Present War," BSY 1941, 209.

2. Interrogation Nav. 76: Admiral Yonai Mitsumasa 17.11.1945, United States Strategic Bombing Survey (hereinafter USSBS) [Pacific], Naval Analysis Division: Interrogations of Japanese Officials, OPNAV-P-03-100, No. 379, 327–28, http://www.ibiblio.org/hyperwar/AAF/USSBS/IJO; J. Ozawa, "The Naval General Staff" *Pacific War Papers*, 31.

3. Interrogation Nav. 7: Vice Admiral Kazutaka Shiraichi 15.10.1945, USSBS: No. 33, 25; M. Chihaya, "Organisation of the Naval General Staff Headquarters in Tokyo" 19.12.1947, *Pacific War Papers*, 37.

4. Marder, *Strategic Illusions 1936–1941*, 4; S. Ienaga, *Japan's Last War: World War II and the Japanese, 1931–1945* (Canberra: Australian National University Press, 1979), 34.

5. Interrogation Nav. 75: Admiral Toyoda Soemu 13–14.11.1945, USSBS No. 378, 314; Oi, "The Japanese Navy in 1941," *Pacific War Papers*, 27; Ienaga, *Japan's Last War*, 34–35.

6. Interrogation Nav. 38: Captain Tashikazu Ohmae 22.10.1945, USSBS No. 160, 177; Interrogation Nav. 13: Captain Watanabe Yasuji 15.10.45, USSBS No. 96, 70.

7. Interrogation Nav. 75: Toyoda 13–14.11.1945, USSBS No. 378, 313; Interrogation Nav. 76: Yonai 17.11.1945, USSBS No. 379, 327–28; Marder,

Strategic Illusions, 1936–1941, 90–91; M. Chihaya, "The Organisation of the Japanese Naval Department," 18.1.1948, *Pacific War Papers,* 45.

8. "47th Liaison Conference, August 16, 1941," in N. Ike (ed.), *Japan's Decision for War: Records of the 1941 Policy Conferences* (Stanford, CT: Stanford University Press, 1967), 121–23; Ienaga, *Japan's Last War,* 43; Marder, *Strategic Illusions, 1936–1941,* 101.

9. Interrogation Nav. 70: Vice Admiral Paul H. Wenneker 11.12.45, USSBS No. 359, 285.

10. H. Agawa, *The Reluctant Admiral: Yamamoto and the Imperial Navy* (Tokyo: Kodansha International, 1979), 28–29.

11. Oi, "The Japanese Navy in 1941," *Pacific War Papers,* 5–6; Marder, *Strategic Illusions, 1936–1941,* 94, 101–3; Interrogation Nav. 38: Ohmae 22.10.1945, USSBS No. 160, 177.

12. Marder, *Strategic Illusions, 1936–1941,* 275; Dull, *Imperial Japanese Navy,* 3.

13. Interrogation Nav. 38: Ohmae 22.10.1945, USSBS No. 177; Oi, "The Japanese Navy in 1941," *Pacific War Papers,* 56.

14. Interrogation Nav. 9: Vice Admiral Kurita Takeo 16–17.10.1945, USSBS No. 47, 52; Macintyre, *The Battle for the Pacific,* 66.

15. Oi, "The Japanese Navy in 1941," *Pacific War Papers,* 6.

16. J. Ozawa, "Development of the Japanese Navy's Operational Concept against America," *Pacific War Papers,* 68–69.

17. Interrogation Nav. 13: Watanabe 15.10.45, USSBS No. 96, 65.

18. Ozawa, "Japanese Navy's Operational Concept against America," *Pacific War Papers,* 70; Fuchida and Okumiya, *Midway,* 43.

19. Interrogation Nav. 38: Ohmae 22.10.1945, USSBS No, 160, 176; "66th Liaison Conference, November 1, 1941," *Japan's Decision for War,* 201–7.

20. Interrogation Nav. 34: Commander Chikataka Nakajima 21.10.1945, USSBS No. 139, 144; "Imperial Conference, November 5 1941," *Japan's Decision for War,* 233; Interrogation Nav. 13: Watanabe 15.10.45, USSBS No. 96, 66–70.

21. M. Chihaya, "Importance of the Japanese Naval Bases Overseas," *Pacific War Papers,* 59–60; Ozawa, "Japanese Navy's Operational Concept against America," *Pacific War Papers,* 69; Interrogation Nav. 34: Nakajima 21.10. 1945, USSBS No 139, 144.

22. "29th Liaison Conference, June 11, 1941," *Japan's Decision for War*, 50; "59th Liaison Conference, October 23, 1941," *Japan's Decision for War*, 184–86; Dull, *Imperial Japanese Navy*, 5.

23. I. Sato, "The Naval Policy of Japan," in A. Richardson and A. Hurd (eds.) *Brassey's Naval Annual 1927* (BSY 1927) (London: W. M. Clowes, 1927) , 79–80.

24. "59th Liaison Conference, October 23, 1941," *Japan's Decision for War*, 186.

25. Chihaya, "Importance of the Japanese Naval Bases Overseas," *Pacific War Papers*, 59–61; "62nd Liaison Conference, October 27, 1941," *Japan's Decision for War*, 191–92.

26. Ozawa, "Japanese Navy's Operational Concept against America," *Pacific War Papers*, 68–70; Agawa, *The Reluctant Admiral*, 195.

27. H. C. Bywater, *Sea Power in the Pacific: A Study of the American-Japanese Naval Problem* (London: Constable, 1921), 254; Interrogation Nav. 4: Captain Aoki Taijiro 9.10.1945, USSBS No. 23, 15; Interrogation Nav. 13: Watanabe 15.10.45, USSBS No. 96, 69; Interrogation Nav. 12: Captain Inoguchi 15.10.1945, USSBS No. 62, 64.

28. "50th Liaison Conference, September 3, 1941," *Japan's Decision for War*, 129–31.

29. Marder, *Strategic Illusions, 1936–1941*, 325–27; "Imperial Conference, November 5, 1941," *Japan's Decision for War*, 233.

30. Agawa, *The Reluctant Admiral*, 267.

31. Ozawa, "Japanese Navy's Operational Concept against America," *Pacific War Papers*, 71.

32. Oi, "The Japanese Navy in 1941," *Pacific War Papers*, 3–5; O. Warner, *Great Sea Battles*, 246.

33. Interrogation Nav. 55: Vice Admiral Ozawa Jisaburo 30.10.1945, USSBS No. 227, 226; Marder, *Strategic Illusions, 1936–1941*, 319.

34. Oi, "The Japanese Navy in 1941," *Pacific War Papers*, 16–17.

35. J. Ozawa, "Outline Development of Tactics and Organisation of the Japanese Carrier Air Force," *Pacific War Papers*, 73–74.

36. Ibid., 74; Rear Admiral E. J. King, "United States Naval Aviation," BSY 1936, 166; Till, *Airpower and the Royal Navy*, 165–66.

37. Oi, "The Japanese Navy in 1941," *Pacific War Papers*, 19; Agawa, *The Reluctant Admiral*, 231.

38. Interrogation Nav. 77: Captain Sonokawa Kamea14.11.1945, USSBS No. 387, 333; Okumiya, Horikoshi, and Caidin, *Zero!*, 15.

39. Marder, *Strategic Illusions, 1936–1941*, 286; Fuchida and Okumiya, *Midway*, 285.
40. Oi, "The Japanese Navy in 1941," *Pacific War Papers*, 22; Interrogation Nav. 64: Rear Admiral Takata Toshitane 1.11.1945, USSBS No. 258, 262.
41. Marder, *Strategic Illusions, 1936–1941*, 288; Macintyre, *The Battle for the Pacific*, 76; Ozawa, "Japanese Navy's Operational Concept against America," *Pacific War Papers*, 71.
42. Oi, "The Japanese Navy in 1941," *Pacific War Papers*, 20–21; Interrogation Nav. 15: Captain Takahashi Chihaya 20.10.1945, USSBS No. 74, 75; Interrogation Nav. 55: Ozawa 30.10.1945, USSBS No. 227, 225; "66th Liaison Conference, November 1, 1941," *Japan's Decision for War*, 207.
43. O'Neill, *Suicide Squads*, 17–18.
44. M. Chihaya, "Concerning the Construction of Japanese Warships," 10.1.1947, *Pacific War Papers*, 83–84; H. Lyon, *The Encyclopaedia of the World's Warships: A Technical Directory of Major Fighting Ships from 1900 to the Present Day* (Turnhout, UK: Leisure Books, 1985), 177.
45. Marder, *Strategic Illusions, 1936–1941*, 8; E. Altham, "Foreign Navies," BSY 1938, 30; Interrogation Nav. 9: Kurita 16–17.10.1945, USSBS No. 47, 52; Interrogation Nav. 72: Vice Admiral Miwa Shigeyoshi 10.10.45, USSBS No. 366, 294.
46. Marder, *Strategic Illusions*, 1936–1941, 301, 309; Oi, "The Japanese Navy in 1941," *Pacific War Papers*, 10, 16; Chihaya, "Concerning the Construction of Japanese Warships," *Pacific War Papers*, 84–85.
47. Interrogation Nav. 72: Miwa 10.10.45, USSBS No. 366, 293; Interrogation Nav. 64: Toshitane 1.11.1945, USSBS No. 258, 266.
48. O'Neill, *Suicide Squads*, 188–89.
49. Ferris, "Student & Master," in Farrell and Hunter (eds.) *Sixty Years On*, 98–99; Till, *Airpower and the Royal Navy*, 63.
50. F. E. McMurtrie, "Foreign Navies," BSY 1941, 73; Stille, *Imperial Japanese Navy Aircraft Carriers*, 17; Ozawa, "Japanese Navy's Operational Concept against America," *Pacific War Papers*, 70.
51. Dull, *Imperial Japanese Navy*, 8; Interrogation Nav. 4: Aoki 9.10.1945, USSBS No. 23, 13; Interrogation Nav. 15: Chihaya 20.10.1945, USSBS No. 74, 76; Interrogation Nav. 64: Takata 1.11.1945, USSBS No. 258, 262; Oi, "The Japanese Navy in 1941," *Pacific War Papers*, 15–16.
52. Marder, *Strategic Illusions, 1936–1941*, 300; Stille, *Imperial Japanese Navy Aircraft Carriers*, 6–7.

53. Interrogation Nav. 55: Ozawa 30.10.1945, USSBS No. 227, 226; Interrogation Nav. 64: Takata 1.11.1945, USSBS No. 258, 266.

54. Oi, "The Japanese Navy in 1941," *Pacific War Papers*, 18–19; Till, *Airpower and the Royal Navy*, 63–64; Ferris, "A British 'Unofficial'" Aviation Mission and Japanese Naval Developments, 1919–1929," in Farrell and Hunter (eds.), *Sixty Years On*, 435; Ferris, "Student & Master," in Farrell and Hunter (eds.) *Sixty Years On*, 95–99.

55. B. Collier, *Japanese Aircraft*, 14–15; Hezlet, *Aircraft and Sea Power*, 116.

56. Ferris, "Student & Master," in Farrell and Hunter (eds.) *Sixty Years On*, 99; Agawa, *The Reluctant Admiral*, 104–5.

57. Oi, "The Japanese Navy in 1941," *Pacific War Papers, 19–20*; Okumiya, Horikoshi, and Caidin, *Zero!*, 40–41; J. Burton, *Fortnight of Infamy: The Collapse of Allied Airpower West of Pearl Harbor* (Annapolis, MD: Naval Institute Press, 2006), 9–11; Collier, *Japanese Aircraft*, 11.

58. W. H. Bartsch, *Doomed at the Start: American Pursuit Pilots in the Philippines, 1941–1942* Williams Ford: Texas A&M University Press, 1995), 42; Ferris, "A British 'Unofficial'" Aviation Mission," 436.

59. Okumiya, Horikoshi, and Caidin, *Zero!*, 21–24; Marder, *Strategic Illusions, 1936–1941*, 306–9; Burton, *Fortnight of Infamy*, 16.

60. Macintyre, *The Battle for the Pacific*, 181; Oi, "The Japanese Navy in 1941," *Pacific War Papers*, 19–21.

61. Interrogation Nav. 31: Rear Admiral Katsumata Seizo 25.10.1945, USSBS No. 129, 135; Interrogation Nav. 15: Takahashi 20.10.1945, USSBS No. 74, 75–76; Okumiya, Horikoshi, and Caidin, *Zero!*, 36, 39.

Chapter 6. Force Z Revisited

1. Marder, *Strategic Illusions, 1936–1941*, 423.

2. Salmaggi and Pallavisini, *2194 Days of War*, 183–222. This chronology has been provided for the same purposes as the chronology in chapter four.

3. Kuantan is located approximately 130 miles southwest of the point Force Z had reached when spotted on 9 December.

4. G. Layton, Despatch 17.12.1941, *Loss of H.M. Ships Prince of Wales and Repulse*, LDNGZT Issue 38214, 26.2.1948, 1237–245, http://www.london.gazette.co.uk/issues/38214/supplements; "The Loss of the Prince of Wales and Repulse, 1941, Memorandum by Admiral Sir Dudley Pound, First Sea Lord, 25 January 1942," Doc. 469, *British Naval Documents 1204–1960*, 850–51.

5. "The Loss of the Prince of Wales and Repulse, 1941," Doc. 469, *British Naval Documents 1204–1960*, 848–49.

6. Marder, *Strategic Illusions, 1936–1941*, 422; Grenfell, *Main Fleet*, 92, 96.

7. Churchill, *The Grand Alliance*, 524–25, 547.

8. "The Loss of the Prince of Wales and Repulse, 1941," Doc. 469, *British Naval Documents 1204–1960*, 848–50; Churchill, *The Grand Alliance*, 547.

9. Dull, *Imperial Japanese Navy*, 38; Kemp, *Key to Victory*, 203; Roskill, *The Defensive*, 567; Marder, *Strategic Illusions, 1936–1941*, 498–500.

10. Cunningham, Despatch 4.8.1941, LDNGZT, 3103–104.

11. Roskill, *Churchill and the Admirals*, 198–200; R. Hough, *The Longest Battle*, 127.

12. L. Kennedy, *Pursuit*, 91.

13. Kemp, *Key to Victory*, 204; Marder, *Strategic Illusions, 1936–1941*, 506.

14. Murfett, "Reflections on an Enduring Theme," in Farrell and Hunter (eds.), *Sixty Years On*, 17–18.

15. Ibid., 16–17. The composition of the Backhouse-Drax squadron mirrored that of the wartime Force H.

16. COSWR No. 119 of the Naval, Military and Air Situation from 0700 December 4th, to 0700 December 11th, 1941, TNA (UK), CAB/66/20/22; COSWR No. 120 of the Naval, Military and Air Situation from 0700 December 12th to 0700 December 18th, 1941, TNA (UK), CAB/66/20/24; Marder, *Strategic Illusions, 1936–1941*, 422.

17. P. Maltby, *Report on the Air Operations during the Campaigns in Malaya and the Netherlands East Indies from 5th December 1941 to 12th March 1942*, LDNGZT Issue 38216, 26.2.1948, 1349–352, 1374, http://www.london.gazette.co.uk/issues/38216/supplements.

18. Interrogation Nav. 15: Takahashi 20.10.1945, USSBS No. 74, 75–76; Interrogation Nav. 55: Ozawa 30.10.1945, USSBS No. 227, 227.

19. Interrogation Nav. 77: Sonokawa14.11.1945, USSBS No. 387, 333; Ozawa, "Tactics and Organisation of the Japanese Carrier Air Force," *Pacific War Papers*, 80–82; Agawa, *The Reluctant Admiral*, 265–67.

20. R. Brooke-Popham, *Despatch on the Far East, Air Chief Marshal Sir Robert Brooke-Popham, CIC Far East (17th October 1940–27th December 1941)*, 28.5.1942, TNA (UK), CAB/66/28/33-0001, 9–10, 20–22; "The Loss of the Prince of Wales and Repulse, 1941," Doc. 469, *British Naval Documents 1204–1960*, 847.

21. Despatch 28.5.1942, CAB/66/28/33-0001, 5–6; Grenfell, *Main Fleet*, 100.

22. "The Situation in the Far East in the Event of Japanese Intervention against Us," Chiefs-of-Staff Appreciation 31.7.1940, TNA (UK), CAB/66/10/33-0001; Brooke-Popham, Despatch 28.5.1942, CAB/66/28/33-0001, 17–19; Maltby, Report 26.2.1948, LDNGZT, 1349; Roskill, *The Defensive*, 562; Murfett, "Reflections on an Enduring Theme," 15.

23. J. A. Collins, Despatch 17.3.1942: *Battle of the Java Sea 27 February 1942*, LDNGZT Issue 38346, 6.7.1948, 3937–948, http://www.london. gazette.co.uk/issues/38346/supplements; Dull, *Imperial Japanese Navy, 1941–1945*, 87.

24. "Assistance to the Dutch in Event of Japanese Agression in the Netherlands East Indies," COS Appreciation 7.8.1940, TNA (UK), CAB/66/10/39-0001, 2–3; Chiefs-of-Staff Appreciation 31.7.1940, CAB/66/10/33-0001, 2.

25. Interrogation Nav. 68: Captain Ihara Mitsugo 10.11.1945, USSBS No. 331, 275–76.

26. "36th Liaison Conference, June 30, 1941," *Japan's Decision for War*, 74; "59th Liaison Conference, October 23, 1941," *Japan's Decision for War*, 186.

27. Murfett, "Reflections on an Enduring Theme," Farrell and Hunter (eds.), *Sixty Years On*, 16–17.

28. Layton, Despatch 17.12.1941, LDNGZT, 1237.

29. Admiral Somerville has been chosen as the hypothetical commander because he assumed command of the Eastern Fleet in March 1942. As commanding officer of the China Fleet, Commodore Collins was on station at the time of these events.

30. "Attack on Enemy Convoys," Sec. XIX: Minor Operations," Forbes and Pound, *Fighting Instructions*, 107–8.

31. N. Kondo, "Some Opinions Concerning the War," 28.2.1948, *Pacific War Papers*, 303.

32. Collins, Despatch 17.3.1942, LDNGZT, 3937–948.

33. Despatch 28.5.1942, CAB/66/28/33-0001, 20–21.

34. Maltby, Report 26.2.1948, LDNGZT, 1376; Burton, *Fortnight of Infamy*, 302.

35. Kondo, "Some Opinions Concerning the War," 28.2.1948, *Pacific War Papers*, 304–5; Okumiya, Horikoshi, and Caidin, *Zero!*, 67.

36. The two other occasions (1942) were the Makassar Strait (24 January) and the Bandung Strait (19–20 February).

37. M. Chihaya, "Essay Concerning the Book Battle Report," 14.2.1947, *Pacific War Papers*, 264; "Some Remarks Made by Japanese Diplomats and Attaches in European Capitals at the End of February," NID Report 31.3.1942, TNA (UK), CAB/66/23/26, 1–2; Dull, *Imperial Japanese Navy*, 55, 559; D. Van der Vat, *The Pacific Campaign: The U.S.-Japanese Naval War 1941–1945* (New York: Simon & Schuster, 1991), 127.

38. Despatch 28.5.1942, CAB/66/28/33-0001, 23; Maltby, Report 26.2.1948, LDNGZT, 1407; COSWR (No. 122) of the Naval, Military and Air Situation from 0700 December 25th to 0700 December 31st, 1941, TNA (UK), CAB/66/23/34, 11–12.

39. Interrogation Nav. 77: Sonokawa14.11.1945, USSBS No. 387: 333–36; Okumiya, Horikoshi, and Caidin, *Zero!*, 62; Interrogation Nav. 15: Takahashi 20.10.1945, USSBS No. 74, 74.

40. Maltby, Report 26.2.1948, LDNGZT, 1407; Burton, *Fortnight of Infamy*, 102; Okumiya, Horikoshi, and Caidin, *Zero!*, 53–56.

41. Maltby, Report 26.2.1948, LDNGZT, 1379; Marder, *Strategic Illusions, 1936–1941*, 230; Grenfell, *Main Fleet*, 210; Till, *Airpower and the Royal Navy*, 184; Brown, *Duels in the Sky*, 99, 210.

42. Ozawa, "Japanese Navy's Operational Concept against America," *Pacific War Papers*, 72; Oi, "The Japanese Navy in 1941," *Pacific War Papers*, 19.

43. Okumiya, Horikoshi, and Caidin, *Zero!*, 60.

44. "To Pound 23.5.1941," Doc. 220, *Cunningham Papers*, vol. 1, *Mediterranean Fleet*, 410.

45. Layton, Despatch 17.12.1941, LDNGZT, 1245–246; "The Loss of the Prince of Wales and Repulse, 1941," Doc. 469, Hattendorf and Pearsall (eds.), *British Naval Documents 1204–1960*, 851.

46. Despatch 28.5.1942, CAB/66/28/33-0001, 20–23; Maltby, Report 26.2.1948, LDNGZT, 1409.

47. Despatch 28.5.1942, CAB/66/28/33-0001, 23; Maltby, Report 26.2.1948, LDNGZT, 1361; Burton, *Fortnight of Infamy*, 290.

48. J. Somerville, "Somerville on the Functions of Force *H*, December 1940," Doc. 118, *The Somerville Papers*, 215.

49. "Plans for the Employment of Naval and Air Forces of the Associated Powers."

50. Marder, *Strategic Illusions, 1936–1941*, 211.

51. Chiefs-of-Staff Appreciation 31.7.1940, CAB/66/10/33-0001, 6; Dull, *Imperial Japanese Navy*, 50–51; "36th Liaison Conference, June 30, 1941," *Japan's Decision for War*, 74.

52. Chiefs-of-Staff Appreciation 31.7.1940, CAB/66/10/33-0001, 6; Oi, "The Japanese Navy in 1941," *Pacific War Papers*,10.

53. Maltby, Report 26.2.1948, LDNGZT, 1389–90; E. R. (Bon) Hall, *Glory in Chaos: The RAAF in the Far East in 1940–1942* (West Coburg, Australia: The Sembawang Association, 1989), 185–90.

54. Collins, Despatch 17.3.1921, LDNGZT, 3945–948; Interrogation Nav. 7: Shiraichi 15.10.1945, 27–28; Interrogation Nav. 15: Takahashi 20.10.1945, 74–76; Okumiya, Horikoshi, and Caidin, *Zero!*, 60, 90–91.

55. Dull, *Imperial Japanese Navy*, 71; Hough, The *Longest Battle*, 143.

56. W. E. Johns and R. A. Kelly, *No Surrender* (London: W. H. Allen, 1989), 56.

57. Gillison, D., *Royal Australian Air Force !939-1942* (Adelaide, Australia: Griffin Press, 1962), 431; On 7 December 2011 the Australian governor general proclaimed 19 February as a National Day of Observance to be known as "Bombing of Darwin Day," Australian Government, Department of Defence, http://www.defence.gov.au/defencenews/stories/2013/feb.

58. Burton, *Fortnight of Infamy*, 67–68.

59. Ferris, "Student and Master," 271.

60. Murfett, "Reflections on an Enduring Theme," 16–17.

61. Collier, *Japanese Aircraft*, 23.

Chapter 7. Supremacy Surrendered

1. Somerville, "Report of Proceedings," paragraph 55.

2. Churchill, *The Grand Alliance*, 551.

3. Chief-of-Staffs Appreciation 31.7.1940, CAB/66/10/33-0001.

4. Churchill, *The Grand Alliance*, 768.

5. Ibid., 770–72.

6. Grenfell, *Main Fleet*, 94, 96.

7. Churchill, *The Grand Alliance*, 768.

8. Ibid., 772; "The Loss of the Prince of Wales and Repulse, 1941," Doc. 469, *British Naval Documents 1204–1960*, 848–49.

9. Churchill, *The Hinge of Fate*, 155–56; J. Somerville, "To Pound," 11.3.42, Doc. 222, *The Somerville Papers*, 392–93.

10. Warner, *Great Sea Battles*, 259.

11. Hough, *The Longest Battle*, 229.

12. Ibid., 226.

13. Churchill, *The Grand Alliance*, 768.
14. Ibid., 580; Somerville, "Report of Proceedings," paragraph 27.
15. Ibid., "To Pound," 23.5.1941, Doc. 220, *The Cunningham Papers*, 410.
16. Rosinski, "Mahan and the Present War," in H. G. Thursfield (ed.), BSY 1941, 204.
17. "Report of Proceedings, 7–11 November 1940," Doc. 94, *The Somerville Papers*, 177–79; "To His Wife," 28.11.1940, Doc. 102, *The Somerville Papers*, 200–201; Cunningham, Despatch 4.8.1941, LDNGZT, 3103–104; Cunningham, Despatch 9.7.1940, LDNGZT, 2643; Tovey, Despatch 27.5.1941, LDNGZT, 4848, 4855; Tovey, Despatch 12.9.1941, LDNGZT, 3169.
18. "To Pound," 11.3.42, Doc. 222, *The Somerville Papers*, 393.
19. Churchill, *The Hinge of Fate*, 156; "To Pound," 11.3.42, Doc. 222, *The Somerville Papers*, 232.
20. "To His Wife," 4.4.1942, Doc. 232, *The Somerville Papers*, 399–401.
21. Churchill, *The Grand Alliance*, 771–74; "The Loss of the Prince of Wales and Repulse, 1941," Doc. 469, *British Naval Documents 1204–1960*, 847–48.
22. Chiefs-of-Staff Appreciation 31.7.1940, CAB/66/10/33-0001, 6; Interrogation Nav. 13: Watanabe 15.10.45, USSBS No. 96, 65; Okumiya, Horikoshi, and Caidin, *Zero!*, 91.
23. Rosinski, "Mahan and the Present War," BSY 1941, 204.
24. Chiefs-of-Staff Appreciation 31.7.1940, CAB/66/10/33-0001, 6; War Cabinet, "Far East Appreciation," 21.2.1942: TNA (UK), CAB/66/22/24-0001, 1; Ozawa, "Tactics and Organisation of the Japanese Carrier Air Force," *Pacific War Papers*, 74.
25. Somerville, "Report of Proceedings," paragraphs 25–30; Churchill, *The Hinge of Fate*, 153, 156; D. Brown, *Carrier Operations*, vol. 1, *The Royal Navy*, 99.
26. Marder, Jacobsen, and Horsefield, *Old Friends*, vol. 2, *Pacific War*, 86; Grove, *Royal Navy Since 1815*, 197; Grenfell, *Main Fleet*, 161; Hough, *The Longest Battle*, 150.
27. Marder, Jacobsen, and Horsfield, *The Pacific War, 1942–1945*, 87; Tomlinson, *Most Dangerous Moment*, 42–44, 185–88.
28. J. Greene, *War at Sea*, 116–18; Grenfell, *Main Fleet*, 173; Tomlinson, *Most Dangerous Moment*, 159–61.

29. Interrogation Nav. 13: Watanabe, 15.10.45, USSBS No. 96, 65; Ozawa, "Tactics and Organisation of the Japanese Carrier Air Force," *Pacific War Papers*, 76; Fuchida and Okumiya, *Midway*, 71.

30. Interrogation Nav. 72: Miwa, 10.10.1945, USSBS No. 366, 298; Marder, Jacobsen, and Horsfield, *Pacific War, 1942–1945*, 87; Taylor, *Second World War*, 135–36.

31. Grenfell, *Main Fleet*, 174; Churchill, *The Gathering Storm*, 475.

32. Polybius, *Histories* 18.24, extract, in G. R. Crane (ed.), Persus Digital Library, Tufts University, http://www.persustufts.edu/hopper/

33. Marder, Jacobsen, and Horsfield, *The Pacific War, 1942–1945*, 125.

34. Somerville, "Report of Proceedings," paragraph 7; Dull, *Imperial Japanese Navy*, 106.

35. Somerville, "Report of Proceedings," paragraph 6.

36. Marder, Jacobsen, and Horsfield, *The Pacific War, 1942–1945*, 119; Collier, *Japanese Aircraft*, 59,120.

37. Marder, Jacobsen, and Horsfield, *The Pacific War, 1942–1945*, 123.

38. "To His Wife," 4.4.1942, Doc. 232, *The Somerville Papers*, 401; Tomlinson, *The Most Dangerous Moment*, 81–82.

39. W. Green, *Famous Fighters of the Second World War* (London: McDonald & Janes, 1978), 275.

40. The Editor of "Flight," "Marine Aviation," BSY 1935, 160.

41. Thursfield, "British Naval Air Progress," BSY 1939, 170–71; Till, *Airpower and the Royal Navy*, 100–101.

42. Somerville, "Report of Proceedings," paragraph 40.

43. Ibid., paragraphs 12, 36, 45.

44. Marder, Jacobsen, and Horsfield, *The Pacific War, 1942–1945*, 123.

45. Somerville, "Report of Proceedings," paragraphs 33, 36.

46. Collins, Despatch 17.3.1942, LDNGZT, 3937–948; Dull, *Imperial Japanese Navy*, 55.

47. Somerville, "Report of Proceedings," paragraph 5.

48. J. Somerville, "To North," 10.4.1942, Doc. 240, *The Somerville Papers*, 407.

49. Marder, Jacobsen, and Horsfield, *The Pacific War, 1942–1945*, 107, 305.

50. Gillison, *Royal Australian Air Force*, 500.

51. J. Somerville, "Pocket Diary 29–31.3.1942," Doc. 229, *The Somerville Papers*, 397.

52. S. Roskill, *The Period of Balance*, 30–32; Hezlet, *Aircraft and Sea Power*, 219; Marder, Jacobsen, and Horsfield, *The Pacific War, 1942–1945*, 93–94.

53. Fuchida and Okumiya, *Midway*, 145–49.

54. Marder, Jacobsen, and Horsfield, *The Pacific War, 1942–1945*, 563; Agawa, *The Reluctant Admiral*, 295.

55. Hough, *The Longest Battle*, 63–68.

56. Marder, *Strategic Illusions*, 136–37.

57. Churchill, *The Grand Alliance*, 767–69; "The Loss of the Prince of Wales and Repulse," 1941, Doc. 469, Hattendorf and Pearsall (eds.), *British Naval Documents 1204–1960*, 847–48.

58. Marder, Jacobsen, and Horsfield, *The Pacific War, 1942–1945*, 139.

59. S. Roskill, *The Period of Balance* (London: H.M.S.O., 1955), 32.

60. C. Barnett, "Roskill, Stephen Wentworth (1903–1980)," Oxford Dictionary of National Biography, 2004, http://dy.doi.org/10.1093/ref.odnb/31628.

61. Dull, *Imperial Japanese Navy*, 106.

62. Churchill, *The Grand Alliance*, 771–74.

63. "Operation HATS, 29 August–5 September 1940," Doc. 90, *The Cunningham Papers*, 141.

64. Hough, *The Longest Battle*, 222.

65. Hezlet, *Aircraft and Sea Power*, 214.

66. Hough, *The Longest Battle*, 151; Dull, *Imperial Japanese Navy*, 105–7.

67. Somerville, "Report of Proceedings," paragraph 7.

68. Hezlet, *Aircraft and Sea Power*, 219.

69. "Pocket Diary 29–31.3.1942," Doc. 229, *The Somerville Papers*, 397.

70. Green, *Famous Fighters*, 55, 232.

71. Greene, *War at Sea*, 170.

72. Marder, Jacobsen, and Horsfield, *The Pacific War, 1942–1945*, 144.

73. Ibid., 555.

Chapter 8. From Juno to Ten-Ichi

1. Bennett, *Naval Battles of World War Two*, 147–48.

2. O'Neill, *Suicide Squads*, 99; J. Winton, *War in the Pacific: Pearl Harbor to Tokyo Bay* (London: Sidgwick & Jackson, 1978), 175.

3. Greene, *War at Sea*, 158; Hough, *The Longest Battle*, 178.

4. Macintyre, *The Battle for the Pacific*, 182; A. Yoshimura, *Battleship Musashi—The Making and Sinking of the World's Biggest Battleship* (Tokyo: Kodansha International, 1999), 153; Greene, *War at Sea*, 154; Bennett, *Naval Battles of World War Two*, 212.

5. Churchill, *The Grand Alliance*, 773–74.

6. Marder, Jacobsen, and Horsfield, *The Pacific War, 1942–1945*, 563; Greene, *War at Sea*, 158.

7. Bennett, *Naval Battles of World War Two*, 176, 214–16, 222–27.

8. Ibid., 120, 172.

9. Collier, *Japanese Aircraft*, 23.

10. Cunningham, Despatch 11.11.1941, LDNGZT, 3592; Cunningham, Despatch 9.7.1940, LDNGZT, 2643; "Somerville's Observations on the Action off Cape Spartiveno," Doc. 117, *The Somerville Papers*, 213.

11. Macintyre, *The Battle for the Pacific*, 178–79; Winton, *War in the Pacific*, 148–49.

12. Greene, *War at Sea*, 154; Van der Vat, *The Pacific Campaign*, 178.

13. Collier, *Japanese Aircraft*, 119.

14. Macintyre, *The Battle of the Atlantic*, 30; D. Brown, *Carrier Operations*, vol. 1, *The Royal Navy*, 13, 18.

15. MacIntyre, *The Battle for the Pacific*, 90.

16. E. Brown, *Duels in the Sky*, 96–98.

17. Collier, *Japanese Aircraft*, 100.

18. Greene, *War at Sea*, 139–41.

19. Van der Vat, *The Pacific Campaign*, 261–62.

20. MacIntyre, *The Battle for the Pacific*, 165.

21. Bennett, *Naval Battles of World War Two*, 217–18.

22. Ibid., 106–7; Hough, *The Longest Battle*, 169–70, 197.

23. MacIntyre, *The Battle for the Pacific*, 59.

24. L. Kennedy, *Pursuit*, 161–62.

25. Greene, *War at Sea*, 162–66.

26. The battles of Samar, Sibuyan Sea, Surigao Strait, and Cape Engano were all collectively grouped under the general heading of Leyte Gulf.

27. MacIntyre, *The Battle for the Pacific*, 212.

28. Agawa, *The Reluctant Admiral*, 300.

29. Winton, *War in the Pacific*, 151–52.

30. Van der Vat, *The Pacific Campaign*, 383.

Chapter 9. Beyond Singapore

1. Taylor, *The Second World War*, 135.

2. Churchill, *The Hinge of Fate*, 8.

3. Ward, "Security: Defending Australia's Empire," Schreuder and Ward (eds.), *Australia's Empire*, 242.

4. D. Day, "The End of Australia's Complacency," in D. Horner (ed.), *The Battles that Shaped Australia—"The Australians" Anniversary Essays* (St. Leonards, Australia: Allen & Unwin, 1994), 29.

5. Churchill, *The Hinge of Fate*, 3.

6. Ward, "Security: Defending Australia's Empire," 243.

7. Cablegram 510: London 23/12/1940, Churchill–Menzies (AA: A1608, AA27/1/1), Doc. 119; J. Robertson and J. McCarthy, *Australian War Strategy 1939-1945—A Documentary History* (St. Lucia: University of QLD Press, 1985), 152.

8. Bennett, *Naval Battles of World War Two*, 114, 120, 139–46.

9. Roskill, *The Defensive*, 7.

10. Ward, "Security: Defending Australia's Empire," 247.

11. Willis, Despatch 8.12.1941, LDNGZT, 4009–12.

12. Grenfell, *Main Fleet*, 174.

13. Raeder, *My Life*, 358–59.

14. Churchill, *The Grand Alliance*, 770–71.

15. Hough, *The Longest Battle*, 225–27.

16. "To Pound," 11.3.42, Doc. 222, *The Somerville Papers*, 393; Okumiya, Horikoshi, and Caidin, *Zero!*, 91.

17. Ward, "Security: Defending Australia's Empire," 233.

18. P. Oppenheim, *The Fragile Forts—The Fixed Defences of Sydney Harbour 1788-1963* (Canberra: Australian Army History Unit, 2004), 101.

19. N. Meaney, "The Yellow Peril: Invasion Scare Novels and Australian Political Culture" in J. Curran and S. Ward (eds.), *Australia and the Wider World—Selected Essays of Neville Meaney* (Sydney: Sydney University Press, 2013), 89.

20. C. H. Kirmess, "The Australian Crisis" (1909), Doc. 82 in N. Meaney, *Australia and the World: A Documentary History from the 1870s to the 1970s* (Melbourne: Longman Cheshire, 1985), 176–77.

21. "Security of Peace: Mr Cook's Hopes," *Sydney Morning Herald*, 26 March 1914, Doc. 103, *Australia and the World*, CPP 1914 Session, vol. 2, no. 33, 207; "Navies Relative Strength in the Pacific. Return Showing Strength of Navies of the Various Powers Now Stationed in the Pacific," Doc. 107, *Australia and the World*, 214–15.

22. "W. M. Hughes Speech on Imperial Conference," Memorandum, Secretary of State for Colonies 16.6.1921, TNA (UK), CAB/23/26.

23. Gillison, *Royal Australian Air Force 1939–1942*, 21.

24. P. Stanley, *Invading Australia: Japan and the Battle for Australia, 1942* (Camberwell, Australia: Penguin Group, 2008), 62; J. McCarthy, *Australia and Imperial Defence 1918–39* (St. Lucia: University of Queensland Press, 1976), 56–57.

25. Albatross [*pseud.*], "Japan and the Defence of Australia" (Melbourne: Robertson & Mullens, 1935), 30, 50.

26. Oppenheim, *The Fragile Forts*, 256.

27. Odgers, *Royal Australian Navy*, 108–9; "Prime Minister of Australia to [British] Prime Minister 22 February 1942," Doc. 255, *Australia and the World*, 475–76.

28. Stanley, *Invading Australia*, 151, 157; P. Burns, *The Brisbane Line Controversy: Political Opportunism Versus National Security*, 1942–45 (St. Leonards, Australia: Allen & Unwin, 1998), 79.

29. Stanley, *Invading Australia*, 172–73.

30. Agawa, *The Reluctant Admiral*, 312.

31. Burns, *The Brisbane Line Controversy*, 42.

32. Stanley, *Invading Australia*, 180; Oppenheim, *The Fragile Forts*, 272; Gillison, *Royal Australian Air Force 1939–42*, 528.

33. Oppenheim, *The Fragile Forts*, 267.

34. Stanley, *Invading Australia*, 156–57.

35. Burns, *The Brisbane Line Controversy*, 8, 103.

Conclusion

1. E. Brown, *Duels in the Sky*, 134.

2. "New Construction Programme, 1942," Memorandum, First Lord of the Admiralty 21.4.1942, TNA (UK), CAB/66/24/3, 3.

BIBLIOGRAPHY

Primary Sources

CABINET DOCUMENTS: THE NATIONAL ARCHIVES, UNITED KINGDOM. http://www.thenationalarchives.gov.uk/.

BRITISH CABINET DOCUMENTS, 1919–30 (CHRONOLOGICAL ORDER)

W. D. Weir. "Memorandum on the Future of the Air Force," 3.1.1919: CAB/24/72-0092.

"Development of Singapore Naval Base," Memorandum, Imperial Defence Committee 16.6.1921: CAB/23/26.

W. S. Churchill. "Report of Committee to Examine Part 1 (Defence Departments) of the Report of the Geddes Committee on National Expenditure," Memorandum 4.2.1922: CAB/24/132-0091.

"Relations between the Navy and the Air Force," Memorandum, First Sea Lord 6.2.1922: CAB/24/132-0100.

"Report of the Committee on National Expenditure," Cabinet Conclusions 17.2.1922: CAB/23/29-0011.

M. Hankey. "The Part of the Air Force in the Future of Imperial Defence," 8.3.1922: CAB/23/29-0016.

M. Hankey. "Air Defence—The Part of the Air Force in the Future of Imperial Defence," Cabinet Conclusions 15.3.1922: CAB/23/29-0018.

"The Relations of the Navy and the Air Force," Cabinet Conclusions 31.7.1923: CAB/23/46-0015.

"Report of a Sub-Committee on National and Imperial Defence," 15.11.1923: CAB/24/162-0061.

W. S. Churchill. "Navy Estimates 1925–1926," Cabinet Memorandum 29.1.1925: CAB/24/171-0039.

W. Bridgeman. "Navy Estimates," Memorandum by the First Lord of the Admiralty 5.2.1925: CAB/24/171-0068.

"Navy Estimates," Memorandum, Chancellor of the Exchequer 7.2.1925: CAB/24/171-0072.

M. Hankey. "The Singapore Base—Defence and Development of the Naval Base," Minutes of the Committee for Imperial Defence 2.8.1926: CAB/23/53.

M. Hankey. "The Singapore Base—Defence and Development of the Naval Base," Minutes of the Committee for Imperial Defence 14.7.1927: CAB/24/188.

Lord Birkenhead. "Report on Cruisers," Naval Programme Committee 14.12.1927: CAB/24/190-0005.

W. Bridgeman. "Navy Estimates 1929," Memorandum by First Lord of the Admiralty 6.12.1928: CAB/24/199-0034.

M. Hankey. "The Singapore Base—Defence and Development of the Naval Base," Minutes of the Committee for Imperial Defence 13.12.1928: CAB/24/199.

W. W. Fisher and G. C. Upcott. "Navy Estimates 1930," Joint Reply by Admiralty-Treasury on Navy Estimates 13.12.1929: CAB/24/209-0014.

P. Snowdon. "Memorandum by Treasury on Financial Aspects of the Naval Conference," 16.12.1929: CAB/24/209-0012.

BRITISH CABINET DOCUMENTS, 1930–39 (CHRONOLOGICAL ORDER)

S. Baldwin, "Imperial Defence Policy," Interim Report by the Ministerial Committee on Disarmament Dealing with Air Defence 16.7.1934: CAB/24/250-0018.

"Defence Policy and Requirements—Singapore Defences," Memorandum by the Committee for Imperial Defence 19.7.1935: CAB/24/256.

S. Baldwin. "Statement Relating to Defence," P.M. Statement to the House of Commons 3.3.1936: CAB/24/260-0029.

Viscount Swindon. "Plan for Further Expansion of First-Line Strength of the Royal Air Force," Memorandum by the Secretary of State for Air 14.1.1937: CAB/24/267-0019.

Viscount Swindon. "Pledges Given as Regards Parity with the German Air Force," Memorandum by the Secretary of State for Air 22.1.1937: CAB/24/267-0028.

Viscount Swindon. "Further Expansion of the First-Line Strength of the Royal Air Force: Parity with the German Air Force," 27.1.1937: CAB/23/87-0006.

T. Inskip. "Progress in Defence Requirements," Memorandum by the Minister for Defence Co-ordination 1.2.1937: CAB/24/267.

T. Inskip. "Progress in Defence Requirements," Memorandum by the Minister for the Co-Ordination of Defence 1.2.1937: CAB/24/267-0041.

T. Inskip. "The Navy and Its Relation to the Fleet Air Arm and Shore-Based Aircraft," Memorandum from the Minister of Co-Ordination of Defence 21.7.1937: CAB/24/270-0044.

T. Inskip, "The Navy and Its Relation to the Fleet Air Arm and Shore-Based Aircraft," Supplementary Memorandum from the Minister of Co-Ordination of Defence 26.7.1937: CAB/24/270-0045.

T. Inskip. "Comparison of the Strength of Great Britain with that of Certain Other Nations as at January 1938," Report by the Chiefs-of-Staff Sub-Committee 3.12.1937: CAB/24/273-0021.

BRITISH CABINET DOCUMENTS, 1939–42 (CHRONOLOGICAL ORDER)

"The Situation in the Far East in the Event of Japanese Intervention against Us," Chiefs-of-Staff Appreciation 31.7.1940: CAB/66/10/33-0001.

"Assistance to the Dutch in Event of Japanese Aggression in the Netherlands East Indies," Chiefs-of-Staff Appreciation 7.8.1940: CAB/66/10/39-0001.

COSWR (No. 119) of the Naval, Military and Air Situation from 0700 December 4th, to 0700 December 11th, 1941: CAB/66/20/22.

COSWR (No. 120) of the Naval, Military and Air Situation from 0700 December 12th to 0700 December 18th, 1941: CAB/66/20/24.

COSWR (No. 122) of the Naval, Military and Air Situation from 0700 December 25th to 0700 December 31st, 1941: CAB/66/23/34.

War Cabinet, "Far East Appreciation," 21.2.1942: CAB/66/22/24-0001.

"Some Remarks Made by Japanese Diplomats and Attaches in European Capitals at the End of February," NID Report 31.3.1942: CAB/66/23/26.

COSWR (No. 136) of the Naval, Military and Air Situation from 0700 April 2nd to 0700 April 9th, 1942: CAB/66/27/6-0001.

R. Brooke-Popham. Despatch on the Far East, Air Chief Marshal Sir Robert Brooke-Popham, CIC Far East (17th October 1940–27th December 1941), 28.5.1942: CAB/66/28/33-0001.

OPERATIONAL DESPATCHES/REPORTS: LONDON GAZETTE

Collins, J. A. Despatch 17.3.1942: *Battle of the Java Sea 27 February 1942*, LDNGZT Issue 38346, 6.7.1948. http://www.london.gazette.co.uk/issues/38346/supplements.

Cunningham, A. Despatch 9.7.1940: *Report of an Action with the Italian Fleet off Calabria*, LDNGZT Issue 38273, 27.4.1948. http://www.london.gazette.co.uk/issues/38273/supplements.

Cunningham, A. Despatch 19.3.1941: *Operation EXCESS*, LDNGZT Issue 38377, 10.8.1948. http://www.london.gazette.co.uk/issues/38377/supplements.

Cunningham, A. Despatch 4.8.1941: *The Battle of Crete*, LDNGZT Issue 38296, 21.5.1948. http://www.london.gazette.co.uk/issues/38296/supplements.

Cunningham, A. Despatch 11.11.1941: *Battle of Matapan*, LDNGZT Issue 38031, 29.7.1947. http://www.london.gazette.co.uk/issues/38031/supplements.

Forbes, C. Despatch 17.7.1940: *Norway Campaign*, LDNGZT Issue 38011, 8.7.1947. http://www.london.gazette.co.uk/issues/38011/supplements.

Harwood, H. Despatch 2.6.1942: *The Battle of Sirte of 22nd March 1942*, LDNGZT Issue 38073, 16.9.1947. http://www.london.gazette.co.uk/issues/38073/supplements.

Layton, G. Despatch 17.12.1941: *Loss of H.M. Ships Prince of Wales and Repulse*, LDNGZT Issue 38214, 26.2.1948. http://www.london.gazette.co.uk/issues/38214/supplements.

Maltby, P. *Report on the Air Operations during the Campaigns in Malaya and the Netherlands East Indies from 5th December 1941 to 12th March 1942*, LDNGZT Issue 38216, 26.2.1948. http://www.london.gazette.co.uk/issues/38216/supplements.

Ramsey, B. Despatch 18.6.1940: *The Evacuation of the Allied Armies from Dunkirk and Neighbouring Beaches*, LDNGZT Issue 38017, 17.6.1947. http://www.london.gazette.co.uk/issues/38017/supplements.

Tovey, J. Despatch 27.5.1941: *Sinking of the German Battleship Bismarck*, LDNGZT Issue 38098, 14.10.1947. http://www.london.gazette.co.uk/issues/38098/supplements.

Tovey, J. Despatch 12.9.1941: *The Carrier Borne Aircraft Attack on Kirkness and Petsamo*, LDNGZT Issue 38300, 25.5.1948. http://www.london.gazette.co.uk/issues/38300/supplements.

Tovey, J. Despatch 20.5.1942: *Convoys to North Russia 1942*, LDNGZT Issue 39041, 13.10.1950. http://www.london.gazette.co.uk/issues/39041/supplements.

Wavell, A. Despatch: Operations in Eastern Theatre, Based on India, from March 1942 to December 31, 1942, LDNGZT Issue 37728, 18.9.1946. (print).

Willis, A. Despatch 8.12.1941, 29.12.1941: *Actions against Raiders*, LD-NGZT Issue 38349, 9.7.1948. http://www.london.gazette.co.uk/issues/38073/supplements.

UNITED STATES STRATEGIC BOMBING SURVEY (USSBS) [PACIFIC], NAVAL ANALYSIS DIVISION: INTERROGATIONS OF JAPANESE OFFICIALS, OPNAV-P-03–100. HTTP://WWW.IBIBLIO.ORG/HYPERWAR/AAF/USSBS/IJO.

Interrogation Nav. 7: Vice Admiral Kazutaka Shiraichi 15.10.1945, USSBS No. 33.

Interrogation Nav. 9: Vice Admiral Kurita Takeo 16–17.10.1945, USSBS No. 47.

Interrogation Nav. 12: Captain Inoguchi Rikibei 15.10.1945, USSBS No. 62.

Interrogation Nav. 13: Captain Watanabe Yasuji 15.10.45, USSBS No. 96.

Interrogation Nav. 4: Captain Aoki Taijiro 9.10.1945, USSBS No. 23.

Interrogation Nav. 31: Rear Admiral Katsumata Seizo 25.10.1945, USSBS No. 129.

Interrogation Nav. 34: Commander Nakajima Chikataka 21.10.1945, USSBS No. 139.

Interrogation Nav. 38: Captain Tashikazu Ohmae Tashikazu 22.10.1945, USSBS No. 160.

Interrogation Nav. 55: Vice Admiral Ozawa Jisaburo 30.10.1945, USSBS No. 227.

Interrogation Nav. 64: Rear Admiral Takata Toshitane 1.11.1945, USSBS No. 258.

Interrogation Nav. 68: Captain Ihara Mitsugo 10.11.1945, USSBS No. 331.

Interrogation Nav. 70: Vice Admiral Paul H. Wenneker 11.12.45, USSBS No. 359.

Interrogation Nav. 15: Captain Chihaya Takahashi 20.10.1945, USSBS No. 74.

Interrogation Nav. 72: Vice Admiral Miwa Shigeyoshi 10.10.45, USSBS No. 366.

Interrogation Nav. 75: Admiral Toyoda Soemu 13–14.11.1945, USSBS No. 378.

Interrogation Nav. 76: Admiral Yonai Mitsumasa 17.11.1945, USSBS No. 379.
Interrogation Nav. 77: Captain Sonokawa Kamea 14.11.1945, USSBS No. 387.

BRASSEY'S NAVAL & SHIPPING ANNUALS

Richardson, A., and A. Hurd, eds. *Brassey's Naval Annual, 1924–28.* London: W. M. Clowes, 1924–28.

Robinson, C. N., and H. M. Ross, eds. *Brassey's Naval Annual, 1931–35.* London: W. M. Clowes, 1931–35.

Robinson, C. N., ed. *Brassey's Naval Annual 1936.* London: William Clowes, 1936.

Thursfield, H. G., ed. *Brassey's Naval Annual, 1937–42.* London: W. M. Clowes, 1937–42.

Other Primary Sources—Print, Electronic, Televised

Albatross (*pseud.*). "Japan and the Defence of Australia." Melbourne: Robertson & Mullens, 1935.

Baumbach, W. *Broken Swastika: The Defeat of the Luftwaffe.* Maidstone, UK: George Mann, 1974.

"British Submarines at War, Part 1, 1939–1942," *Campaign Summaries of World War 2,* http://www.navalhistory.net/ww2CampaignsBritishSubs.htr/.

Churchill, W. S. *The Second World War.* Vol. 1, *The Gathering Storm.* London: Cassell, 1948.

Churchill, W. S. *The Second World War.* Vol. 2, *Their Finest Hour.* London: Cassell, 1949.

Churchill, W. S. *The Second World War.* Vol. 3, *The Grand Alliance.* London: Cassell, 1950.

Churchill, W. S. *The Second World War.* Vol. 4, *The Hinge of Fate.* London: Cassell, 1951.

Doenitz, K. *The World at War: Episode Ten*—"Wolfpack: U-Boats in the Atlantic 1939–1944." Interview with BBC Television, 1973. DVD recording.

Forbes, C., and D. Pound. *The Fighting Instructions 1939.* (C.B. 4027) ADM 239/261. http://www.admirals.org.uk/records/adm/adm239.

Fuchida, M., and M. Okumiya. *Midway: The Battle that Doomed Japan.* Annapolis, MD: Naval Institute Press, 1992.

Goldstein, D. M., and K. V. Dillon, eds. *The Pacific War Papers: Japanese Documents of World War II.* Dulles, VA: Potomac Books, 2004.

Ike, N., ed. *Japan's Decision for War: Records of the 1941 Policy Conferences.* Stanford, CT: Stanford University Press, 1967.

Knight, R. J. B. *British Naval Documents 1204–1960*, edited by J. B. Hattendorf and A. W. H. Pearsall. Aldershot, UK: Scolar Press for the Navy Records Society, 1993.

Mahan, Capt. A. T., USN. *Naval Strategy—Compared and Contrasted with the Principles and Practices of Military Operations on Land.* London: Sampson Low Marston, 1911.

Meaney, N. *Australia and the World: A Documentary History from the 1870s to the 1970s.* Melbourne: Longman Cheshire, 1985.

Okumiya, M., J. Horikoshi, and M. Caidin. *Zero! The Story of Japan's Air War in the Pacific 1941–45.* New York: Ballentine Books, 1973.

Raeder, E. *My Life.* Annapolis, MD: Naval Institute Press, 1960.

Ranft, B., ed. *The Beatty Papers: Selections from the Private and Official Correspondence of Admiral of the Fleet Earl Beatty.* Vol. 2, *1916–1927.* Aldershot, UK: Scolar Press for the Navy Records Society, 1995.

Robertson, J., and J. McCarthy. *Australian War Strategy 1939–1945—A Documentary History.* St. Lucia: University of QLD Press, 1985.

Simpson, M., ed. *The Cunningham Papers: Selections from the Private and Official Correspondence of Admiral of the Fleet Viscount Cunningham of Hydenhope.* Vol. 1, *The Mediterranean Fleet, 1939–1942.* Aldershot, UK: Ashgate—Navy Records Society, 1999.

Simpson, M. (ed.). *The Somerville Papers: Selections from the Private and Official Correspondence of Admiral of the Fleet Sir James Somerville, G.C.B., C.B.E., D.S.O./edited by Michael Simpson with the Assistance of John Somerville.* Aldershot, UK: Scolar Press for the Navy Records Society, 1995.

Somerville, J. "Report of Proceedings of Eastern Fleet from 29th March to 13th April 1942," Office of the British Naval Commander-in-Chief, Eastern Fleet 18th April 1942, Number 4. S/4682. http://www.naval-history.net/xDKWD-EF1942-Introduction.ht.

Speer, A. *Inside the Third Reich: Memoirs by Albert Speer.* New York: Bonanza Books, 1982.

Secondary Sources

Agawa, H. *The Reluctant Admiral: Yamamoto and the Imperial Navy*. Tokyo: Kodansha International, 1979.

Andrew, C. *The Defence of the Realm: The Authorised History of MI5*. London: Penguin Books, 2009.

Barber, N. *Sinister Twilight: The Fall of Singapore*. Glasgow: Collins, 1976.

Barnett, C. "Roskill, Stephen Wentworth (1903–1980)," Oxford Dictionary of National Biography, 2004. http://dy.doi.org/10.1093/ref.odnb/31628.

Bartsch, W. H. *Doomed at the Start: American Pursuit Pilots in the Philippines, 1941–1942*. College Station: Texas A&M University Press, 1995.

The Battleships. (DVD), Australian Broadcasting Corporation, 2002, accessed 10.07.2011.

Bekker, C. *Hitler's Naval War*. London, MacDonald & Jane's, 1974.

Bennett, G. *Naval Battles of World War Two*. Barnsley, UK: Pen & Sword, 2003.

Bowyer, C. *History of the RAF*. London: Bison Books, 1977.

Boyle, A. *Trenchard*. London: Collins, 1962.

Brown, D. *Carrier Operations of World War II*. Vol. 1, *The Royal Navy*. London, Ian Allen: 1974.

Brown, E. M. *Duels in the Sky: World War II Naval Aircraft in Combat*. Annapolis, MD: Naval Institute Press, 1988.

Burns, P. *The Brisbane Line Controversy: Political Opportunism Versus National Security, 1942–45*. St. Leonards, Australia: Allen & Unwin, 1998.

Burton, J. *Fortnight of Infamy: The Collapse of Allied Airpower West of Pearl Harbor*. Annapolis, MD: Naval Institute Press, 2006.

Butler, J. R. M. *Grand Strategy*. Vol. 1, *Rearmament Policy*. London: Her Majesty's Stationery Office (hereinafter H.M.S.O.), 1976.

Butler, J. R. M. *Grand Strategy*. Vol. 2, *September 1939–June 1941*. London: H.M.S.O., 1957.

Butler, J. R. M. *Grand Strategy*. Vol. 3, Part 2, *June 1941–August 1942*. London: H.M.S.O., 1964.

Bywater, H. C. *Sea Power in the Pacific: A Study of the American-Japanese Naval Problem*. London: Constable, 1921.

C. Cantrill. "UK Expenditure 1880–1914." http://www.ukpublicspending.co.uk.

Carlton, M. *First Victory 1914: HMAS Sydney's Hunt for the German Raider Emden*. North Sydney: William Heinemann, 2013.

Casey, L. S. *Naval Aircraft*. London: Phoebus, 1977.

Cherpak, E. M. *Register of the Herbert Rosinski Papers*. Newport, RI: Naval Historical Collection, 1988. http://www.usnwc.edu/Academics/Library/RightsideLinks/Naval.

Collier, B. *Japanese Aircraft of World War II*. New York: Mayflower Books, 1979.

Cornwall, J. *Hitler's Scientists—Science, War and the Devil's Pact*. London: Penguin Books, 2003.

Curran, J., and S. Ward, eds. *Australia and the Wider World—Selected Essays of Neville Meaney*. Sydney: Sydney University Press, 2013.

Day, D. *The Great Betrayal—Britain, Australia and the Onset of Pacific War 1939–42*. North Ryde, Australia: Angus & Robertson, 1988.

Dull, P. S. *A Battle History of the Imperial Japanese Navy: 1941–1945*. Annapolis, MD: Naval Institute Press, 1975.

Farrell, B., and S. Hunter, eds. *Sixty Years On: The Fall of Singapore Revisited*. Singapore: Eastern Universities Press, 2003.

Gibbs, N. H. *Grand Strategy*. Vol. 1, *Rearmament Policy*. London: H.M.S.O., 1976.

Gillison, D. *Royal Australian Air Force 1939–1942*. Adelaide, Australia: Griffin Press, 1962.

Green, W. *Famous Fighters of the Second World War*. London: McDonald & Janes, 1978.

Greene, J. *War at Sea: Pearl Harbor to Midway*. New York: Gallery Books, 1988.

Grenfell, R. *Main Fleet to Singapore: An Account of Naval Actions of the Last War*. Singapore: Oxford University Press, 1987.

Grove, E. *The Royal Navy Since 1815: A New Short History*. New York: Palgrave Macmillan, 2005.

Gunston, B. *German, Italian and Japanese Fighters of World War II*. London: Lansdowne Press, 1980.

Hall, E. R. (Bon). *Glory in Chaos: The RAAF in the Far East in 1940–1942*. West Coburg, Australia: The Sembawang Association, 1989.

Hezlet, A. *Aircraft and Sea Power*. London: Wyman & Co., 1970.

Hillsborough, R. *Samurai Revolution: The Dawn of Modern Japan Seen through the Eyes of the Shogun's Last Samurai*. Tokyo: Tuttle Publishing, 2014.

Horner, D., ed. *The Battles that Shaped Australia—"The Australians" Anniversary Essays*. St. Leonards, Australia: Allen & Unwin, 1994.

Hough, R. *The Longest Battle: The War at Sea 1939–45*. London: Cassell, 2003.

Ienaga, S. *Japan's Last War: World War II and the Japanese, 1931–1945*. Canberra: Australian National University Press, 1979.

Jane's Fighting Aircraft of World War II. London: Random House, 2001.

Johns, W. E., and R. A. Kelly. *No Surrender*. London: W. H. Allen, 1989.

Kemp, P. K. *Key to Victory: The Triumph of British Sea Power in World War II*. Boston: Little, Brown, 1957.

Kennedy, L. *Pursuit: The Sinking of the Bismarck*. London: Cassell, 1974.

Kennedy, P. M. *The Rise and Fall of British Naval Mastery*. London: Macmillan Press, 1983.

Lambert, A., ed. *Naval History: 1850–Present*. Vol. 2. Aldershot, UK: Ashgate Publishing, 2003.

Lyon, H. *The Encyclopaedia of the World's Warships: A Technical Directory of Major Fighting Ships from 1900 to the Present Day*. Turnhout, UK: Leisure Books, 1985.

Macintyre, D. *The Battle of the Atlantic*. London: Severn House, 1975.

Macintyre, D. *The Battle for the Pacific*. London: Angus & Robertson, 1966.

MacKay, R. F. *Balfour: Intellectual Statesman*. Oxford: Oxford University Press, 1985.

Marder, A. J. *Old Friends, New Enemies: The Royal Navy and the Imperial Japanese Navy*. Vol. 1, *Strategic Illusions, 1936–1941*. Oxford: Clarendon Press, 1981.

Marder, A. J., M. Jacobsen, and J. Horsfield. *Old Friends, New Enemies: The Royal Navy and the Imperial Japanese Navy*. Vol. 2, *The Pacific War, 1942–1945*. Oxford: Clarendon Press, 1990

McCarthy, J. *Australia and Imperial Defence 1918–39*. St. Lucia: University of Queensland Press, 1976.

Meaney, N. *A History of Australian Defence and Foreign Policy*. Vol. 1, *The Search for Security in the Pacific*. Sydney: Sydney University Press, 1976.

Montgomery Hyde, H. *British Air Policy between the Wars 1918–1939*. London: William Heinemann, 1976.

Murray, W. *Luftwaffe*. London: George Allen & Unwin, 1985.

Neilson, K., and G. Kennedy, eds. *Far Flung Lines: Studies in Imperial Defence in Honour of Donald McKenzie Schurman*. London: Frank Cass, 1996.

Odgers, G. *The Royal Australian Navy: An Illustrated History*. Hornsby, Australia: Child & Henry, 1982.

O'Neill, R. *Suicide Squads: The Men and Machines of World War Two Special Operations.* London: Salamander, 1999.

Oppenheim, P. *The Fragile Forts—The Fixed Defences of Sydney Harbour 1788–1963.* Canberra: Australian Army History Unit, 2004.

Parkinson, R. *The Late Victorian Navy—The Pre-Dreadnought Era and the Origins of the First World War.* Woolbridge, UK: The Boydell Press, 2008.

Polybius, *Histories* 18.24, extract in G. R. Crane, ed., Persus Digital Library, Tufts University. http://www.persustufts.edu/hopper/.

Preston, A. *Aircraft Carriers.* London: Bison Books, 1979.

Reynolds, D. *Britannia Overruled—British Policy and World Power in the 20th Century.* London: Longman 2000.

Richards, D. *RAF Bomber Command in the Second World War: The Hardest Victory.* London: Classic Penguin, 2001.

Richards, D., and H. St. George Saunders. *Royal Air Force 1939–1945.* Vol. 2, *The Fight Avails.* London: H.M.S.O., 1975.

Roskill, S. *Churchill and the Admirals.* London: Collins, 1977.

Roskill, S. *The War at Sea, 1939–1945.* Vol. 2, *The Defensive.* London: H.M.S.O., 1954.

Roskill, S. *The War at Sea, 1939–1945.* Vol. 3, *The Period of Balance.* London: H.M.S.O., 1955.

Salmaggi, C., and A. Pallavisini. *2194 Days of War—An Illustrated Chronology of the Second World War.* London: Windward, 1977.

Schreuder, D. M., and S. Ward, eds. *Australia's Empire.* Oxford: Oxford University Press, 2008.

Schull, J. *Far Distant Ships: An Official Account of Canadian Naval Operations in World War II.* Ottawa: King's Printer, 1952.

Shepherd, E. C. *The Air Force of Today.* Glasgow: Blackie & Son, 1939.

Stanley, P. *Invading Australia: Japan and the Battle for Australia, 1942.* Camberwell: Australia Penguin Group, 2008.

Stille, M. *Imperial Japanese Navy Aircraft Carriers 1921–45.* Oxford: Osprey Publishing, 2005.

Taylor, A. J. P. *The Second World War: An Illustrated History.* London: Penguin, 1976.

Terraine, J. *White Heat: The New Warfare 1914–18.* London: Book Club Associates, 1982.

Till, G. *Airpower and the Royal Navy 1914–1945—A Historical Survey.* London: Jane's Publishing, 1979.

Tomlinson, M. *The Most Dangerous Moment*. London: William Kimber, 1976.

Tusa, A., and J. Tusa. *The Nuremberg Trial*. London: Macmillan London, 1983.

Van der Vat, D. *The Pacific Campaign: The U.S.-Japanese Naval War 1941–1945*. New York: Simon & Schuster, 1991.

Warner, O. *Great Sea Battles*. London: Spring Books, 1963.

Williamson, P. *National Crisis and National Government: British Politics, the Economy and Empire 1926–1932*. Cambridge: Cambridge University Press, 1992.

Winton, J. *War in the Pacific: Pearl Harbor to Tokyo Bay*. London: Sidgwick & Jackson, 1978.

Yoshimura, A. *Battleship Musashi—The Making and Sinking of the World's Biggest Battleship*. Tokyo: Kodansha International, 1999.

INDEX

ABOUT THE AUTHOR

Angus Britts is a qualified historian from Australia who specializes in military studies and who has enjoyed a background in the subject since his childhood in the 1970s. His studies have included politics, international relations, and a variety of historical subjects.